CUTTY SARK

THE LAST OF THE TEA CLIPPERS

CUTTY SARK

THE LAST OF THE TEA CLIPPERS

150th Anniversary Edition

Foreword
HRH The Duke of Edinburgh

Preface
Dr Kevin Fewster AM

Author
Eric Kentley

Picture Editor
Jessica Lewis

ROYAL
MUSEUMS
GREENWICH

ADLARD
COLES
NAUTICAL

Adlard Coles Nautical
An imprint of Bloomsbury Publishing Plc
50 Bedford Square
London WC1B 3DP
UK
29 Earlsfort Terrace
Dublin 2, Ireland
www.bloomsbury.com
www.adlardcoles.com

Published in association with Royal Museums Greenwich, the group name for the National Maritime Museum,
Royal Observatory Greenwich, Queen's House and *Cutty Sark*.
www.rmg.co.uk

British Library Cataloguing in Publication Data:
A catalogue record for this book is available
from the British Library.

ISBN 9781472959539

10 9 8 7 6 5 4 3 2

Printed in China by C&C Offset Printing Company.

Previous pages:
'*Cutty Sark at Sunset*, by John Everett, early twentieth century.

A complete set of picture credits can be found on page 198.

Contents

Foreword

This is the story of a very famous sailing ship, and when you read it, it is worth bearing in mind that before her time every merchant ship on the oceans was driven by the wind. Ships driven by steam were already common by the time she was built, but after her time all merchant ships are driven by engines. 'Cutty Sark' is, therefore, the last representative of a very long tradition. Needless to say, at the time when she was built, no one imagined that she might, one day, become a museum piece. The Cutty Sark Preservation Society saved her from the scrap yard in the 1950s and restored her for exhibition, but she was built to last for only about thirty years; not for two or three hundred years.

Her active life was fairly dramatic, but no-one could have foreseen what she would have to go through, even after she had been placed in a specially built dry-dock at Greenwich. In some ways, the devastating fire in 2007, which nearly destroyed her, turned out to be her saviour. The massive 6 year re-building program, made possible by many generous donors, has ensured that she can now look forward to many years as an historic object as well as a memorial to the age of sail, and to the men who 'went down to the sea' in sailing ships.

HRH The Duke of Edinburgh and
Commander Steele, Captain-
Superintendent of HMS Worcester
on the 'tween deck of *Cutty Sark*,
28th May 1953.

CUTTY SARK

DESIGNED BY

Hercules Linton for John Willis & Son

BUILT BY

Scott & Linton of Dumbarton, Scotland

LAUNCHED

22nd November 1869

PORT OF REGISTRY

London

REGISTRATION NUMBER

63557

HULL LENGTH

212½ feet (65 metres)

EXTREME LENGTH

280 feet (86 metres)

BEAM

36 feet (11 metres)

DEPTH

22½ feet (7 metres)

MAXIMUM RECORDED SPEED

17½ knots (20 mph, 32.5 kph)

Preface

As the very last of the tea clippers, the importance of *Cutty Sark* to the nation's history cannot be understated. The original owner of *Cutty Sark*, John Willis, commissioned her with the hope and expectation that she would become the fastest ship in the world. While he anticipated both generating sizeable financial profits and gaining acclaim, he certainly could not have expected her to have survived into the 21st century. I am sure that he would be delighted to see his prized ship treasured by people from all over the world, visited by millions and hailed as the finest example of the golden age of sailing.

As Director of Royal Museums Greenwich, I have been involved with *Cutty Sark* since my appointment in 2007. From her incredible 2006–12 Conservation Project, through to her award-winning visitor experience today, the ship continues to inspire new generations of visitors, and I am proud that so many of the visitors we welcome on board are families with young children. We continue to seek to engage all of our audiences, and a visit to *Cutty Sark* really does provide something for everyone – she has become a must-see attraction and, more than ever before, truly lives up to her standing as the jewel in the crown of the Maritime Greenwich World Heritage Site.

The story of *Cutty Sark* did not end when she arrived in Greenwich more than sixty years ago. She has now welcomed more than 17 million visitors on board since opening to the public in 1957, including nearly two million since 2012. In 2019 *Cutty Sark* celebrates her 150th anniversary. For a ship designed to last no more than thirty years or so, this is a remarkable achievement and one that Royal Museums Greenwich will ensure is a milestone to remember. The continued support of our key stakeholders is vital to our ongoing work to preserve *Cutty Sark* for future generations and we look forward to welcoming new supporters throughout the ship's 150th year.

Dr Kevin Fewster AM
Director, Royal Museums Greenwich

Introduction

On a November afternoon in 1869 a new ship slid down the slipway into the River Leven. Named *Cutty Sark*, she was built for one purpose – to transport tea from China to London as quickly as possible.

Cutty Sark was launched in the middle of Britain's 'imperial century'. A great spirit of entrepreneurism had been backed by successive governments, the latest being the Liberal administration led, for the first time, by William Gladstone (Member of Parliament for Greenwich). Restrictions on trade, protectionism and high taxes were seen as the causes of poverty: free trade was the cure.

The defeat of the combined French and Spanish fleets at Trafalgar in 1805 is often regarded as the beginning of a century of supremacy at sea for Britain; but the boom in British seaborne trade began well before this and, indeed, underpinned

Fig. 1 *Squally Weather*, by Montague Dawson, *c.* 1958.

Fig. 2 An early advertisement for tea.

the huge costs of the Royal Navy that protected it through the long French wars of 1793 to 1815. London, the port of registry for the new ship, had seen a succession of new docks built in the early 1800s, including the West India Docks (1802), London Docks (1805) and the East India Docks (1806). The Royal Victoria Docks had opened in 1855, and in the year before *Cutty Sark* was launched, the Millwall Docks had been completed.

Britain was unrivalled: Germany had yet to be united and the United States, although on the ascent, was some years away from challenging her. Materials poured in from across the Empire: jute and cotton from India, the Empire's 'jewel in the crown', gold and copper from newly found deposits in Australia, sugar from the West Indies. Yet few, if any, of the hundreds of British and American tea clippers would have been built if it had not primarily been for events in the 35 years before *Cutty Sark*'s launch. Most significant of these were the so-called Opium Wars. Now almost forgotten in Britain, but taught to every Chinese child as the time when the humiliation of their country by foreigners began, these two conflicts, ignited by the flimsiest of reasons, forced the Chinese to open all their major ports to foreigners, making the tea trade possible.

Tea imports into Britain and her colonies were originally monopolised by the Honourable East India Company (later the British or simply East India Company), almost from the moment in the seventeenth century that tea reached British shores. This monopoly was taken away in 1834 after the free-trade lobby successfully argued that the East India Company was keeping tea prices artificially high. However, the *supply* of tea remained a Chinese monopoly. Even after tea plants were discovered in Assam in the 1830s, and production began in India, it was not until towards the end of the nineteenth century that China ceased to be the world's foremost exporter of tea.

The combination of falling prices and a strong push from the Temperance Movement in the early nineteenth century led to tea – once a luxury drink for the aristocracy – becoming immensely popular at all levels of society. Demand soared but soon hit a problem: the Chinese, although content to export tea, silks and porcelain, had no interest in importing goods from the West. They demanded payment in silver, creating an ever-increasing trade imbalance. Attempting to redress this, the East India Company began growing and processing opium in Bengal, and selling it to merchants to smuggle into China. The silver that had paid for the tea would now find its way back to the West. These opium supplies began to reach China in 1781, reaching a huge scale between 1821 and 1837. Inevitably, it resulted in an enormous addiction problem.

The Chinese authorities prohibited the sale of opium in 1799 but were unable to enforce the ban. In 1839, they made a further and particularly determined effort, seizing and destroying most of that year's opium imports at Guangzhou (Canton). The merchant lobby in Britain argued that this was a 'violation' of free trade, and the government was persuaded to take the strongest possible action. The First Anglo-Chinese War – popularly known as the First Opium War – began that year.

After the British attacked Guangzhou and occupied Shanghai, the Chinese emperor was forced to sign the Treaty of Nanking (Nanjing) in 1842. This ceded Hong Kong to the British and opened up a number of ports to Western traders for the first time – most notably Fuzhou (Foochow) and Shanghai. (These were particularly important because Western tea merchants soon discovered that tea was available earlier in the year further up the coast from Guangzhou, and from 1853 onwards Fuzhou and Shanghai became the principal tea ports.) But China's humiliation was not over. The arrest in 1856 of the crew of a Hong Kong-registered vessel, the *Arrow*, on suspicion of piracy and smuggling, was used by the British as another excuse for war. This time they were joined by the French and even American and Russian forces. This Second Anglo-Chinese War was ended by the Treaty of Tientsin (Tianjin), which was finally ratified in 1860. As well as being forced to legalise the opium trade and pay

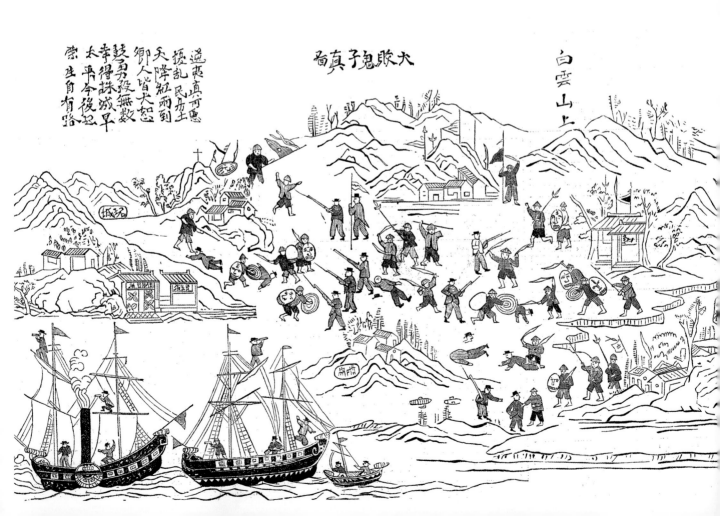

Fig. 4 The main tea ports of China in the late nineteenth century.

a huge amount of compensation (in silver, of course) the Chinese were also obliged to open up yet more ports on the Changjiang (Yangtze) River. Of these, the most important was the tea capital of China, Hankou (Hankow) – 586 miles from the sea and at the centre of a vast inland canal network.

The result was a huge number of ships, built in Britain and America, to take advantage of the opening up of the Chinese ports. As the supply of tea grew, a fashion arose for 'fresh' tea, and particularly for the very first of the year's crop (very like the competition to drink the first bottles of Beaujolais Nouveau which began a hundred years later). It was a fad (tea is, after all, a dry product with a shelf life of about three years) but Victorians relished novelty, and the ship-owners and tea merchants were happy to satisfy it.

From 1861, a premium of 10 shillings for each ton of tea was paid to the first ship of the year to land her cargo in London, some of which would end up in the pockets of the crew. Competition between ships was intense, never more so than in the Great Tea Race of 1866. On 30th May, the clipper *Ariel*, which had loaded in Fuzhou, reached the open sea. She was almost a day behind another vessel, *Fiery Cross*, and closely followed by *Serica* and *Taeping*. *Taitsing* was another day behind. *Fiery Cross* kept her lead through the south-west monsoon to the Sunda Strait, the way into the Indian Ocean between the islands of Sumatra and Java, and the ships then became separated. At one point there were five days between them. By the time she rounded Africa and was up to the equator, *Ariel* had caught up with *Fiery Cross* (although well out of sight) but so had *Taeping*. Finally *Ariel* reached the Kent coast, after 99 days and 15,000 miles under sail, just 10 minutes ahead of *Taeping*, only for *Taeping* to find a tug more quickly and snatch back the lead. *Ariel*'s crew may have still felt that they could tie up in London first, since their ship was making for the East India Docks while *Taeping* was heading further up the Thames to the London Docks. But *Ariel* was a little deeper in draft than *Taeping* and had to endure a frustrating wait for the tide to

rise before she could enter the docks. As a result *Taeping* managed to start unloading her cargo 20 minutes ahead of *Ariel*. However, she did not take all the premium: the owners of the two vessels feared that the merchants would realise that the tea market was about to be flooded, not just by their two ships but also by all those just behind, and then use any dispute about the result of the race as an excuse not to pay the premium. So they secretly agreed not to argue about whether the race was to the Thames or to the dock or to the quayside, but to split the bonus.

It was the last time the premium was offered. Yet nothing could stop the rivalry among the crews and their owners to make the season's fastest passage, or that between ship-owners to build the fastest vessel in the trade.

This was the context for which *Cutty Sark* was built and, of her type, she was one of the most advanced: her rigging was of wire, not hemp rope; her steering mechanism was an ingenious space-saving device, not one that occupied vital cargo space; and behind her wooden hull planks was a finely fashioned and strong skeleton of iron.

Probably no one on the Leven riverside that day would have thought it strange that a sailing ship was being launched, even though steamships were commonplace long before 1869 – the Peninsular and Oriental Steamship Navigation Company had been running regular steamers to Australia and the Far East for over 10 years. Moreover, no one would have predicted the impact of the Suez Canal, opened just five days earlier and which, with the steamer, was to bring the end of the tea clipper within a relatively short time. *Cutty Sark* was one of the very last tea clippers constructed: only four clippers were built in the following year of 1870, and only three more after that. The short flowering of the type would soon be over.

In addition, few on the Leven riverside in 1869 would have predicted that this new ship would become one of the most famous in the world, and no one would have predicted that she would still be with us a century and a half later.

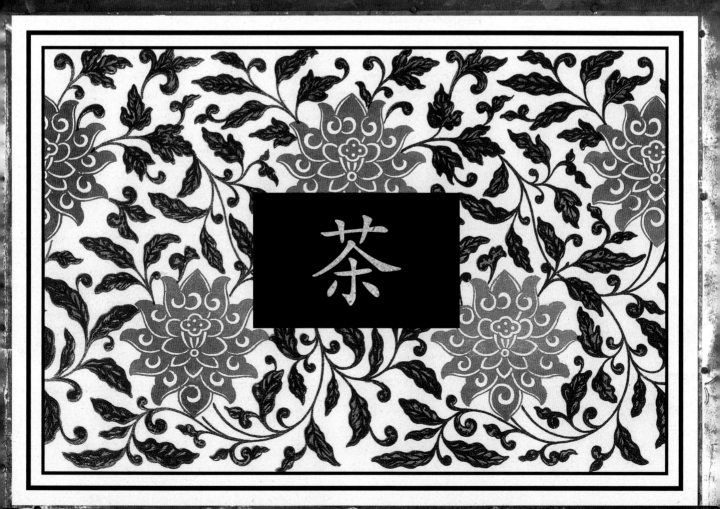

Building *Cutty Sark*

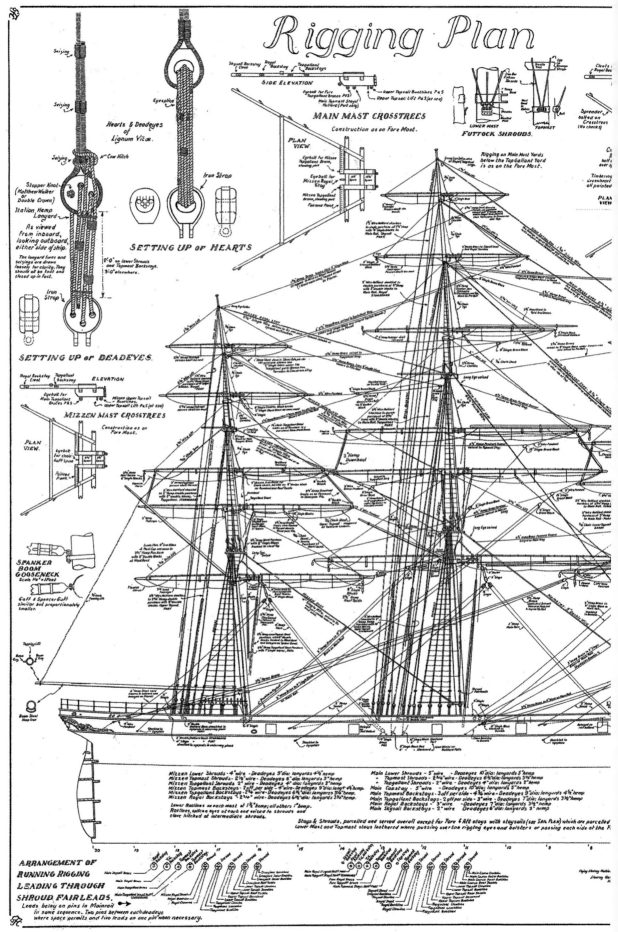

Rigging Plan

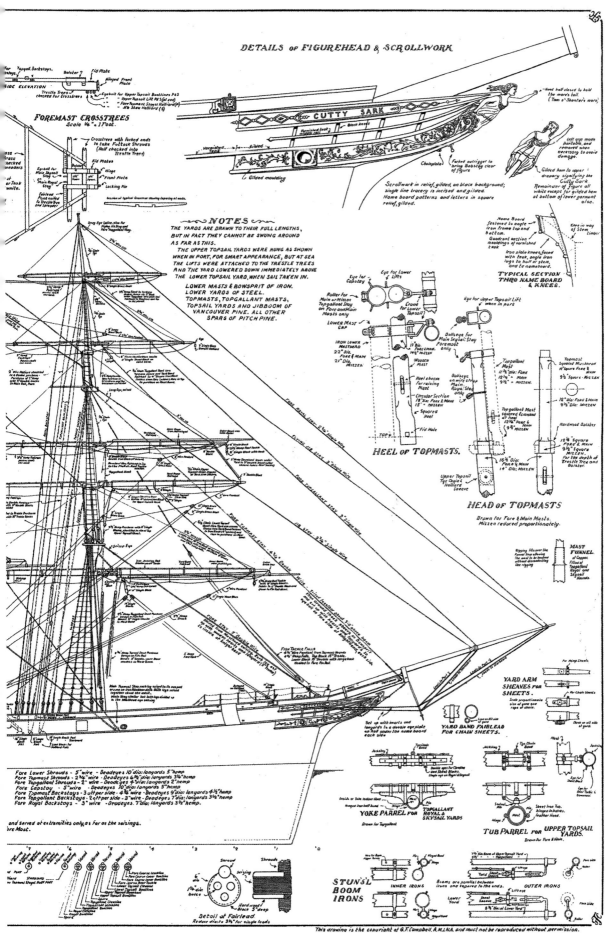

DETAILS of FIGUREHEAD & SCROLLWORK

FOREMAST CROSSTREES
Scale ¼" = 1 Foot

CUTTY SARK

NOTES
THE YARDS ARE DRAWN TO THEIR FULL LENGTHS,
BUT IN FACT THEY CANNOT BE SWUNG AROUND
AS FAR AS THIS.
THE UPPER TOPSAIL YARDS WERE HUNG AS SHOWN
WHEN IN PORT, FOR SMART APPEARANCE, BUT AT SEA
THE LIFTS WERE ATTACHED TO THE TRESTLE TREES
AND THE YARD LOWERED DOWN IMMEDIATELY ABOVE
THE LOWER TOPSAIL YARD, WHEN SAIL TAKEN IN.

LOWER MASTS & BOWSPRIT OF IRON.
LOWER YARDS OF STEEL.
TOPMASTS, TOPGALLANT MASTS,
TOPSAIL YARDS AND JIBBOOM OF
VANCOUVER PINE. ALL OTHER
SPARS OF PITCH PINE.

HEEL of TOPMASTS.

HEAD of TOPMASTS
Drawn for Fore & Main Masts.
Mizzen reduced proportionately.

MAST FUNNEL.

YARD ARM SHEAVES for SHEETS.

YARD BAND FAIRLEAD FOR CHAIN SHEETS.

YOKE PARREL for TOPGALLANT ROYAL & SKYSAIL YARDS

TUB PARREL for UPPER TOPSAIL YARDS.

Fore Lower Shrouds - 5" wire · Deadeyes 10"dia: lanyards 5" hemp
Fore Topmast Shrouds - 2¾" wire · Deadeyes 5½"dia: lanyards 3¾" hemp
Fore Topgallant Shrouds - 2" wire · Deadeyes 4"dia: lanyards 2" hemp
Fore Capstay - Deadeyes 10"dia: lanyards 5" hemp
Fore Topmast Backstays - 3 off upper side · 4½" wire · Deadeyes 9"dia: lanyards 4½" hemp
Fore Topgallant Backstays - 2 off upper side - 3" wire · Deadeyes 7"dia: lanyards 3½" hemp
Fore Royal Backstays - 3" wire · Deadeyes 7"dia: lanyards 3½" hemp.

and served at extremities only, as far as the seizings.

STUN'SL BOOM IRONS

INNER IRONS

OUTER IRONS

Detail of Fairlead

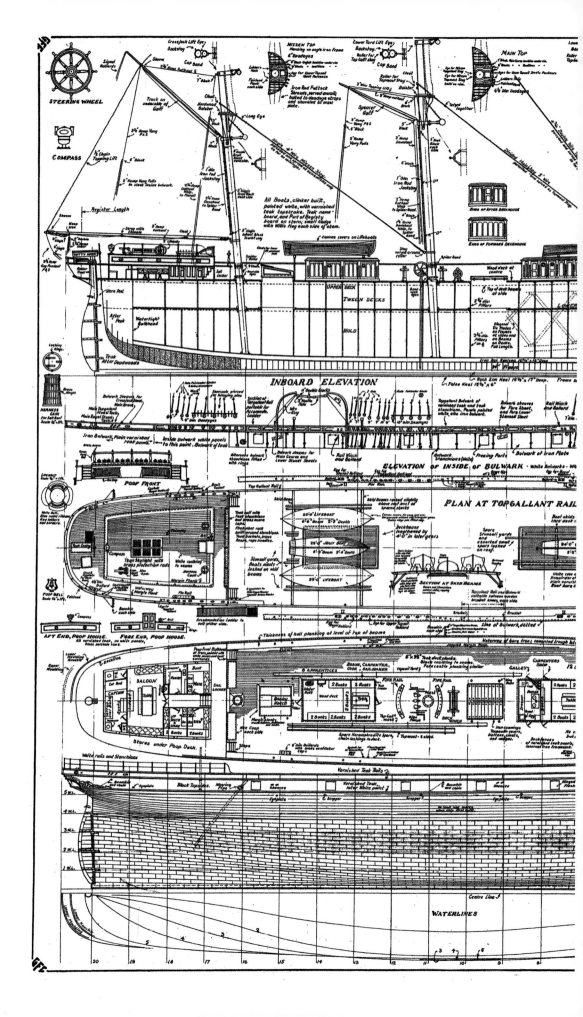

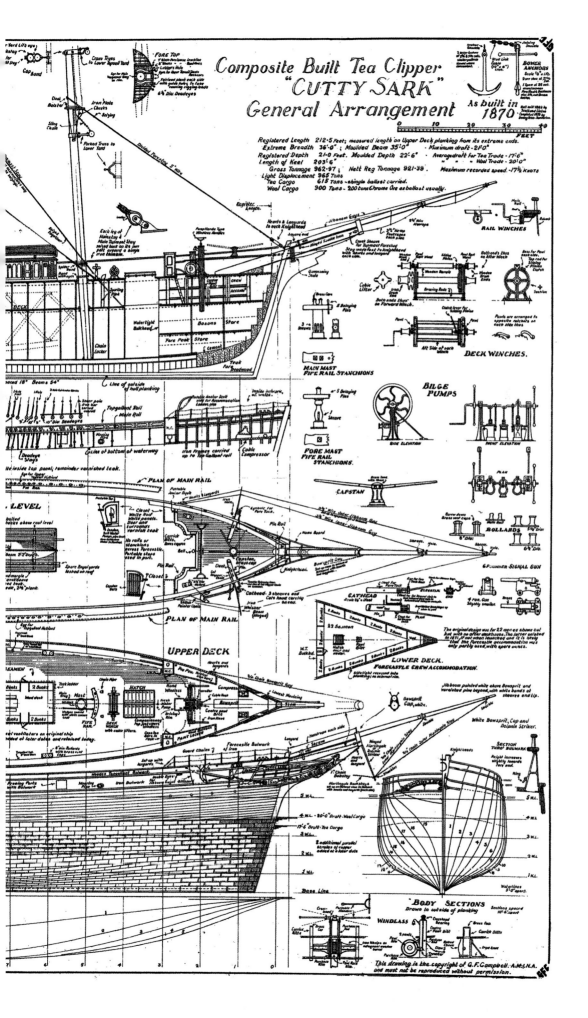

Composite Built Tea Clipper "CUTTY SARK"
General Arrangement As built in 1870

Registered Length 212·5 Feet; measured length on Upper Deck planking from its extreme ends.
Extreme Breadth 36'·0"; Moulded Beam 35'·0" · Maximum draft· 21'·0"
Registered Depth 21·0 Feet. Moulded Depth 22'·6" · Average draft for Tea Trade· 17'·6"
Length of Keel 203'·6" · Wool Trade· 20'·0"
Gross Tonnage 962·97; Nett Reg Tonnage 921·39. Maximum recorded speed·17½ KNOTS
Light Displacement 965 Tons
Tea Cargo 615 Tons - shingle ballast carried.
Wool Cargo 900 Tons - 200 tons Chrome Ore as ballast usually.

RAIL WINCHES

DECK WINCHES.

MAIN MAST FIFE RAIL STANCHIONS

FORE MAST FIFE RAIL STANCHIONS.

BILGE PUMPS

CAPSTAN

BOLLARDS

6 POUNDER SIGNAL GUN

PLAN OF MAIN RAIL.

CATHEAD

LOWER DECK. FORECASTLE CREW ACCOMMODATION.

22 Seamen

UPPER DECK

BODY SECTIONS Drawn to outside of planking

WINDLASS

This drawing is the copyright of G.F. Campbell; A.M.I.N.A. and must not be reproduced without permission.

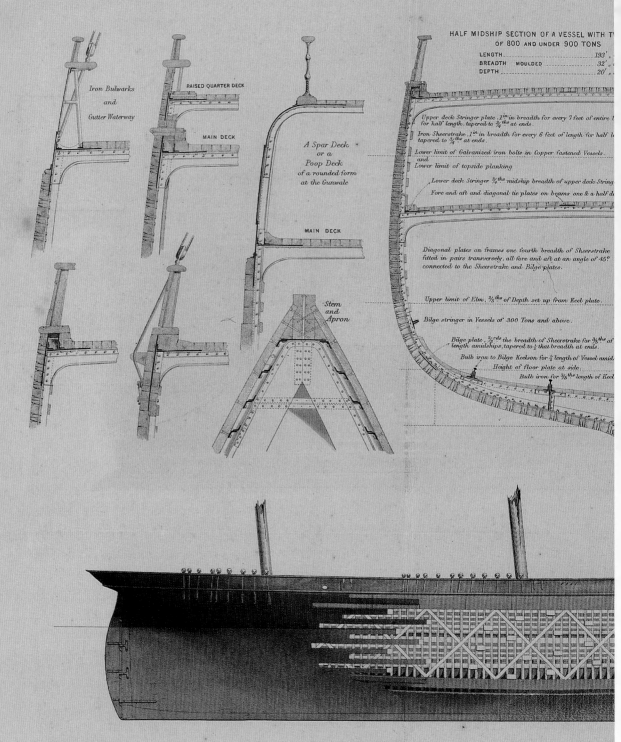

HALF MIDSHIP SECTION OF A VESSEL WITH T
OF 800 AND UNDER 900 TONS

LENGTH .... 193'
BREADTH MOULDED .... 32'
DEPTH .... 20'

*Iron Bulwarks
and
Gutter Waterway*

RAISED QUARTER DECK

MAIN DECK

*A Spar Deck
or a
Poop Deck
of a rounded form
at the Gunwale*

MAIN DECK

*Stem
and
Apron*

Upper deck Stringer plate, 1ᵗʰ in breadth for every 7 feet of entire
for half length, tapered to ¾ths at ends.

Iron Sheerstrake, 1ᵗʰ in breadth for every 6 feet of length for half le
tapered to ¾ths at ends.

Lower limit of Galvanized iron bolts in Copper fastened Vessels.
and
Lower limit of topside planking

Lower deck Stringer ¾ths midship breadth of upper deck String

Fore and aft and diagonal tie plates on beams one & a half d

Diagonal plates on frames one fourth breadth of Sheerstrake
fitted in pairs transversely, all fore and aft at an angle of 45°
connected to the Sheerstrake and Bilge plates.

Upper limit of Elm, ⅖ths of Depth set up from Keel plate.

Bilge stringer in Vessels of 300 Tons and above.

Bilge plate, ⅔rds the breadth of Sheerstrake for ¾ths of the
length amidships, tapered to ½ that breadth at ends.

Bulb iron to Bilge Keelson for ½ length of Vessel amid
Height of floor plate at side.
Bulb iron for ¾ths the length of Keel

Drawn by H. Cornish, Lloyd's Surveyor

Printed by Robᵗ Edmᵈ Tayl

CUTTY SARK: THE LAST OF THE TEA CLIPPERS

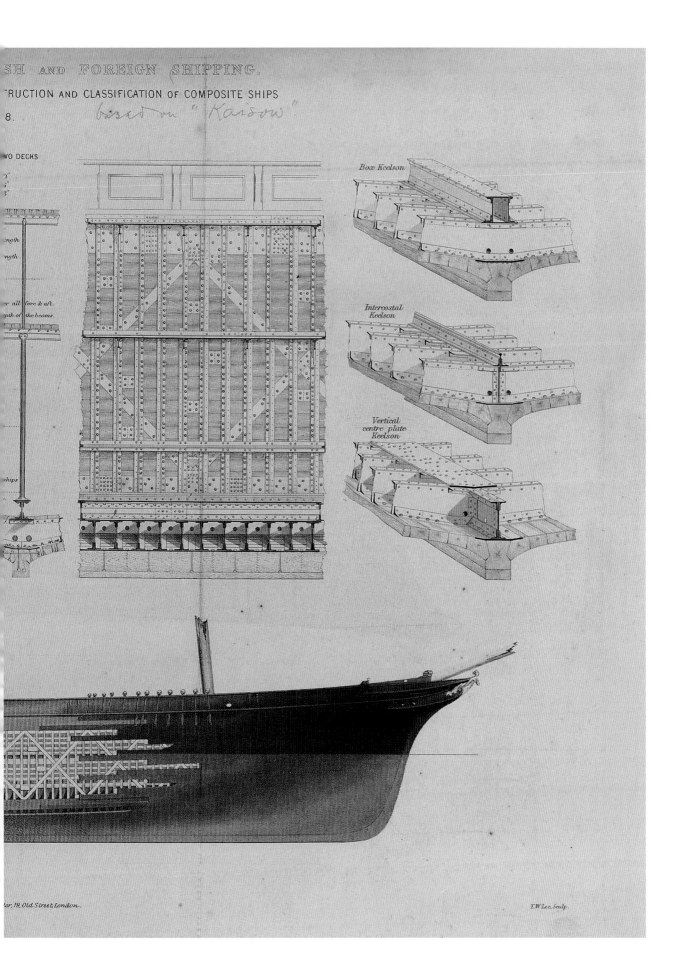

based on "Kaisow"

WO DECKS

Box Keelson

Intercostal
Keelson

Vertical
centre plate
Keelson

tor, 19, Old Street, London.

T.W.Lee, Sculp.

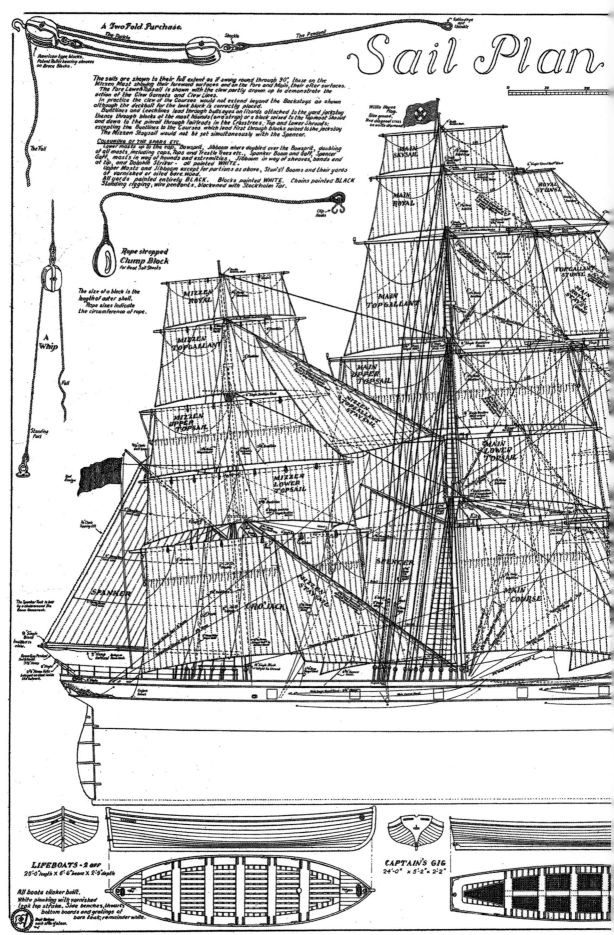

CUTTY SARK: THE LAST OF THE TEA CLIPPERS

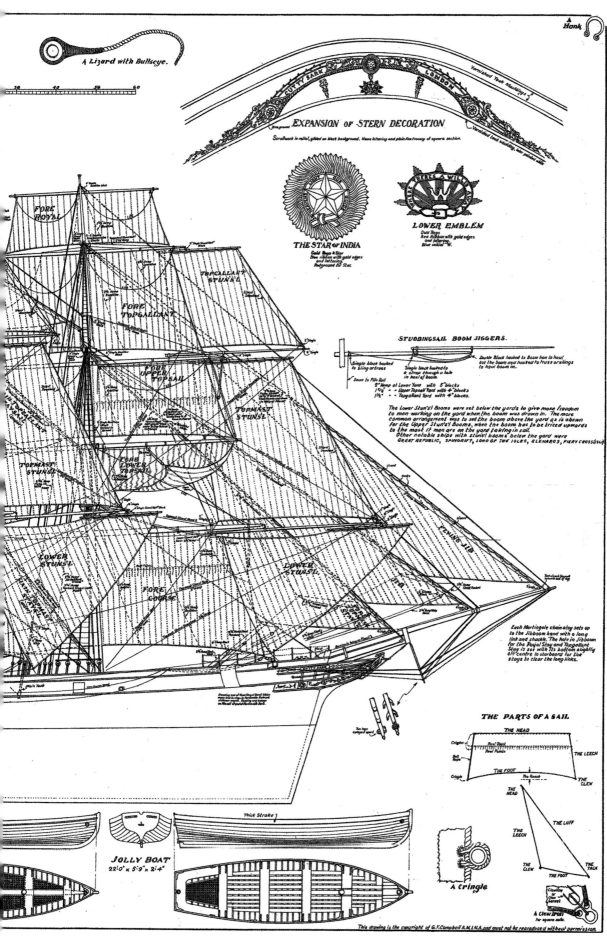

A Lizard with Bullseye.

Hank

EXPANSION OF STERN DECORATION

Scrollwork in relief, gilded on black background. Name lettering and plain line tracery of square section.

THE STAR OF INDIA
Gold Rays & Star
Blue ribbon with gold edges
and lettering.
Background (to) Star.

LOWER EMBLEM
Gold Rays
Red Ribbon with gold edges
and lettering.
Blue initial W.

STUDDINGSAIL BOOM JIGGERS.

The Lower Stun's'l Booms were set below the yards to give more freedom
to men working on the yard when the boom was drawn in. The more
common arrangement was to set the boom above the yard as is shown
for the Upper Stun's'l Booms, when the boom has to be triced upwards
to the mast if men are on the yard taking in sail.
Other notable ships with stuns'l booms below the yard were
GREAT REPUBLIC, SPINDRIFT, LORD OF THE ISLES, GLENAROS, FIERY CROSS &c.

Each Martingale chain stay sets up
to the Jibboom band with a long
link and shackle. The hole in Jibboom
for the Royal Stay and Topgallant
Stay is set with its bottom slightly
off centre to starboard for the
stays to clear the long links.

THE PARTS OF A SAIL

A Cringle

JOLLY BOAT
22'·0" x 5'·9" x 2'·4"

A Clew Iron
for square sails.

This drawing is the copyright of G.F.Campbell R.M.I.N.A. and must not be reproduced without permission.

The rise of the clipper

S ince tea imports began in the mid-seventeenth century, the British had been content for it to be brought at a leisurely pace in 'East Indiamen' – the ships of the East India Company. In design, these vessels were not very different to the warships of the period – large, bluff-bowed vessels, their shape in plan often described as 'cod's head and mackerel tail'. They were built to carry large quantities of cargo, not for speed and looked very much the same for nearly two hundred years.

But Victorian Britain was a very different place to that of Charles II. Railways and telegrams were shrinking the world and suddenly speed was desirable in everything. One manifestation of this was the demand for the first of the season's China tea, which had to be brought to London by a fast ship.

For as long as there have been Customs officials to evade – and smugglers to catch – there have been fast vessels. During the War of 1812 between Britain and the United States, shipbuilders around Chesapeake Bay on the eastern seaboard of the United States developed types of brigs and schooners that were particularly successful in evading the Royal Navy. The vessels were known as Baltimore clippers, the word 'clipper' coming from the American expression 'to go at a clip' – that is, go quickly. A couple of decades later, their design led American shipbuilders to rethink some of their assumptions about the shape of ships and they began to incorporate some of the qualities of Baltimore clippers into larger vessels. A new type of ship emerged, one with a long, narrow hull and tall, raking masts: the clipper ship was born.

Previous pages:
Fig. 6 *Cutty Sark*, by Frederick Tudgay, 1872. This detailed ship's portrait originally belonged to *Cutty Sark*'s owner, John Willis.

Fig. 7 *The East Indiaman Triton*, by William John Huggins, 1839. For almost two centuries East Indiamen brought tea to Britain. The end of the East India Company's monopoly in 1834 opened up the trade and inadvertently led to the development of the clipper.

Then in 1848 gold was discovered at Sutter's Mill in California and, suddenly, hundreds of thousands of people wanted to travel west. The transcontinental railway would not be completed for another 20 years, so the way to reach California was either a four- to six-month trek by wagon-train through country inhabited by hostile Native Americans or a (usually) quicker westward journey in a fast sailing ship round Cape Horn. For American shipbuilders who could produce clipper ships large enough for an economic number of passengers and tough enough to round the Horn against the prevailing winds, this was a boom time.

American ship-owners in this trade had a problem, over and above that of their crews deserting to the goldfields: once their vessels reached California there was no freight and very few passengers to take back to the East Coast. Rather than return empty, some enterprising owners hit on the idea of sending their ships from California across the Pacific to China. There they could pick up a tea cargo, sail with the prevailing winds around the Cape of Good Hope, and unload at the ports on the eastern seaboard of the United States.

One American clipper, however, chose London rather than New York to land her tea cargo. This was *Oriental*. She arrived in 1850, only a year after the British Parliament had repealed the Navigation Acts, which had for two centuries restricted the transport of goods between Britain and her colonies to British ships. *Oriental* was a threat to British shipping, not just as a foreign ship bringing a tea cargo into the capital, but also because she was a new type of fast ship that the British had yet to develop. It is no wonder that the Admiralty requested permission to record her lines (her shape) before she departed.

So confident were the Americans of their superiority in ship design over the British that, in 1852, the American Navigation Club of Boston challenged British ship-owners to a race to China for a prize of £10,000. The challenge was not accepted.

However, innovation was not exclusive to the Americans. In Aberdeen, Alexander Hall & Sons had developed their own prototype for a new style of ship. It was a fast vessel but, equally importantly to ship-owners, it was also a tax-efficient one. Up until 1854, ships were assessed for dues by taking their length and multiplying this figure by a notional percentage for depth (actually measuring the depth of a vessel was always troublesome). This was, of course, an incentive to build ships as deep as possible and, although such ships had a large carrying capacity, they became ever slower. But in 1854 the rules changed: dues were now to be calculated

Fig. 8 Drawing showing the lines, body plan and longitudinal half-breadth for *Oriental* (1849), an American clipper. *Oriental* was the first of a new breed of clipper, designed for speed. She arrived in London from Hong Kong with her cargo of tea in 1850, in just 97 days, shaking British ship-owners out of their complacency.

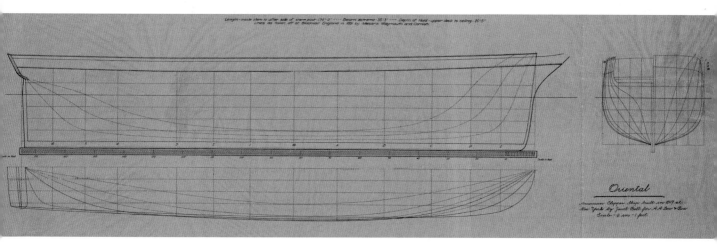

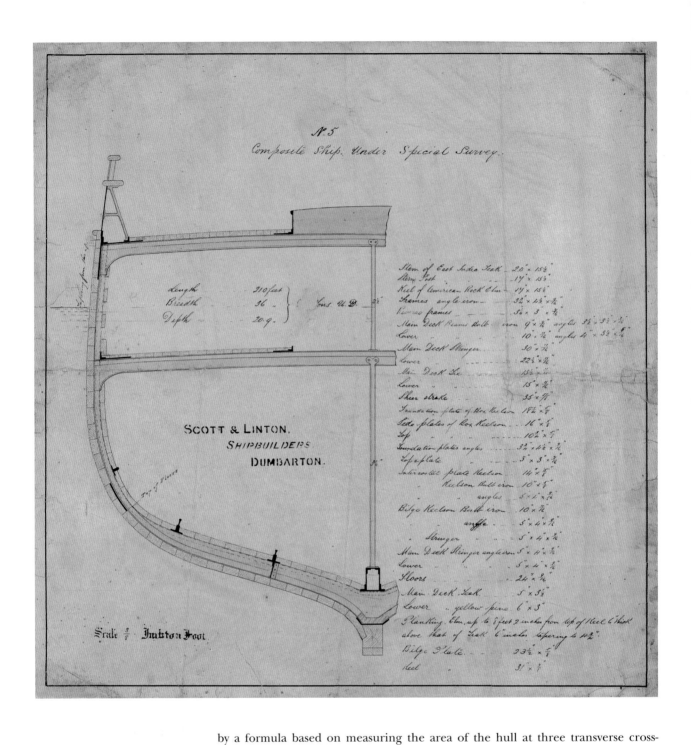

No 5

Composite Ship Under Special Survey.

Length — 210 feet
Breadth — 36 "
Depth — 20.9 "

Tons U.D. __ 2¼

SCOTT & LINTON,
SHIPBUILDERS
DUMBARTON.

Stem of East India Teak — 20" × 15½"
Stern Post — 17" × 15½"
Keel of American Rock Elm — 17" × 15½"
Frames angle iron — 3½" × 4½" × ½"
Reverse frames — 3½" × 3" × ½"
Main Deck Beams Bulb iron 9" × ½" angles 3½" × 3½" × ½"
Lower — 10" × ½" angles 4" × 3½" × ½"
Main Deck Stringer — 30" × ½"
Lower — 22½" × ½"
Main Deck Tie — 13½" × ½"
Lower — 15" × ½"
Sheer strake — 33" × ⅞"
Foundation plate of Box Keelson 18½" × ½"
Side plates of Box Keelson — 16" × ⅝"
Top — 10½" × ⅝"
Foundation plates angle — 3½" × 4½" × ½"
Top a plate — 3" × 3" × ½"
Intercostal plate Keelson — 14" × ⅝"
Keelson Bulb iron 10" × ⅝"
angles 5" × 4" × ½"
Bilge Keelson Bulb iron — 10" × ½"
angle — 5" × 4" × ½"
Stringer — 5" × 4" × ½"
Main Deck Stringer angle iron 5" × 4" × ½"
Lower — 5" × 4" × ½"
Floors — 24" × ⅜"
Main Deck Teak — 5" × 3½"
Lower yellow pine 6" × 3"
Planking Elm up to 3 feet 2 inches from top of Keel 6 Thick
above that of Teak 6 inches tapering to 4½"
Bilge Plate — 23½" × ⅝"
Keel — 31" × ⅞"

Scale ⅜ Inch to a Foot

Fig. 9 Half-midship section for *Cutty Sark*, by Hercules Linton. Completed before the ship was named, this plan show the vessel's composite construction in great detail.

by a formula based on measuring the area of the hull at three transverse cross-sections. The most advantageous shape now became one with the smallest possible cross-sectional areas. Little could be done to make the cross-section in the middle of the ship small without significantly reducing her carrying capacity; but the aft section could be made smaller and, if the bow was long and pointed, the forward section could be smaller still. Alexander Hall & Sons perfected the long, curving, sharp bow – the 'Aberdeen bow' – that became characteristic of the clippers. It was, however, the accumulation of features – the long, narrow hull; the sharp, extended bow; raking masts; and the very, very large sail area – that defined the clipper. In some vessels these features were particularly exaggerated: these were the extreme clippers, of which *Cutty Sark* was one.

These clipper ships were not simply designed for speed and profitability: an obvious aesthetic element was also included. The high bulwarks hid the raised poop and anchor decks and even the roofs of the deckhouses, so that from the side only the sheer – or rather the swoop of the topgallant rail – was visible. Combined with their raked masts, this gave them a yacht-like appearance. Rock elm and teak – durable, dense woods from outposts of the Empire in Canada and India, respectively – were commonly used for hull planking. But *Cutty Sark* went a step further with a teak main deck, rather than common pine. With her extensive brass fittings, black hull and 'gold' decorative scheme, capped with a white figurehead and white lower masts, she was a splendid-looking ship among a handsome company.

Not all British clippers were built for the tea trade. Like the California gold rush, the Australian gold rush of the 1850s led to a similar demand for emigrant clippers. But British clippers tended to be smaller than their American counterparts, partly because the former had to cross the sandbars at the mouths of the major Chinese rivers while the latter were built to sail against the winds around Cape Horn. However, because the hulls of the British ships were planked with hardwoods from the colonies rather than softwood, they were less prone to damage and lasted considerably longer than their American rivals.

It is possible that American clippers could have posed a significant threat to the British ships in the tea trade, had it not been for the 'Panic' of 1857 – the very first international financial crisis, precipitated in some measure by the sinking of the paddle steamer *Central America* with the loss of $2 million worth of Californian gold (and 246 lives). The Panic pushed the USA into a deep recession, from which it did not fully recover until after the Civil War (1861–65). A huge number of American ships found themselves laid up or broken up because there were no cargoes to carry. The effect of the Panic was much less keenly felt in Britain, leaving ship-owners on the eastern side of the Atlantic to compete for tea trade supremacy largely among themselves.

The builders

In his book *The Tea Clippers*, David MacGregor identifies 277 British-built sailing vessels engaged in the China tea trade between 1824 and 1876, constructed in at least 89 different yards. Of them all, the most prolific builders were Alexander Hall & Sons, which constructed twice as many vessels as its nearest competitor outside Aberdeen, Robert Steele & Co. of Greenock (see Table 1).

Most of the vessels the Aberdeen yards produced were wooden. A few iron clippers were built before 1870 but anti-fouling treatments for iron hulls were not advanced, so they were not popular among ship-owners who wanted fast vessels which did not require frequent docking to have their bottoms scraped free of weed and barnacles. There was also a belief among ship-owners that changes in humidity in an iron hull would cause a tea cargo to 'sweat' and spoil.

It was not long, however, before effective anti-fouling solutions were found and, despite the reservations, from 1870 onwards iron rapidly took over as the preferred material. But for six years or so before this, an entirely different construction technique became extremely popular. This was composite construction: the ship's hull

TABLE 1
Leading builders of vessels for the China tea trade
(analysis of data in MacGregor, 1985)

Alexander Hall & Sons, Aberdeen	34
Walter Hood, Aberdeen	17
Robert Steele & Co., Greenock	16
Alexander Stephen & Sons, Dundee and Glasgow	14
William Pile, Sunderland	14
T. & J. Brocklebank, Whitehaven	11
Alexander Duthie, Aberdeen	9
Thomas Bilbe & Co., Rotherhithe, London	8
Charles Connell, Glasgow	7

TABLE 2
**Vessels for the China trade –
construction method**
(analysis of data in MacGregor, 1985)

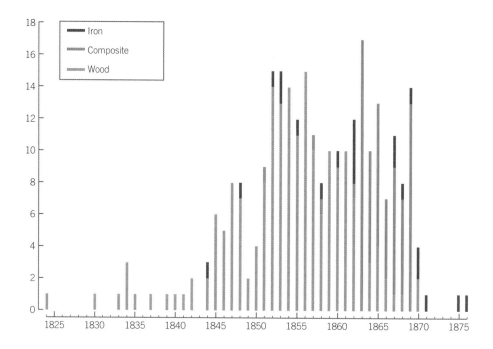

TABLE 3
**Building locations of composite
clippers for the China trade,
1863–70**
(analysis of data in MacGregor, 1985)

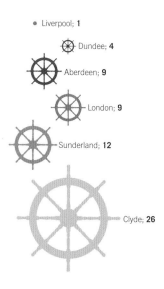

Liverpool; **1**

Dundee; **4**

Aberdeen; **9**

London; **9**

Sunderland; **12**

Clyde; **26**

was wooden but the planks were fastened to an iron skeleton of frames, beams and diagonal cross-bracing (which also extended under the decks). The resulting ship was very strong and rigid. Even more importantly, the iron framework took up substantially less space than the bulky frames, beams and knees of a wooden ship. Virtually unknown before 1860, by 1864 its advantages were so self-evident that composite construction was by far the most dominant method for building new clippers until 1870.

Like ships built entirely of wood, these composite ships had their timber hull planking sheathed with metal plates to prevent fouling and worm attacks on the wood. If weed, barnacles and molluscs attach themselves to a hull, they will slow it down. If wood-boring shipworm (the mollusc *Teredo navalis*) takes hold, a ship can sink. Keeping these creatures off was a centuries-old problem that had only been solved in the middle of the previous century. The answer was to sheath the hull in copper plates. But copper was, and remains, expensive and during the early 1800s there was much interest in developing a cheaper alternative. The successful substitute, patented in 1832, was 'yellow metal', also known as Muntz metal, after its developer, the Birmingham metal-roller George Fredrick Muntz. It is brass, composed of almost 60 per cent copper and 40 per cent zinc, with a trace of iron. On *Cutty Sark*, both the sheathing and the bolts that secured the planking to the frames were of Muntz metal.

The change in construction from wood to composite resulted in a shift in the relative importance of shipbuilding centres: Aberdeen, although still significant, had lost its pre-eminence to the emerging industrial centres of Britain with access to the sea – London, Sunderland and, most importantly, to the shipyards of the Clyde.

The Clyde, shipyards and clippers

From Glasgow to the open sea, the River Clyde flows for around 25 miles. Along this stretch, fishing and small coasting vessels have been built for centuries, but for most of its history Scotland traded mainly with England and the Continent, so there was little demand for large ships. Besides, the Clyde was very shallow in places, only 2 feet (0.6 metres) at some points, which made it an unpromising location for one of the world's greatest centres of shipbuilding.

The spur to change from rural riverside to industrial complex was the unification of Scotland and England in 1706–07. The two Acts of Union brought to Scotland the protection of the Navigation Acts: now Scottish-owned ships could carry produce to all the British colonies. Glasgow, hitherto disadvantaged by being on the west coast – away from the markets of the Continent – was now seen as a port with one of the shortest routes to the eastern seaboard of North America. The effect was immediate and explosive: from just eight ships owned by Clyde merchants in 1707, five years later the number had risen to 1,123. Glasgow's merchants quickly grew rich from trade in the products of the transatlantic slave plantations – sugar, raw cotton and, above all, tobacco from Maryland and Virginia.

The merchants survived the collapse of the tobacco trade caused by the American War of Independence (1775–83) by increasing their focus on Caribbean produce – sugar, rum and raw cotton. But cotton, in particular, needs large vessels to make its transport profitable, so the Clyde itself had to be deepened to enable its unloading in Glasgow, not further downstream. This was a long project, but by 1840 dredging gave a spring-tide depth of 18 feet (5.5 metres). And the profits from the resulting growth in trade went into financial institutions, factories and mines, placing the area in an enviable position for the advancing Industrial Revolution.

While shipping boomed, local shipbuilding remained a relatively minor industry throughout the eighteenth and early nineteenth century. Scott's and Robert Steele, both of Greenock and both destined to become major constructors, were founded in 1711 and 1765 respectively; not to build ships for the transatlantic trade, but to build boats for the fishing industry. Soon even this was under threat – the loss of the American colonies had meant the seemingly endless supply of white oak for shipbuilding was cut off. Some firms, like Scott's, partially solved the problem by opening yards in Canada. But the key to the Clyde's future lay elsewhere:

Fig. 10 Map of the River Leven at Dumbarton in 1860. The shipyard of Scott & Linton would be located in the Wood Ship Building Yard (the Woodyard).

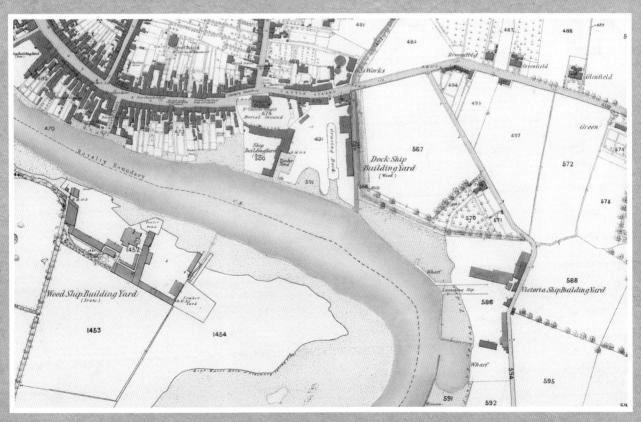

The Clyde, shipyards and clippers cont.

not in North American timber supplies from across the Atlantic but in the iron found in nearby Lanarkshire. The future lay not in wooden vessels but in iron ships and industrial production. In 1819, the barge *Vulcan*, the first entirely iron vessel, was launched into the Monklands Canal (dug to bring coal from Monklands to Glasgow); eight years later the Clyde's first ship with a steam engine, *Agalia*, was launched.

The builder of *Agalia* was David Napier. Yet, like his cousin Robert Napier, widely thought of as the 'father of Clyde shipbuilding', David was not primarily a shipbuilder but an engineer; that is, an engine maker. This pattern of such marine engineers becoming shipbuilders was repeated all along the Clyde and a great many of the Clyde yards were both shipbuilders and engine makers. For example, John Brown – now associated with the great ships like the first *Queen Mary* – was established in Govan in 1847 as an engine and boiler works, which started building ships in 1851. Similarly, Caird & Co. began by building engines for ships of the Peninsular & Oriental Steam Navigation Co., but by 1840 it was building ships in its own right. As E.C. Smith put it: 'It is the art of boiler-making that leads to the art of iron shipbuilding.'

Iron tea clippers emerged only at the very end of the clipper era, but it was the development of the composite ship – of wooden planking secured to an iron frame – that drew ship-owners to the Clyde and

other industrial centres, where iron-working skills were best, and away from the wooden shipbuilding yards on the Scottish east coast such as Aberdeen and Dundee. The wily shipbuilders Alexander Stephen & Co., founded in 1750 at Burghead, Grampian, and later with yards in Aberdeen, Arbroath and Dundee, opened another in Glasgow in 1851. Between then and 1869 this yard produced 136 ships, of which seven were clippers (the same number as produced by its Dundee yard). In 1861 one of Alexander Stephen & Co.'s yard managers at Glasgow, Charles Connell, left to set up his own company and, of the 68 ships he then built up to 1869, five were clippers.

Even Robert Steele of Greenock, the most prolific of the Clyde tea-clipper builders, launched only 16 among their total of 106 vessels produced between 1855 and 1869. However, these did include some of the most famous tea clippers such as *Taeping*, *Ariel* and *Serica*, all of which competed in the Great Tea Race of 1866.

Many of the Clyde yards – Barclay, Curle & Co., Charles Scott & Co., Duncan, Reid, Lawrie, Randolph, Elder & Co., William Simons and W.H. Rowan – built just one or two clippers. Of the 69 vessels that A. & J. Inglis built between its foundation in 1863 and 1869, only one – *Norman Court* – was a tea clipper.

A single clipper – *Gauntlet* – was built by Denny & Rankine at Dumbarton but not one by Denny Brothers, the company that played a minor role in *Cutty Sark*'s story. The Denny family had been shipbuilding at Dumbarton from at least 1818 but the company was founded when three brothers, William, Peter and Alexander, went into formal partnership in 1844. It was on their land – the Woodyard at Dumbarton – that *Cutty Sark* was built.

In total, 51 tea clippers were built on the Clyde, one more than the Aberdeen yards of Alexander Hall and William Hood together. But whereas the Aberdeen vessels were predominantly wooden, most of the Clyde's were of composite construction. In terms of overall numbers of Clyde-built ships, the clippers were not a significant proportion. That said, *Cutty Sark*, with her intricately shaped iron frames, some still visibly stamped 'Monklands' and 'Glasgow best' (although the latter was a quality standard rather than a mark of origin), is a tangible piece of the river's story as part of what was, within living memory, the world's greatest shipbuilding centre.

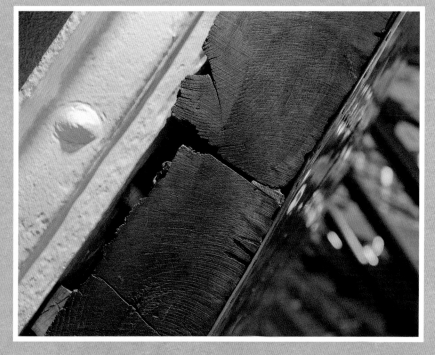

John Willis & Son, ship-owners

Among the shipping companies competing in the China tea trade, although not a competitor in the Great Race of 1866, was John Willis & Son. The founder, John Willis (1791–1862), a native of St Abb's Head in the Scottish Borders, had migrated to London sometime between 1825 and 1829. He apparently worked his way up from seaman to captain and eventually to ship-owner, his ships specialising in importing sugar from Demerara (now part of Guyana). Nicknamed 'Old Stormy', he is thought to have been the inspiration for the sea shanty *Old Stormalong*:

Stormy he is dead and done,
To my way, hay, storm along, John,
O Stormy was a good old man,
Ay, ay, ay, Mister Stormalong:

We dug his grave with a silver spade,
To my way, hay, storm along, John,
And lowered him down with a golden chain,
Ay, ay, ay, Mister Stormalong:
I wish I was old Stormy's son,
To my way, hay, storm along, John,
I'd build a ship of a thousand ton,
Ay, ay, ay, Mister Stormalong:
I'd fill her with New England rum,
To my way, hay, storm along, John,
And all my shellbacks they'd have some,
Ay, ay, ay, Mister Stormalong …etc.

The 'son' in John Willis & Son was another John, but sometimes known as Jock. Born in 1817, he was the eldest of eight children, and at the age of 18 became master of the Willis ship *Demerara Planter*.

However, around this time, the final abolition of slavery in Demerara combined with a growth in popularity of beet-sugar to make cane-sugar a significantly less profitable product. Like many other merchant and shipping companies at the time, John Willis & Son turned eastwards and in 1847 Willis junior brought back his first tea cargo in the barque *Borderer*. He made two more voyages before retiring, six years later, from the sea altogether to concentrate on the business of ship-owning.

With his distinctive white top hat, Willis junior was an easily recognised figure in the City of London. It was said that whenever one of his ships was due to depart, he would go down to the dock from his office at 18 East India Chambers, Leadenhall Street,

Fig. 11 John Willis (1817–99). Also known as 'White Hat' Willis, he commissioned the building of *Cutty Sark* in 1869.

Fig. 12 *Blackadder* (1870) at moorings in Brisbane, Australia, late nineteenth century. *Blackadder*, an iron clipper built in Greenwich and launched the year after *Cutty Sark*, was another of John Willis' fleet of tea ships.

to raise this hat and shout 'Goodbye, my lads!' – bidding farewell to a crew that might not return for 10 months or more. Yet he was not known for generosity towards his employees and was among the group of ship-owners who opposed the demands of the dockers in the London Dock Strike of 1889.

John Willis senior died in July 1862, leaving John junior to run the business. It is not clear how much his other son, Robert (who died in 1889), was involved, but he owned a number of shares in the company's vessels, although always fewer than his older brother.

Throughout the company's history, John Willis & Son managed a total of 29 vessels, but no more than 14 at any one time. All were sailing vessels: most were ships but a few were barques. (Unlike full-rigged ships, these had fore-and-aft sails rather than square sails on their aftermost mast: they were a little slower but needed a smaller crew.)

TABLE 4

Number of vessels in the Willis fleet

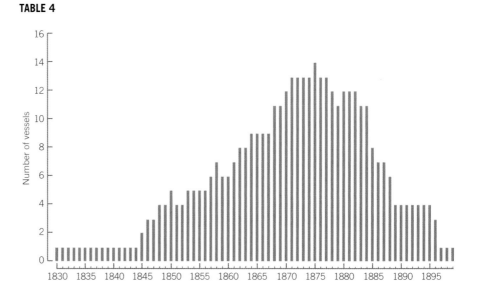

The fates of 27 of the Willis vessels are known and reveal the precarious nature of ship ownership in the nineteenth century (see Table 5). Of all the Willis vessels, 10 are known to have worked in the China tea trade (see Table 6). As can be seen in the names of these vessels, the Willises' Scottish roots were never forgotten. Even their house flag bore more than a passing resemblance to the St Andrew's saltire, the national flag of Scotland.

TABLE 5   The fate of Willis ships

Sold	9
Lost or missing	8
Wrecked or abandoned	6
Condemned or broken up	4
	27

TABLE 6   Willis ships in the China tea trade

NAME	DATE OF LAUNCH	BUILDER	TYPE	FATE
Borderer	1845	William Pile, Sunderland	wood (barque)	abandoned 1860
St Abbs	1848	William Pile, Sunderland	wood (barque)	wrecked, 1855
Merse	1853	William Pile, Sunderland	wood	wrecked, 1877
Lammermuir	1856	William Pile, Sunderland	wood	wrecked, tea-laden, 1859
Lauderdale	1858	Bilbe & Perry, Rotherhithe	composite	missing, 1877
Whiteadder	1862	Bilbe & Co., Rotherhithe	wood with iron beams	broken up, 1884
Lammermuir	1864	J. Pile, Hartlepool	wood	missing, 1876
Cutty Sark	1869	Scott & Linton, Dumbarton	composite	sold, 1895
Hallowe'en	1870	Maudslay, Sons & Field, Greenwich	iron	wrecked, 1887
Blackadder	1870	Maudslay, Sons & Field, Greenwich	iron	wrecked, 1905

Jock Willis' favourite ship is thought to have been *The Tweed* – most likely because of her speed. The writer Joseph Conrad served under one of her former masters, 'Captain S—':

> Our captain was a man famous for the quick passages he had been used to make in the old *Tweed*, a ship famous the world over for her speed. *The Tweed* had been a wooden vessel, and he brought the tradition of quick passages with him… [*The Tweed* was] a ship, I have heard, heavy to look at but of phenomenal speed. In the middle sixties she had beaten by a day and a half the steam mail-boat from Hong Kong to Singapore.
>
> *The Mirror of the Sea* (1906, pp.9–12)

The Tweed was too large for the tea trade – it was on the Australia run that she excelled – but there are two very remarkable points about her. First, she was not designed as a merchant vessel – she had been a naval frigate named *Punjaub*; and, secondly, she was not originally a sailing ship at all but had been a paddle steamer.

Fig. 13 Plan of mid-section of *Punjaub*. John Willis bought *Punjaub*, a paddle steamer, in 1862 and converted her into a sailing ship, *The Tweed*. She was one of the fastest ships of the age.

The vessel was designed by Oliver Lang junior of Deptford Dockyard (who also designed the Royal Yacht *Victoria and Albert*, launched in 1855) but she was built in Bombay (Mumbai) in 1854 for the Indian Marine of the East India Company, Bombay. *Punjaub* had taken part in the bombardment of Bushehr in 1856 during the Anglo-Persian War (1856–57, fought to prevent the Persians annexing the strategic Afghan town of Herat). In 1862, she and her sister ship, *Assaye*, were taken to England to be converted from paddle steamers into screw steamers. For some reason this plan was abandoned and in the same year both vessels were bought by John Willis for £44,000. He promptly resold *Assaye* for £40,000 and removed the engines from *Punjaub*, selling them for £12,000. *Punjaub* was then converted into a sailing ship and renamed *The Tweed*.

Basil Lubbock, in his book *The Log of the Cutty Sark*, states that Willis, after appointing Hercules Linton to design the ship that would become *Cutty Sark*, took Linton to see *The Tweed* in dry-dock. As a result, *Cutty Sark* was given the same design of bow as *The Tweed*, if not something of her hull lines as well. At first sight, the plans of *Punjaub/The Tweed*, with a beautifully curving stem, seem quite unlike *Cutty Sark*, with her straight stem and uniquely sharp forefoot. But recently a close comparison was made by Alan Platt and Bob Sexton, which revealed that despite the differences in the sizes of the two vessels, and allowing for the differently shaped stems, they share the same shape in the forward quarter of the hull. (Curiously, Lubbock's papers, now at the National Maritime Museum at Greenwich, include an interview with Linton's partner, William Scott-Moncrieff, which records him saying he had never heard *The Tweed* mentioned during the time of *Cutty Sark*'s contract and construction.)

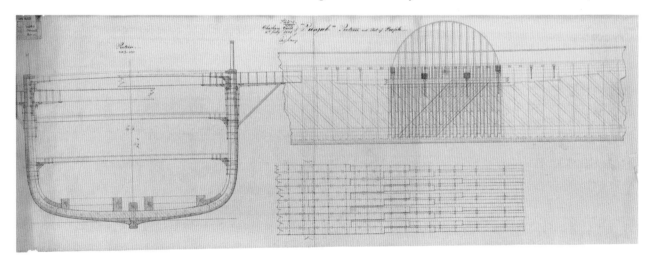

Construction

Before *Cutty Sark*, Willis had never ordered a vessel from a Clyde shipyard. By 1868, however, almost all new ships for the China trade were being built using composite construction, and the Clyde shipyards were producing more composite-built tea clippers than anywhere else in the country.

Robert Steele & Co. of Greenock and Alexander Stephen & Co. of Glasgow were the most prolific of the Clyde builders. Yet instead of choosing one of these two, or even one of the more minor yards, Willis selected a firm that had been in

The triumph of steam

The sail, as well as being one of mankind's greatest inventions, was also one of the earliest. Evidence of sails has been found from around 5000BC, which, presumably coincidentally, is about the same time as the wheeled vehicle is known to have existed. The sail evolved relatively little – a seaman in ancient Egypt would have understood the principles of *Cutty Sark*'s rig; vessels simply increased in size, more sails were added and their shapes refined. But relatively suddenly, after seven millennia of this slow evolution, the sailing ship was displaced by the steamer as the primary military and commercial vessel. However, this displacement was not achieved without something of a struggle.

From their simple prototypes in the early 1800s, largely restricted to plying canals, steam vessels developed rapidly and by 1818 they were in use in the Mediterranean. Twenty years later, a regular transatlantic steamship service was in operation. But their early engines were relatively inefficient, requiring huge quantities of coal. When, in 1838, the paddle steamer *Sirius* (despite a four-day head start) narrowly beat Isambard Kingdom Brunel's *Great Western* across the Atlantic she famously had to burn cabin furniture, spare yards and even a mast to keep her boilers going.

But all that changed between 1850 and 1870 when several technological breakthroughs were made, including the introduction of the compound engine (later developed into the triple-expansion engine), super-heaters and forced-draught boilers. The construction of boilers also improved and they could now work at higher pressures. Equally importantly, the screw propeller was conclusively proved to be more efficient than paddle wheels

CANAL of SUEZ. - TUSSUN curve.

where manoeuvrability was not an issue. These innovations greatly reduced coal consumption and, consequently, the number of stokers required, so costs fell and the profitability of steam rose.

This profitability was given a further boost by the opening of the Suez Canal in 1869, which saw the number of steamers in the British fleet rise from 17 per cent of total registered tonnage in that year to 31 per cent in 1874.

It is perhaps something of a misnomer to describe these new vessels as 'steamers'. They all carried masts and sails. Even Brunel's massive *Great Eastern*, launched in 1858, whose bunkers could hold enough coal to reach Australia and get back without refuelling, was also designed to carry sails on six masts. It would be almost the end of the nineteenth century before 'auxiliary sail' was finally abandoned: the mid-century steamers could and did take advantage of the winds when favourable; but they also

had the means to continue under power only when it was not. In either case, journey times could be cut by staggering amounts. *Sirius*' transatlantic voyage from Cork to New York (essentially a publicity stunt, given that she was designed as a small Irish Sea packet and was fairly soon back in that role) took just over 18 days: a sailing ship at the time might take 40.

The steamers' advance was slightly hampered by the time taken to establish stations for coaling and fresh water (for the boilers) around the world. These included Aden (a British possession since 1836 at the southern end of the Red Sea), Singapore and Hong Kong. Moreover, there was no more efficient way of transporting coal than by sailing ship, which did not consume any. Furthermore, the improvement to the steam engines encouraged owners to build larger and larger ships, and it took time to construct quays big enough to receive them. Yet still the sailing ship had more capacity in

SAILING SHIP ROUTE - - - ->   SUEZ CANAL ROUTE - - - ->

LONDON

SHANGHAI

SUEZ

respect to its tonnage: none was taken up accommodating engines and bunkers.

The sailing ships perhaps owed their final unexpected resurgence to an international economic downturn, the so-called Long Depression of 1874. There was suddenly too much shipping capacity and freight rates fell. As a result, some steamers even had their engines removed and became sail-only. The durability of the sailing ship was also helped by a certain class of owner – individuals like John Willis, who had built their shipping companies based on their own experience as captains. Mature men by this time, these owners understood wind and tide, not boiler pressures and coal-consumption statistics.

There may also have been an innate conservatism among certain merchants, particularly those in the China tea trade, and a prejudice against the new technology (as there had been against iron ships). But more important to the merchants was the fact that sailing ships had lower freight rates than the steamers. However, there was also another class of ship-owner: the strict businessman with no direct personal experience of the sea who wanted the most profitable means of transport – and that was proving to be the steamship. In the same year that *Cutty Sark* was launched, the Ocean Steam Ship Company's *Agamemnon* brought over 2.5 million pounds (1,100 tonnes) of tea from Hankou after only 77 days at sea: this was twice as much as *Cutty Sark* ever carried and 32 days more quickly.

Cutty Sark was one of the last sailing ships loading tea in the late 1870s. Most of her contemporaries had left to find other bulk cargoes like wool. The steamers had not yet entered this trade in significant numbers, although they would soon do so. The few clippers that by then survived were forced to

look for cargoes of such low value that they would not attract competition, and did not need the steamers' exclusive advantage of running to predictable voyage timetables.

It was for this very purpose that ships powered only by sail continued to be built. The era of the clipper had passed and the next and final evolution in commercial sail were the huge four-masted barques, the so-called 'windjammers', half as long again as *Cutty Sark*. This type of vessel began to appear in the mid-1870s and continued to be built into the very early 1900s. Whereas the clippers had been designed for speed and to carry high-value cargoes, these barques were true bulk carriers for low-value freights, usually from small, remote ports where coal and water were limited. Their vast holds were often filled with grain from Australia or guano (seabird droppings mined as a source of nitrates, mainly for fertiliser and explosives) from South America. Their numbers dwindled over the years but some continued to trade well into the twentieth century. Although Eric Newby's entertaining account of his 1938–39 Australian voyage in the *Moshulu* is titled The Last Grain Race, this is misleading: the final year in which these large ships sailed commercially was 1949.

Several examples of these barques survive, scattered and lovingly preserved around the world, including *Moshulu* in Philadelphia, the three-masted *Glenlee* in Glasgow, *Passat* in Travemünde (north Germany), *Pommern* at Mariehamn in the Åland Islands (Finland) and *Falls of Clyde* in Honolulu. It is another tribute to the quality of Scottish shipbuilders that, of these, only the Hamburg-built *Passat* was not launched on the Clyde. That all still exist is equally a tribute to the enduring appeal of the sailing ship. Of the Victorian merchant steamers that drove clippers out of the tea and wool trades, not one has been preserved.

Fig. 15 Sailing ships still had to make the long journey around Africa, around the Cape of Good Hope, whereas steamships could enjoy a shorter and more direct route through the Suez Canal.

business for less than a year and had launched only a single vessel – and that was a steamship. The firm was Scott & Linton.

Hercules Linton was born in 1836 at Inverbervie, a coastal town in north-east Scotland, 25 miles to the south of Aberdeen. He was the son of Alexander Linton, who later became a surveyor for Lloyd's Register of Shipping. Although no clipper ship is credited to Hercules except *Cutty Sark*, he would have been familiar with the requirement of a ship for the China tea trade. He was apprenticed from 1st January 1855 until 1860 to the Aberdeen shipbuilders Alexander Hall & Sons. During his time there, the firm built eight vessels for the China trade (see Table 7).

In 1862 Linton joined the Liverpool Underwriters' Registry for Iron Vessels (a rival to Lloyd's Register) as one of their surveyors on the east coast – an area stretching from Hull to Kirkaldy. It included the busy shipyards of Sunderland where a number of composite ships for the tea trade were built (see Table 8), although it is not known if Linton actually surveyed them.

As well as surveying, Linton found time to undertake some private design work. He drew up the plans for at least one iron screw steamer, *Lady Alice Kenlis*, a vessel 130 feet (40 metres) in length that was launched in December 1867 by Swan of Maryhill. Three months later, he entered into partnership with William Dundas

Fig. 16 Hercules Linton (1836–1900), designer of *Cutty Sark*.

TABLE 7
Alexander Hall & Sons' ships for the China trade, 1856–60

SHIP	YEAR OF LAUNCH
Friar Tuck	1855
Sea Star	1855
Robin Hood	1856
Ziba	1858
Chaa-sze	1860
Flying Spur	1860
Ocean Mail	1860
Pegasus	1860

TABLE 8
Composite ships for the China trade built in Sunderland, 1863–68

SHIP	YEAR OF LAUNCH	SHIPBUILDER
Pak Wan	1863	George Peverall
Coral Nymph	1864	William Pile
Lennox Castle	1865	G.S. Moore & Co.
Maitland	1865	William Pile
Cleta	1866	Gardner
Elmstone	1866	Moore
Jungfrau	1867	Doxford
Undine	1867	William Pile
Lucia	1868	Blumer

Fig. 17 Original profile and plan for *Cutty Sark*, by John Rennie. Rennie was chief draughtsman for Scott & Linton who built the ship. The plan shows the original configuration of *Cutty Sark*, with a single deckhouse and accommodation in the fo'c's'le.

Scott-Moncrieff, a talented and energetic engineer and the firm of Scott & Linton was established.

It began by renting part of a site called the Woodyard, owned by the shipbuilders William Denny & Bros, at Dumbarton, on the lower part of the River Leven, for £200 a year (see page 27). However, by April 1869, to cope with the orders on its books, the firm was renting the whole site and, in total, had contracts to build nine vessels (see Table 9).

The agreement to build the new ship that would become *Cutty Sark* was signed by Scott & Linton on 29th January 1869 and by John Willis & Son in London on 1st February. She was to be built under the supervision of a surveyor appointed by

TABLE 9
Vessels built by Scott & Linton
(from Brettle, 1969)

NAME	TYPE	OWNER	PRICE	LAUNCH	NOTE
Camel	steamship	J. Bibby & Co.	£980	October 1868	
Jura	steamship	A. McKechnie	£1,275	24th May 1869	
[Unknown]	twin screw tug	A. Leslie	£620	7th April 1869	
[Unknown]	composite twin screw steamer				Sent to Japan in pieces
Snowdon	paddle steamer	W.R. Preston & Co.	£2,700	16th April 1869	
Giao	paddle steamer	Donna Maria	£2,225	9th June 1869	Destined for the Amazon
Invereshie	iron sailing ship	I. & K. Grant	£10,700	6th November 1869	East India trade – wrecked at Madras 1872
Cutty Sark	composite sailing ship	J. Willis	£16,150	22nd November 1869	China trade
Linn Fern	composite sailing three-masted schooner		£2,475	18th January 1870	South American trade

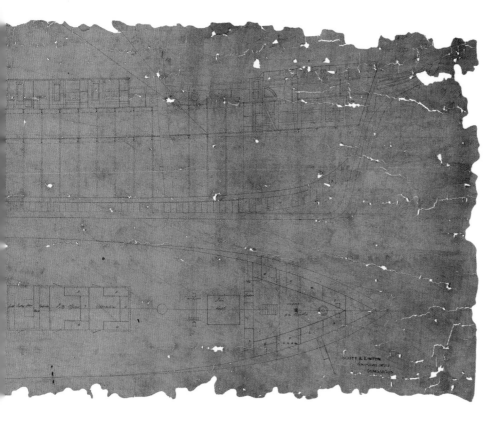

Willis (he chose Captain George Moodie, assisted by Henry Henderson, later to be the ship's first master and carpenter respectively) who was entitled to examine the vessel, materials and workmanship, and progress of the work, but without taking away any of Scott & Linton's responsibilities. The vessel was to be completed by 30th July 1869: if it failed to deliver on time for any other reasons than delays caused by agreed alterations or shipyard strikes, Scott & Linton was to pay £5 a day.

For the ship, Willis would pay £17 a ton but only up to a maximum of 950 tons. The price of the ship was therefore £16,150, to be paid in eight instalments:

£500 on execution of the agreement
£1,500 when the keel was laid and the stem- and stern-posts properly in place
£2,000 when the vessel was in frame and the beams riveted
£1,000 when the vessel was ready for planking
£2,500 when the vessel was caulked, coppered and ready for launching
£2,500 when the vessel was launched

The balance of £6,150 – 38 per cent of the price – would only be paid on completion of the ship 'with sails bent and compasses adjusted' to the satisfaction of Willis' surveyor.

It was a hard bargain. Not only would £17 a ton be difficult to achieve but the schedule of payments would give the young company huge problems with cash flow. Willis must have been aware that Scott & Linton were running a risk of bankruptcy and presumably he took measures to ensure his investment was protected.

The specification for *Cutty Sark* has been preserved by Dumbarton Public Library and is reproduced in full in Appendix A. It details everything Scott & Linton was expected to supply, right down to the ivory-handled dessert knives. It also reveals that the ship was quite well armed with at least one carriage-mounted gun, six muskets (with bayonets), six pistols and 12 cutlasses. These were partly to defend the ship against pirates who, although *Cutty Sark* never encountered any, were a persistent

Fig. 18 William Dundas Scott-Moncrieff (1846–1924), partner of Hercules Linton of Scott & Linton, builders of *Cutty Sark*.

Fig. 19 John Rennie (1842–1918), chief draughtsman at Scott & Linton, builders of *Cutty Sark*.

problem in the South China Sea. The only occasions on which weapons are known to have been broken out was to enforce discipline among the crew.

Exactly how Linton, or any other nineteenth-century ship designer, set about designing a ship has never been fully documented. Fred Walker, the historian of shipbuilding on the Clyde and a naval architect himself, suggested the following: like most naval architects, and particularly one who had been a surveyor, Linton would have built up a collection of ship plans and would be aware of the hull characteristics of the record-breaking ships (both British and American). He would be able to define optimum dimensions for a ship that could achieve disparate requirements: maximum speed for a high-value cargo and enough capacity for a sufficient quantity of cargo, but without so great a draught as to hamper crossing the sandbars at the mouths of the Yangtze and Min rivers. It is possible that he started with a few preliminary drawings, followed by some early calculations, and then made a half-block model.

Half-models were a widely used design tool. They were made either of a solid block of timber, or from a number of boards – often of inexpensive pine – fixed together, one on top of the other, and then carefully shaped to the desired form of one side of the ship. It would probably be a small model, perhaps a couple of feet long (which would give a convenient scale of 1: 96, ⅛th inch to the foot), and otherwise very simple. Such models were nevertheless an excellent way of checking the 'fairness' of the lines – the smooth transition of the complex shape of a vessel. Four half-block models of Linton's survive but, sadly, not one of *Cutty Sark*. On two models made in the 1870s, Linton carefully applied strips of wood over the model to give the appearance of a planked vessel – which suggests how highly he valued them, firstly as a tool and secondly as objects of beauty.

With the model finished, the transverse shape at each of a number of regularly spaced points would be taken and transferred to paper. This would allow the final lines plan and body plan to be drawn up. These shapes would be to the inside of planking – they would determine the shape of the frames. (Modern practice, by contrast, is to draw lines plans to the outside of planking or plating, because hydrostatic calculations and tank testing play such an important role.) The lines plan, body plan and the sail plan were drawn up by Chief Draughtsman John Rennie, later to become the Naval Constructor and Instructor for the Chinese government in Shanghai.

Linton would have been aware of a form of tank testing: this technique had been used at Alexander Hall's yard. A scale-model hull was pulled across a pool of

water in a glass-walled tank about 10 feet (3 metres) long. The water was covered with about 2 inches (50 millimetres) of red turpentine so that the naval architect could see the turbulence created. However, there is no evidence that Linton used this technique himself, although his time at Hall's would have given him a good awareness of the complexity of hydrodynamics and the basics of hull configuration. (The world's first commercial testing tank was opened in 1882 by Denny, almost next door to Scott & Linton's old yard.)

According to Lubbock, the model was shown to Lloyd's surveyors Harry Cornish and Bernard Waymouth (designer of the successful Aberdeen-built composite clipper *Thermopylae*) who were allegedly shocked by the knife-like 'entrance' (bow), which they thought would restrict the ship's power, but the design was approved by Willis. Unlike *The Tweed*, and every clipper ship in China trade, *Cutty Sark* has a completely straight stem-post (which meets the keel at a sharp angle), not rounded to the least degree.

Cutty Sark's keel was probably laid in February 1869. She was built under special survey and classed A1 at Lloyd's for 16 years. The First Entry Report was signed by W.T. Mumford and Alexander Linton – Hercules' father.

However, the surveyors do not appear to have been completely convinced by Linton's designs and they insisted that additional bilge plates ($10 \times 5/8$th inches from bulkhead to bulkhead) were fitted, as well as five additional beams at the fore-end and four at the aft, to prevent 'panting' (planking moving in and out in a rough sea). This was not accepted by Linton without a struggle and it led to a serious delay. This in turn delayed payments from Willis. The promised completion date in July was missed and by late August the company was in difficulties. In the first week of September work in the yard was partially suspended. Scott & Linton's creditors now took over the three ships on the stocks – *Invereshie, Linn Fern* and *Cutty Sark* – and were forced to complete the vessels themselves. According to his biographer, Robert Brettle, Hercules Linton always held the view that William Denny & Bros had played a significant role in the downfall of Scott & Linton.

Cutty Sark was finally launched on 22nd November 1869. A small note appeared in the *Dumbarton Herald* three days later:

On Monday afternoon there was launched from the shipbuilding yard of Messrs Scott & Linton, a handsome composite clipper ship of the following

Following pages:
Fig. 21 *Cutty Sark*'s Certificate of Registry and reverse, 1869. This was issued a week before the ship's maiden voyage. The document details the vessel's name, number, specification and ownership.

Fig. 20 *Cutty Sark* on the stocks (left) during construction in Dumbarton in 1869, by Hercules Linton.

CERTIFICATE OF BRITISH REGISTRY.

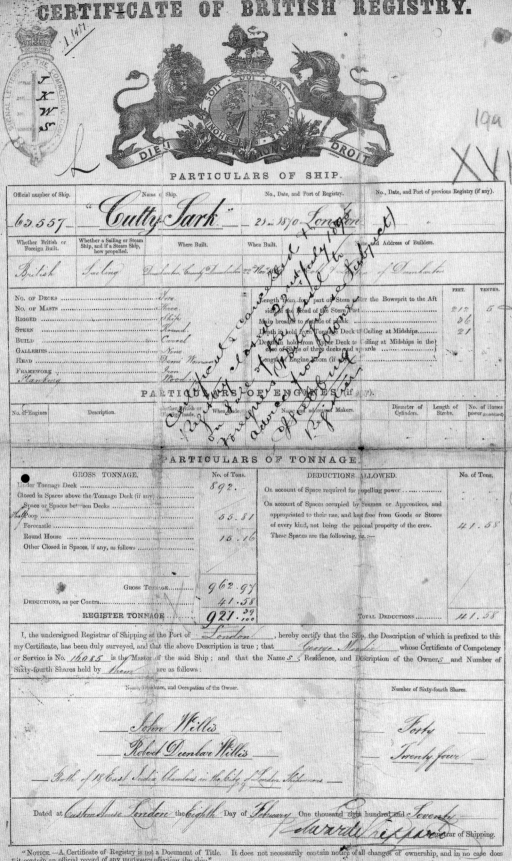

PARTICULARS OF SHIP.

Official number of Ship.	Name of Ship.	No., Date, and Port of Registry.	No., Date, and Port of previous Registry (if any).
62,557	"Cutty Sark"	25. 1870 London	

Whether British or Foreign Built.	Whether a Sailing or Steam Ship, and if a Steam Ship, how propelled.	Where Built.	When Built.	Name and Address of Builders.
British	Sailing	Dumbarton, County of Dumbarton	22 Nov. 1869	Scott & Linton of Dumbarton

					FEET.	TENTHS.
NO. OF DECKS	Two	Length from fore part of Stem under the Bowsprit to the Aft side of the Head of the Stern Post			212	5
NO. OF MASTS	Three	Main breadth to outside of plank			36	
RIGGED	Ship	Depth in hold from Tonnage Deck to Ceiling at Midships			21	
STERN	Round	Depth in hold from Upper Deck to Ceiling at Midships in the case of Ships of three decks and upwards				
BUILD	Carvel	Length of Engine Room (if any)				
GALLERIES	None					
HEAD	Demi Woman					
FRAMEWORK	Iron					
Planking	Wood					

PARTICULARS OF ENGINES (if any).

No. of Engines	Description.	Whether British or Foreign made.	When Made.	Name and address of Makers.	Diameter of Cylinders.	Length of Stroke.	No. of Horses power (combined)

PARTICULARS OF TONNAGE.

GROSS TONNAGE.	No. of Tons.	DEDUCTIONS ALLOWED.	No. of Tons.
Under Tonnage Deck	892	On account of Space required for propelling power	
Closed in Spaces above the Tonnage Deck (if any)		On account of Spaces occupied by Seamen or Apprentices, and appropriated to their use, and kept free from Goods or Stores of every kind, not being the personal property of the crew. These Spaces are the following, viz.:—	41.58
Space or Spaces between Decks			
Half Poop	55.81		
Forecastle			
Round House	15.16		
Other Closed in Spaces, if any, as follows			
GROSS TONNAGE	962.97		
DEDUCTIONS, as per Contra	41.58		
REGISTER TONNAGE	921.39	TOTAL DEDUCTIONS	41.58

I, the undersigned Registrar of Shipping at the Port of London, hereby certify that the Ship, the Description of which is prefixed to this my Certificate, has been duly surveyed, and that the above Description is true; that George Moodie whose Certificate of Competency or Service is No. 16085 is the Master of the said Ship; and that the Name s, Residence, and Description of the Owner s and Number of Sixty-fourth Shares held by them are as follows:

Name, Residence, and Occupation of the Owner.	Number of Sixty-fourth Shares.
John Willis	Forty
Robert Dunbar Willis	Twenty four
Both of 18 East India Chambers in the City of London, Merchants	

Dated at Custom House London the Eighth Day of February One thousand eight hundred and Seventy

Edward Shepard, Registrar of Shipping.

Custom House written 6 Novr 1872 I hereby
certify that Francis William Miller's certificate 23947
now granted — Willm McPher
Custom House London 4 November 1873. I hereby certify that William
Miller's certificate No 23886 is now granted. — Geo Kivon for Registrar

I hereby certify that Registered owner whose certificate of competency
No. 26960 (5b of 5) has this day been appointed Master in the
of William Prince — Geo Lyon for Registrar
British Consulate General
New York April 25th 18
Master

Custom House London 17 March 1896 — William Prosper Clayton
Geo 89125 is own Master — Geo Lyon for Registrar

H. M. Customs London — I hereby certify that, on the 8th day of Feb
1895, John Richards of 37 Winnghton Road, Balham, County of Lond
Gentleman, is registered Sole Owner of the Vessel within described
— Registrar of Shipping
Port of Lond

£ 9 1 4

dimensions: —length, 210 feet; beam, 36 feet; depth of hold, 20 feet 9 inches, and about 250 tons burthen. As she left the ways she was named the "Cutty Sark" by Mrs Moody [sic], wife of Captain Moody. The Cutty Sark is intended for the China tea trade, and is expected by her owners to be one of the fastest ships engaged in that traffic.

The ship was moved to Denny's wet dock on the Leven for masting and then towed to Greenock on 20th December for her running rigging to be set up. She left Scotland on 13th January 1870. Two weeks later, she was taking on her first cargo in London's East India Docks.

The ship was registered on 8th February 1870, giving her the official number 63557. Ownership of a vessel was, and remains to this day, divided into 64 shares: the Certificate of Registry records the division between John Willis (40) and his brother Robert (24).

On 12th April 1870 (when *Cutty Sark* was rounding the Cape of Good Hope – her log position for that day was 43°35′S 31°50′E), an auction was held at the Woodyard of all the machinery and tools of Scott & Linton. Everything sold, including Linton's models and drawings, almost certainly many relating to *Cutty Sark*.

It remains something of a mystery why Willis chose 'Cutty Sark' as the name for his new ship. It was not unique to the clipper. David MacGregor in *The Tea Clippers* mentions a Siamese barque with this name trading between Hong Kong and Bangkok at the end of the 1860s. There was a *Cutty Sark* yacht on the Thames in the 1870s, and racehorses in the 1840s and 1870s also bore the name.

Most of the Willis vessels were named after rivers or towns around the Eyemouth area from which the family hailed, after family members, or ports with which they traded. *Hallowe'en* and *Cutty Sark* are the exceptions.

The phrase 'cutty sark' comes from Robert Burns' narrative poem *Tam O'Shanter*, first published in 1791. It tells us that the end of every market day in Ayr finds Tam O'Shanter drunk and relates the story of what happens when he rides his faithful horse, Maggie, home after dark.

Tam rides the few miles to Alloway but is suddenly surprised to see lights shining from the church. Curious, he urges Maggie forward for a closer look. Peering through a window he sees that the church altar has been desecrated and the building is full of warlocks and witches dancing to a tune played on the bagpipes by the Devil himself.

The witches are all repulsive old hags, except one – Nannie, a young beauty cavorting in a 'cutty sark', a short shift:

> There was ae winsome wench and walie, […]
> Her cutty-sark o' Paisley harn,
> That while a lassie she had worn,
> In longitude tho' sorely scanty,
> It was her best, and she was vauntie.—

Tam, overwhelmed by the sight of Nannie in her revealing outfit, cannot help but cry out:

> 'Weel done, cutty-sark!'

Fig. 22 Hercules Linton's sketch for *Cutty Sark*'s figurehead.

The witches and warlocks now spot Tam and a wild chase begins, with Nannie at the head of the pursuers. Tam urges Maggie to race for the Alloway bridge because he knows that witches cannot cross running water. Just as they reach the bridge's keystone, Nannie manages to grab Maggie's tail but horse and rider press on and escape, leaving Maggie's tail in Nannie's hand.

It is not surprising that a patriotic Scotsman-in-exile like John Willis should take a name for his ship from the writings of his country's greatest poet. That said, the reason why he chose to name the vessel after the undergarment of a witch, a creature unable to cross water, will never be known.

The ship's figurehead is Nannie, the witch in the poem (carved, according to Basil Lubbock, not in Scotland – nor by 'Allan' as the specification stated – but in Blackwall by Frederick Hellyer, 1821–1906, one of a then very well-known family of ship-carvers), dressed in a 'cutty sark' with her arm outstretched. One of the duties of the ship's apprentices, whenever she was in port, was to place a wad of unpicked rope in her hand to represent poor Maggie's tail. When first carved, the figurehead was in line with Burns' concept of Nannie as a beautiful young woman. Sadly, the original Nannie was lost during *Cutty Sark*'s eventful career at sea – though there are conflicting reports as to precisely when this occurred and whether more than one figurehead was lost over her time afloat. The current head resembles rather more a hag than a pretty girl. It is thought that this replacement was copied in the 1950s for the replica figurehead now attached to the ship.

Linton's designs for the stern decoration of the ship show Tam on Maggie on one side of a dancing Nannie, and the Devil playing the bagpipes on the other. Writing in the 1920s, just after the ship had been recovered and moored in Falmouth, C. Neapean

Longridge stated: '… the design of the original carving is irretrievably lost, but was said to have shocked our Victorian ancestors.' It is not certain that Linton's scheme was ever realised. Clearly, the restorers of the 1920s did not believe so. Similarly, it is thought that Linton's original designs were only rediscovered after the work of the 1950s carvers was complete. At the time of writing, the condition of the replica Nannie is due to be assessed. Depending on the outcome, an entirely new Nannie may be required. Should this be the case, Linton's original designs will be called upon.

Another stern decoration that Linton designed, which has been preserved on *Cutty Sark* today, included the dreadful pun, 'Where there's a Willis a way'. Below it, although not part of Linton's scheme, was the emblem of the Most Exalted Order of the Star of India. This was probably copied, or perhaps even taken, from Willis' favourite ship, *The Tweed*, when she had been the Indian Marine's *Punjaub*.

The order has no known connection with Willis – it was established in 1861 by Queen Victoria to reward conspicuous merit and loyalty and was mainly awarded to maharajas and senior military officers working in India – but the Order's motto, which forms part of the decoration, could not be more fitting for any ship navigating by the sun and the stars: 'Heaven's light our guide.'

With all her sails flying, *Cutty Sark* carried nearly 32,300 square feet (3,000 square metres) of canvas. Like most sailing ships of the time, to save labour, she carried a lower and an upper topsail rather than a single huge topsail, on all three masts. Above

the upper topgallant, each mast carried a royal, and above this on the main mast was a single skysail. Apart from the courses (the lowest or main sails on each mast), the spanker (the fore-and-aft sail on the mizzen mast) and the skysail, all other sails were said to be of the same size and thus interchangeable.

Although all masts except the lower foremast have been replaced (a process which began after the 1916 dismasting) and her deck equipment was reconstructed in the 1950s, the ship still retains the original steering mechanism linking the wheel with the rudder. It demonstrates the increased influence of engineers in ship design. The steering wheel is fixed to a very large screw. One half of the screw has a left-handed thread, on which there is a nut. This nut is linked by a connecting rod to the starboard end of the cross-head which is fixed to the top of the rudder. On the other half of the screw, which has a right-handed thread, another nut is linked by a rod to the port side of the cross-head. When the wheel is turned to starboard, the two nuts move apart, the starboard rod pushing its end of the crosshead forward, the port rod pulling its end back, turning the rudder. When the wheel is turned to port, the two nuts move towards each other – the port rod now pushing, and the starboard rod pulling – and the rudder moves in the opposite direction. It is an ingenious system, taking no space within the ship, unlike the tiller system of earlier large vessels.

Tam O'Shanter by Robert Burns

When chapmen billies leave the street,
And drouthy neebors neebors meet,
As market-days are wearing late,
And folk begin to tak the gate;
While we sit bousing at the nappy,
And gettin fou, and unco happy,
We think na on the long Scots miles,
The waters, mosies, slaps and styles,
That lie between us and our hame,
Where sits our sulky, sullen dame,
Gathering her brows, like gathering storm
Nursing her wrath to keep it warm.

This truth fand honest Tam o'Shanter,
As he frae Ayr ae night did canter;
(Auld Ayr, whom ne'er a town surpasses
For honest men and bonnie lasses.)

O Tam ! hadst thou but been sae wise
As taen thy ain wife Kate's advice !
She tauld thee weel, thou was a skellum,
A bletherin, blusterin, drunken blellum;
That frae November till October,
Ae market-day thou was na sober:
That ilka melder, wi' the miller,
Thou sat as long as thou had siller
That every naig was ca'd a shoe on,
The smith and thee gat roarin fou on:
That at the L—d's house, even on Sunday,
Thou drank wi' Kirkton Jean till Monday.
She prophesied that, late or soon,
Thou wad be found deep-drown'd in Doon;
Or catch'd wi' warlocks in the mirk
By Aloway's old haunted kirk.

Ah, gentle dames! it gars me greet,
To think how mony counsels sweet,
How mony lengthen'd sage advices,
The husband frae the wife despises!

But to our tale : —Ae market-night,
Tam had got planted unco right,

Fast by an ingle bleezing finely,
Wi' reamin swats that drank divinely;
And at his elbow, souter Johnie,
His ancient, trusty, drouthy cronie;
Tam lo'ed him like a vera brither,
They had been fou for weeks tegither. —
The night drave on wi' sangs and clatter,
And ay the ale was growing better:
The landlady and Tam grew gracious,
With favours secret, sweet, and precious;
The souter tauld his queerest stories;
The landlord's laugh was ready chorus:
The storm without might rair and rustle,
Tam did na mind the storm a whistle. —
Care, mad to see a man sae happy,
E'en drown'd himself amang the nappy:
As bees flee hame, wi' lades o' treasure,
The minutes wing'd their way wi' pleasure:
Kings may be blest, but Tam was glorious;
O'er a' the ills o' life victorious!

But pleasures are like poppies spread,
You sieze the flower, its bloom is shed;
Or like the snow falls in the river,
A moment white—then melts for ever;
Or like the borealis race,
That flit ere you can point their place;
Or like the rainbow's lovely form,
Evanishing amid the storm. —
Nae man can tether time or tide,
The hour approaches Tam maun ride;
That hour o' night's black arch the kcy
   stane,
That dreary hour he mounts his beast in;
And sic a night he takes the road in
 As ne'er poor sinner was abroad in.

The wind blew, as 'twad blawn its last;
The rattling showers rose on the blast;
The speedy gleams the darkness swallow'd,
Loud, deep, and lang, the thunder
   bellow'd;

That night a child might understand
The deil had business on his hand,
   Weel mounted on his grey meere, Meg,
A better never lifted leg,
Tam skelpit on thro' dub and mire,
Despising wind, and rain, and fire
Whyles holding fast his gude blue bonnet;
Whyles crooning o'er an auld Scots
   sonnet;
Whyles glowring round wi' prudent cares,
Lest bogles catch him unawares;
Kirk-Alloway was drawing nigh,
Where ghaists and houlets nightly cry.

By this time he was cross the ford,
Where in the snaw the chapman smoor'd;
And past the bilks and meikle stane,
Where drunken Charlie brak's neck-bane;
And thro' the whins, and by the cairn,
Where hunters fand the murder'd bairn;
And near the tree, aboon the well,
Where Mungo's mither hang'd hersel:
Before him, Doon pours all his floods;
The doubling storm roars thro' the woods;
The lightnings flash from pole to pole!
Near, and more near, the thunders roll;
When, glimmering thro' groaning trees,
Kirk-Aloway seem'd in a bleeze;
Thro' ilka bore the beams were glancing,
And loud resounded mirth and dancing.

Inspiring, bold John Barleycorn!
What dangers thou canst make us scorn:
Wi' tippeny, we fear nae evil;
Wi' usquebae, we'll face the devil!
The swats sae ream'd in Tammie's noddle,
Fair-play, he car'd na deils a boddle:
But Maggy stood, right fair astonish'd,
Till by the heel and hand admonish'd,
She ventur'd forward on the light,
And, wow ! Tam saw an unco sight!

Warlocks and witches in a dance,
Nae cotillon brent new frae France,
But hornpipes, jigs, strathspeys and reels,
Put life and mettle in their heels. —
A winnock-bunter in the East,
There fat auld Nick in shape o' beast;
A towzie tyke, black, grim, and large;
To gie them music was his charge :
He screw'd the pipes and gart them skirl,
Till roof and rafters a' did dirl. —
Coffins stood round, like open presses,
That shaw'd the dead in their last dresses;
And (by some deevilish cantraip slight)
Each in its cauld hand held a light;
By which heroic Tam was able
To note upon the haly table,
A murderer's banes, in gibbet-airns;
Twa-span-lang, wee, unchristen'd bairns;
A thief, new cutted frae a rape,
Wi' his last gasp his gab did gape;
Five tomahawks, wi' blood red-rusted;
Five scymitars, wi' murder crusted;
A garter which a babe had strangled;
A knife a father's throat had mangled,
Whom his ain son of life bereft,
The grey hairs yet stak to the heft:
Wi' mair of horrible and awefu',
That even to name wad be unlawfu';
Three lawyers' tongues, turn'd inside out,
Wi' lies seem'd like a beggar's clout;
Three priest's hearts, rotten, black as muck,
Lay stinking, vile, in every neuk.

As Tammie glowr'd, amaz'd and curious,
The mirth and fun grew fast and furious:
The piper loud and louder blew;
The dancers quick, and quicker flew;
They reel'd, they set, they cross'd , they
    cleekit,
Till ilka Carlin swat and reekit,
And coost her duddies on the wark,
And linket at it in her sark.—

Now Tam! O Tam! had thae been queans,
A' plump and strappin in their teens!
Their sarks, instead o' creeshie flainen,
Been snaw-white, seventeen-hunder linen;
Thir breeks o' mine, my only pair,
That ance were plush o' gude blue hair,
I wad hae gien them off my hurdies
For ae blink o' the bonie burdies!
But withered beldams, auld and droll,
Rigwoodie hags wad spean a foal,
Loupin and slingin on a crumock,
I wonder did na turn thy stomach. —

But Tam kend what was what fu' brawlie;
There was ae winsome wench and walie,
That night enlisted in the core,
(Lang after kend on Carrick shore;
For mony a beast to dead she shot,
And perish'd mony a bonnie boat,
And shook baith meikle corn and bear
And kept the country-side in fear) —
Her cutty-sark o' Paisley harn,
That while a lassie she had worn,
In longitude tho' sorely scanty,
It was her best, and she was vauntie.—
Ah! little thought thy reverend graunie,
That sark she coft for her wee Nannie
Wi' twa pund Scots ('twas a' her riches)
Should ever grac'd a dance o' witches!

But here my Muse her wing maun cour,
Sic flights are far beyond her power;
To sing how Nannie lap and flang,
(A souple jad she was and strang,)
And how Tam stood like ane bewitch'd,
And thought his very een enrich'd ;
Even Satan glowr'd, and fidg'd sa' fain,
And hotch'd, and blew wi' might and
    main;
Till first ae caper— syne anither —
Tam lost his reason a' thegither,
And roars out—"Weel done, cutty-sark!"

And in an instant all was dark:
And scarcely had he Maggie rallied,
When the hellish legion out sallied.

As bees bizz out wi' angry fyke,
When plundering herds assail their byke;
As open pussie's mortal foes,
When, pop, she starts before their nose
As eager rins the market-croud,
When "catch the thief !" resounds aloud;
So Maggy rins, the witches follow,
Wi' mony an eldrich shout and hollo. —

Ah Tam ! ah Tam ! thou'll get thy fairin!
In hell they'll roast thee like a herrin!
In vain thy Kate awaits thy comin,
Kate soon will be a woefu' woman!!!
Now, do thy speedy utmost, Meg!
And win the key-stane o' the brig;
There at them thou thy tail may toss,
A running stream they dare na cross!
But ere the key-stane she could make,
The fient a tail she had to shake;
For Nannie, far before the rest,
Hard upon noble Maggy prest,
And flew at Tam with furious ettle,
But little kend she Maggy's mettle!
Ae spring brought off her master hale,
But left behind her ain gray tail:
The carlin claught her by the rump,
And left poor Maggy scarce a stump.

Now wha this Tale o' truth shall read,
Ilk man and mother's son, take heed:
Whene'er to drink you are inclin'd',
Or cutty-sarks rin in your mind,
Think, ye may buy the joys o'er dear;
Remember TAM O' SHANTER'S
    MEARE!

Tam O'Shanter is considered by many to be Burns' finest poem. Based on an old folk tale, the catalyst that transformed it from story to verse was an Englishman, Captain Francis Grose. He was a jovial antiquarian who had published *Antiquities of England and Wales* in six volumes between 1773 and 1789 and, on their completion, turned his attention to Scotland. During his researches there he met Burns, who was much taken with the little fat man – 'O' stature short, but genius bright' – and it was the poet's suggestion that a drawing of the ruins of Alloway church be included in Grose's new book. The antiquarian agreed, on condition that Burns provided a witches' tale to go with it. Burns replied in a letter of June 1790 that he could remember only three about the church, which he then related: the second gives the essence of the Tam O'Shanter story. However, in this version the farmer is not named and the witch's 'sark' is described as 'short' rather than 'cutty'. Very soon afterwards, Burns had developed the tale

into the celebrated narrative poem and the version reproduced here appeared in Grose's posthumously published second volume of *The Antiquities of Scotland* in 1798, with the following note to accompany the illustration of the church ruins:

> [Alloway] church is also famous for being the place wherein the witches and warlocks used to hold their infernal meetings, or sabbaths, and prepare their magical unctions; here too they used to amuse themselves with dancing to the pipes of the muckle-horned Deel. Diverse stories of these horrid rites are still current; one of which my worthy friend Mr. Burns has here favoured me with in verse.

The poem was, however, first published earlier, in the March 1791 edition of the *Edinburgh Magazine*, a few weeks before Grose died while researching the antiquities of Ireland.

The American academic Douglas Short suggests that *Tam O'Shanter* may not have been Burns' first poem involving a short sark. He proposes that Burns was the author of the bawdy poem 'Daniel Macleese' (itself a retelling of the folksong *Tam o' the Linn*) where the consequences of being dressed in a sark, given to the wearer when she was considerably smaller, are made very explicitly.

Fig. 23 *Tam O'Shanter pursued by Nannie*, unknown artist. A depiction of Robert Burns' epic poem, *Tam O'Shanter*. Farmer Tam is chased by Nannie the witch, who wears a 'cutty sark', the inspiration for the ship's name.

Previous pages:
Fig. 24 Sailmaker mending canvas on board *Cutty Sark*, by Captain Woodget, 1880s.

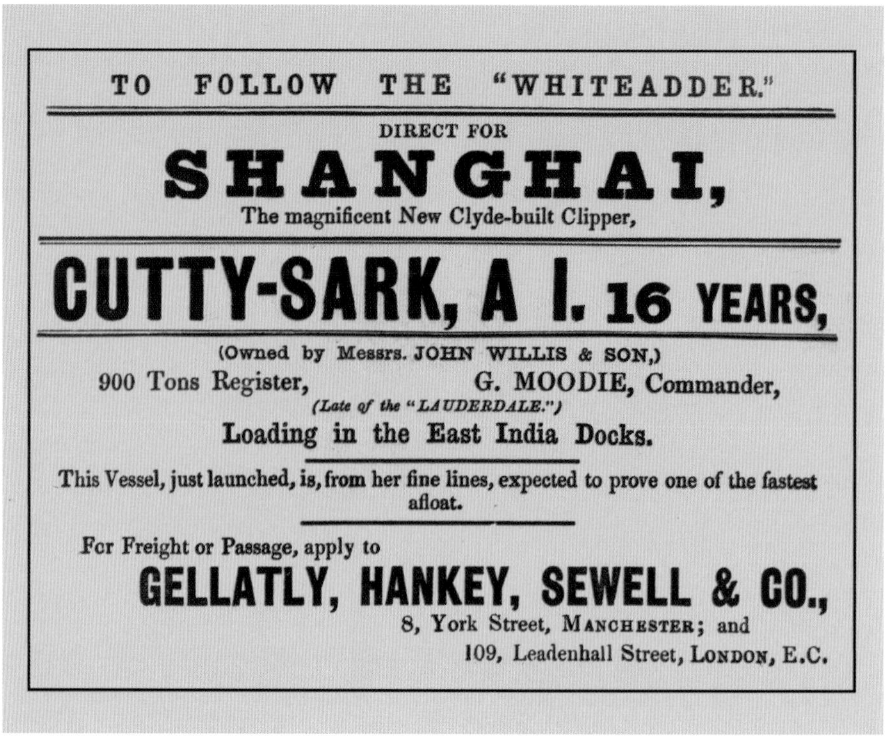

Fig. 25 Advert for *Cutty Sark*'s maiden voyage in 1870 to Shanghai. This advertisement promotes her A1 classification from Lloyd's and demonstrates John Willis' high expectations of his new ship.

> TO FOLLOW THE "WHITEADDER."
>
> DIRECT FOR
>
> # SHANGHAI,
>
> The magnificent New Clyde-built Clipper,
>
> # CUTTY-SARK, A I. 16 YEARS,
>
> (Owned by Messrs. JOHN WILLIS & SON,)
>
> 900 Tons Register, G. MOODIE, Commander,
>
> *(Late of the "LAUDERDALE.")*
>
> Loading in the East India Docks.
>
> This Vessel, just launched, is, from her fine lines, expected to prove one of the fastest afloat.
>
> For Freight or Passage, apply to
>
> # GELLATLY, HANKEY, SEWELL & CO.,
>
> 8, York Street, MANCHESTER; and
>
> 109, Leadenhall Street, LONDON, E.C.

The Tea Voyages

Around midnight on 15th February 1870, *Cutty Sark* left London on her maiden voyage, under Captain Moodie, with a general cargo – including large amounts of wine, spirits and beer – in her hold. Once beyond the English Channel, she headed towards the Canary Islands then almost across the Atlantic, turning south-east, into the South Atlantic, going as far as 44°25′S to pick up the Roaring Forties to whisk her round the Cape of Good Hope. She then turned north-eastwards, heading for the narrow Sunda Strait. Anchoring off Anjer, a town on the western tip of Java, mail for home was dropped off, then *Cutty Sark* entered the South China Sea, sailing to the east of Borneo then to the west of Taiwan. Finally, on 31st May, after three and a half months at sea, she reached Shanghai.

Fig. 26 Shanghai, China, by John Thomson, 1871. It was here that *Cutty Sark* loaded her early tea cargoes.

Compared to some of the later voyages, when many weeks were spent looking for a cargo, *Cutty Sark* spent just 25 days in China, although the actual loading took only two or three days. On her first voyages, the cargo was nearly 600 tons, enough to make some one hundred and fifty million cups of tea.

Skilled Chinese stevedores made use of every available inch of the hold, carefully arranging 10,335 chests, 1,790 half-chests, 621 boxes and 2,256 packages (as well as six tea boxes for Captain Moodie), and using pebbles to ensure a tight fit against the sides of the ship so that it would not shift in even the highest seas. Bamboo matting covered with canvas made sure that the tea was kept dry if water seeped through from the main deck. Records have been destroyed that would have told us exactly which types of tea *Cutty Sark* carried, but they were probably predominantly black varieties. Bohea, Souchong and Pekoe were popular at the time, along with 'Congou', a general word for black tea. Among the green teas, favourites with the British were Hyson, Gunpowder (so-called because its leaves are rolled like pellets) and Twankay, a cheap variety of tea, which gave its name (first recorded in 1861) to the mother of the pantomime hero Aladdin.

Fig. 27 Xie (Alexandra) Kitchin as a Chinese tea merchant, *c.* 1876. Taken by Charles Lutwidge Dodgson, better known as Lewis Carroll, at his studio in Oxford. The photograph shows how ornately the tea chests were decorated.

The freight charge was £3. 10s. a ton, which would have given Willis a gross profit of over £2,000, or around £152,000 in today's values. But, assuming a London price of 2s. 6d a pound for 'fine tea', the retail value of the cargo would have been around £90,000 – over £6 million today.

She was the first ship to get away from Shanghai that year but she was not the first ship away from China: both *Taeping* and *Deerhound* had left Guangzhou earlier in June. *Titania*, which had loaded at Hankou, had crossed the sandbar at Boashan (then Wusong) seven days before.

Nevertheless, the crew was confident enough to bet the crew of *Serica* – one of the last wooden clippers built on the Clyde – £20 that they would reach London first. Before she reached Anjer again (hugging the coast of China much more closely than on the voyage out), the first death on board occurred when Able Seaman Fisher succumbed to dysentery. Once past Anjer, *Cutty Sark* picked up the trade winds to take her almost straight across the Indian Ocean to Madagascar. Then, hugging the

Fig. 28 Unloading tea ships in the East India docks. *Cutty Sark* unloaded her tea cargoes here, two miles downriver from her current berth in Greenwich. On each voyage she brought around 600 tons of tea from China.

South African coastline, she entered the Atlantic once more and on 13th October she was back in London's East India Docks, 110 days out from China. This was a good performance (enough to beat *Serica*, which came in 11 days later) and she maintained her position in fourth place overall, but she did not make the fastest passage that year from Shanghai: both *Thermopylae* and *Undine* were five days faster.

After just 23 days in London, *Cutty Sark* was off again. Even though Moodie chose a slightly longer route, passing Timor rather than Anjer, he shaved 16 days off the time of his previous voyage. However, arriving in February was well before the first tea crop was available, so Moodie filled in the time with a little 'tramping'. He sailed down to Hong Kong, then onto Bangkok where he picked up a rice cargo, which he took back to Hong Kong. Returning to Shanghai, he then sailed back down the coast to Fuzhou for a cargo of poles, to take back to Shanghai. The tea was now ready but the freight being offered (£3 for 50 cubic feet) was so bad that *Cutty Sark*'s agents, Jardine Matheson & Co., sent the ship back to Fuzhou again. The prospect was no better there and the ship went back to Shanghai yet again and loaded at the £3 rate. When she reached London, again 110 days later, the *Cutty Sark* had been away for more than 13 months.

Her next departure from China was on 17th June 1872. Just behind her was Aberdeen White Star Line's *Thermopylae*, built just a year before *Cutty Sark* and already attracting attention as one of the fastest clippers. Her previous two homeward voyages had taken 105 and 103 days: there was now a unique opportunity to compare their performances in exactly the same weather conditions.

Leaving Shanghai, *Cutty Sark* crossed the Boashan sandbar first, but with *Thermopylae* close behind her. *Thermopylae* was spotted nine days later when the two ships reached Hong Kong. *Cutty Sark* managed to pull ahead, but stopped at Anjer to pick up mail while *Thermopylae* sailed on. However, once in the Indian Ocean, *Cutty Sark* not only caught up her rival but was 400 miles ahead by the time she neared the South African coast.

Tea from China

Long ago (around 2737BC) and far away in China, the 'father of Chinese medicine' Shen Nung (who was also the emperor) was suffering after having sampled one too many of his herbal experiments. He was about to cure himself with some plain boiled water when a few leaves from a nearby tree fell in. When he tried the slightly bitter liquid, he began to feel better and realised that he had discovered a restorative drink.

The leaves were from a *Camellia sinensis* tree, the single species native to the southern half of China. All teas come from this species, although almost 260 varieties are now cultivated in China alone. The bush grows in hot and very wet climates (it needs rainfall of at least 60 inches, about 150 centimetres, a year) and at altitudes up to 8,200 feet (2,500 metres). It is happiest on hillsides in acidic soils. Tea is harvested three times a year, with the spring harvest producing the highest quality. As they have been for millennia, the bushes are plucked by hand, with only a new bud and the top two leaves being picked.

China produces three principal types of tea: green, black and oolong, the difference between them being the degree of fermentation of the leaves. For green tea, the leaves are heated to dry them quickly, to minimise fermentation; they are then rolled and dried ('white tea' is processed in the same way but dried more quickly). For black tea, the leaves are first withered on racks to remove moisture; they are then rolled to release the enzymes which give the flavour, before being left to ferment. Finally, they are dried. In the case of one of the most famous black teas from China, Lapsang Souchong, the heat for both withering and drying is provided by pinewood fires that give its distinctive smoky taste. Oolong tea is half-way between green and black: it is only partially fermented; the makers interrupt the natural wilting to dry and roll the leaves.

Green tea has always been the most popular in China; black tea is usually only drunk in winter or if one is unwell. Originally, tea was taken as a soup; only during the Han dynasty (206BC–AD220) did it become a beverage. Heavily taxed and in limited supply, tea was only drunk at court. However, during the Southern and Northern Dynasties period (AD420–589), Buddhist monks recognised tea's stimulating qualities and began to cultivate it around their temples. As a result, propagation and growing methods improved and new varieties emerged. At this time, tea was moulded into blocks, or bricks, for transport, which were later heated to break them up. The leaves were then pounded and added to boiling water along with salt, spices and onions – a method of preparation still found in Tibet, which has been importing tea from almost a thousand miles away since the sixth century AD.

During the Tang dynasty (618–907), the first tea-houses appeared and the drinking process became more sophisticated. In 780, the great poet-philosopher, Lu Yu, completed his book *Cha Ching* (*The Classic of Tea*), the result of 20 years' study of the drink's origin, history, cultivation, preparation and consumption.

The production of loose tea – not in block form – began during the Song

Fig. 29 *Camellia sinensis*, the tea plant. All teas come from this species, although almost 260 varieties are grown in China alone.

TEA.

THEA SINENSIS.

Tea from China cont.

Fig. 30 A painting set in Guangzhou, by an unknown Chinese artist, 1790–1820, depicts the entire tea production process, from picking the tea, to drying the leaves and finally packing the tea into chests. The chests are loaded onto sampans to be taken up river to the waiting Western ships.

Fig. 31 Tea production in China, *c.* 1885. Finished black tea is packed into chests ready for shipping.

Fig. 32 Tea production in China, *c.* 1885. Porters carry the beautifully decorated tea chests to the ports for shipping.

CUTTY SARK: THE LAST OF THE TEA CLIPPERS

Fig. 33 Catherine of Braganza, by or after Dirk Stoop, *c.* 1660–61. Catherine, the Portuguese wife of Charles II, made drinking tea fashionable in Britain after she married the king in 1662.

dynasty (960–1279) when yet more, cheaper and more simply made varieties emerged. At the same time, the tea drunk by the court became even more refined – pounded to a powder and whisked in hot water to a delicate froth, a style still drunk in Japan in the *chanoyu* ('hot water for tea') ceremony.

Under the Ming dynasty (1368–1644) the manufacture of tea blocks ended and loose tea production expanded. Tea was no longer whisked but infused: kettles and teapots suddenly began to appear.

The first reference to tea that reached the West was in the book *Relations of India and China*, written by the Arab merchant Suleiman al-Tajir in 851, but it would take another 700 years before tea itself reached Europe. The Jesuit priest Jasper de Cruz was the first European to write about tea in 1560, 17 years before the Portuguese were allowed to establish a trading port at Macao. From there, tea was shipped to Lisbon, where it quickly became highly fashionable. The Dutch followed shortly afterwards: the *VOC – Vereenigde Oost-Indische Compagnie* (the Dutch East India Company) – delivered its first tea cargo to Amsterdam in 1606.

Tea did not reach Britain until the mid-seventeenth century. The first advertisement for it in England appeared in 1658. Two years later, Samuel Pepys, a man always ready to try new things, recorded in his diary on 25th September 1660: 'I did send for a cup of tee (a China drink) of which I never had drank before...'.

Although Pepys probably drank tea imported from the Netherlands, it was a Portuguese princess who made tea drinking popular among the British aristocracy. In 1662 Charles II married Catherine of Braganza. Her dowry included a chest of tea (as well as the

territories of Tangier and Bombay). Catherine's influence on tea drinking in England was recorded in a poem in honour of her birthday, written by Edmund Waller in 1663.

Venus her Myrtle, Phoebus has his bays;
Tea both excels, which she vouchsafes
   to praise.
The best of Queens, the best of herbs,
   we owe
To that bold nation which the way did
   show
To the fair region where the sun doth rise,
Whose rich productions we so justly prize.
The Muse's friend, tea does our fancy aid,
Regress those vapours which the head
   invade,
And keep the palace of the soul serene,
Fit on her birthday to salute the Queen.

With tea rising in popularity, the British government banned Dutch tea imports and gave the home monopoly to the British East India Company (founded in 1600), which unloaded its first tea consignment in 1669. However, 'banning' was not the same as 'stopping'. As the demand for tea expanded so did its smuggling, principally from the Netherlands. This became so widespread that it is thought at least as much tea reached Britain illegally as was unloaded by East Indiamen (the ships of the East India Company), possibly more.

Tea's growth in popularity was given an early boost by the coffee-houses, which were emerging in the late 1600s. London's first tea-room, Tom's Tea Cabin, was opened by Thomas Twining in 1706 and – unlike the coffee-houses – it admitted women.

Tea from China cont.

The supply of tea was more reliable than that of coffee (from Ethiopia or the Ottoman Empire), even though China was not part of the nascent British Empire. It none the less remained very expensive, not least because it was heavily taxed: even in 1689 a pound (0.45 kilogrammes) of tea cost the equivalent of a worker's weekly wage. Ironically, it was smuggling that brought the cost down. This was proving such a threat to the East India Company's monopoly that in 1784 the government introduced the Commutation Act, slashing the tax on tea from 119 per cent to 12½ per cent: smuggling of it disappeared and consumption began an exponential increase.

Tea was big business and sharp practices emerged. In 1818 more than 20 London grocers were convicted of selling tea adulterated with ash and blackthorn leaves, and re-dried old leaves. Even the Chinese were found to be adulterating tea leaves with cyanide and gypsum to make the green leaves look greener. This has been suggested as one reason why black tea became the more popular form, well before its cultivation began in India as a 'British imperial' crop. Other reasons probably include the fact that (as in anything consumed primarily for pleasure) tastes tend to settle where widest affordability, availability and acceptability meet in the middling- to lower-standard ranges, which are usually simpler and/or stronger than the subtle, limited and most expensive premium crop.

TABLE 10 **Tea Imports into Britain** *(weight in pounds)*

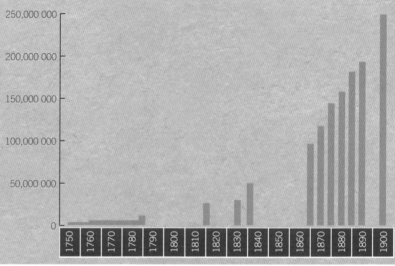

Fig. 34 Two gossiping women taking tea, by S. Jenner, *c.* 1850. By the time Cutty Sark was trading in tea, 30,000 tons of it entered Britain each year and, thanks to the low tax on tea, it was affordable to almost everyone.

Then disaster struck: *Cutty Sark* was hit by such a heavy sea that the rudder broke away. By chance, John Willis' brother Robert (who owned 24/64ths of the ship) was on board. He demanded that Moodie make for Port Elizabeth, the nearest harbour, but Moodie refused, perhaps knowing that Port Elizabeth did not have the facilities for a quick repair. Even though the ship could no longer be steered properly and the sea remained rough, the ship's carpenter, Henry Henderson, set about making a jury (temporary) rudder. A makeshift forge was set up on the main deck to make fashion the fittings. Moodie's son, Alexander, an apprentice on board, later recalled:

> It was fortunate the two stowaways [found earlier on the voyage] were of some use, the English one was a carpenter and the Scotch one was a blacksmith. I was at the forge, and a lovely time I had of it, to keep it upright. I failed once – a heavy roll and I found myself against the after house with the forge on my bosom. I had to outshirt [sic] to get quit of the red hot cinders – I have the marks of them yet. The blacksmith was holding on to the bar, the water took the feet from him and he sailed away past the end of the house, holding the red hot bar as far away as possible, and just escaped the sailmaker's face who was sitting on the doorstep. To my surprise the blacksmith wanted to know why I did not save the fire. I told him I was just in as much of a hurry to get the fire off my chest as he was to keep the red hot bar off his nose.

Nevertheless, after five days, they succeeded in hanging the rudder. This was an amazing feat considering the lowest fixing was 15 feet (5 metres) below the water but, by this time, *Thermopylae* was 500 miles ahead. The repair to *Cutty Sark* was also not perfect and she lost even more time in the South Atlantic.

Fig. 35 *Thermopylao,* by F.I. Soroncon, late eighteenth century. *Cutty Sark* raced her great rival *Thermopylae* from China on just one occasion in 1872.

Thermopylae reached London after 115 days at sea and *Cutty Sark* came in nine days later. Despite this, it was the demonstration of seamanship by *Cutty Sark*'s captain and crew, rather than *Thermopylae*'s victory, that would be remembered. Willis, uncharacteristically, gave £50 to Henderson as a reward for saving his ship, and his ingenuity became a model used by the Board of Trade as an example of how to rig a jury rudder. Moodie, however, was so furious with Robert Willis' behaviour that he immediately resigned and went to work on steamships.

It was around this time that a second deckhouse was added to the main deck. The original arrangement accommodated the petty officers in a deckhouse forward of the main mast and the seamen in 22 berths in the fo'c's'le (although stamped onto a beam is the wording 'Certified to accommodate 20 seamen'). For some reason – possibly the difficulty of getting all hands on deck quickly (as the only way out was up a single ladder) – another deckhouse was added, aft of the mainmast. The apprentices and petty officers were moved into it, leaving the forward deckhouse for the seamen. The galley and carpenter's workshop remained where they were. It also meant that the vacated fo'c's'le was free for additional cargo, and the fact that the figure '921' stamped on a beam under the main hatch to denote her net tonnage was over-stamped with the figure '938' may mark this change of use. However, some seamen had their bunks in the fo'c's'le in 1880, and it may be that it was never completely vacated.

Captain Moodie's replacement was the shore superintendent for the Willis fleet, Francis Moore. He had retired from the sea but had already been persuaded by John Willis to captain *Blackadder* on a single voyage, and now agreed to do the same for *Cutty Sark*.

This voyage was not directly to China but via Australia, to discharge a general cargo. Perhaps typically, not all of it arrived. This included a bale of corn sacks, delivered short; and brandy, four bottles of wine and champagne, pillaged. Even sardines disappeared.

The ship's arrival in Melbourne was noted by the local paper, *The Age*, on 13th February 1873:

> The China tea clipper *Cutty Sark* made her first appearance in Australian
> waters yesterday, but she has not maintained the reputation for swiftness
> which she earned when trading between the China ports and London.
> This is, however, attributable to the baffling and contrary winds which she
> experienced during several portions of her voyage out. She is, however, a
> powerful looking ship, and, like most of the tea ships, looks much larger in the
> water than she really is. […] Of the voyage out Captain Moore reports that he
> left London on the 26th of November, but did not clear Start Point until 4th
> of December. After this, strong westerly winds were experienced for nine days,
> so that but little progress was made. A slant of wind from N.N.E., however,
> carried her as far as the Cape of Verde Islands, when strong N.E. trades were
> met with, and carried to 4.30 deg. North, when light variable winds and calms
> were experienced for a period of four days, The equator was crossed on 23rd
> December in long 28.31 deg. west. The S.E. trades were very scant, being S.S.E.
> for the first eight days, after which southerly breezes lasted until the meridian
> of Greenwich was passed, which was on the 18th of January in lat. 47 S.

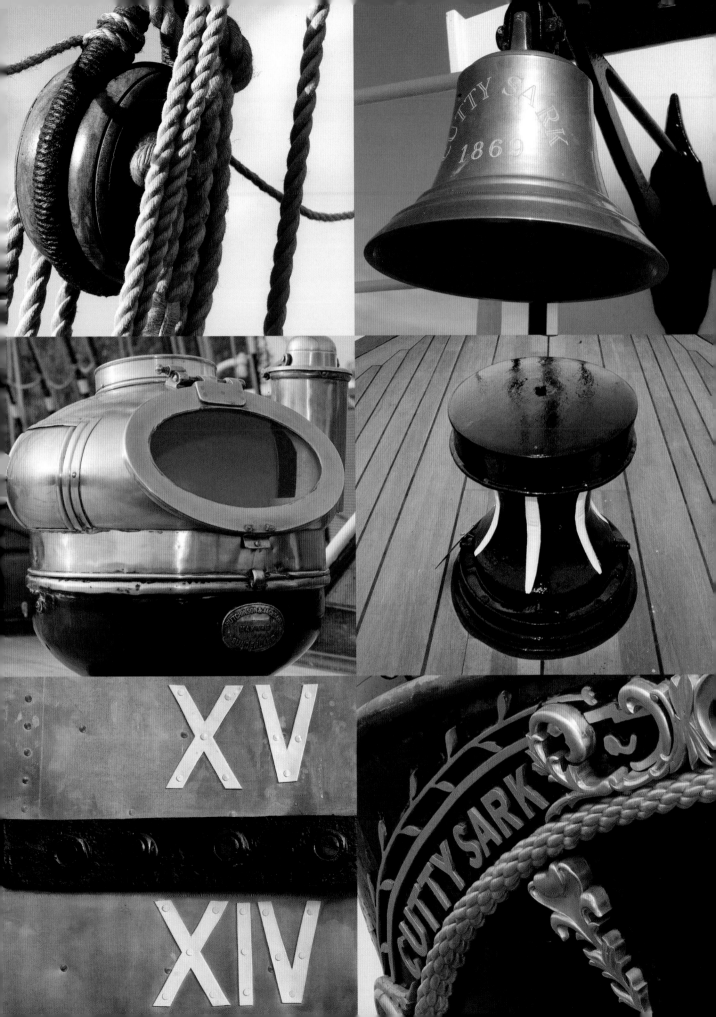

The easting was run down between the 46th and 47th parallels of south lat., moderate winds from the westward being experienced to the coast. The greatest day's work logged was 320 miles. The *Cutty Sark* will, in all probability, discharge at the Sandringle Railway Pier.

In Australia she picked up 1,200 tons of coal to take to Shanghai for the steamers and this pattern of collecting coal from Australia for China was to be repeated on all the subsequent outward tea voyages. It certainly made the outward voyages more profitable, but it led to a problem: desertions. Men were engaged to work the ship all the way to China and back to London – that constituted a voyage – but many jumped ship, particularly in Sydney. The prospect of a free passage to a land in the middle of a gold rush was too tempting. In 1876 for example, 12 of the 16 able seamen deserted. It was an issue faced by all the ships calling at Australian ports and consequently there was a great demand for seamen in Australia. In turn, this meant that they commanded higher rates of pay than those who had signed on in London, which caused some resentment.

Cutty Sark's return from China that year was disappointing; just two days less than Moodie had taken, with a broken rudder to contend with, the previous year.

Moore was allowed to retire again and the ship's next master was William Edward Tiptaft, a Scot from the same area as the Willis family. After discharging his Sydney coal in Shanghai, he took *Cutty Sark* up the Yangtze to Hankou for the first time. Even though she made the homeward passage in 119 days, including several under tow down the river, it was still the best time for three years.

The ship's departure in 1875 was delayed by a collision at Gravesend with another vessel, *Somersetshire*, which cost *Cutty Sark* an anchor, a substantial length of chain and her main topgallant mast, and a return to London for repairs. Finally under way, Able Seaman William Hart was lost overboard before the ship cleared the Isle of Wight. However, once in the open seas the ship set a new record of 2,163 nautical miles in six days.

Fig. 37 Hankou. This was the great tea port of China, several hundred miles up the Yangtze River. *Cutty Sark* loaded tea here every year between 1874 and 1877.

Returning to London at the end of September 1876, she was, for the first time, the first ship home with the season's tea.

She was again first home in 1877, leaving Hankou with 1.3 million pounds (600,000 kilogrammes) of tea. But this was the last cargo of Chinese tea she would carry.

On 3rd November 1877, *Cutty Sark* sailed from London just in time to catch that year's great winter gale. She anchored in the Downs (off the east Kent coast) on the 8th. During the storms that blew on the 10th and 11th, she lost both anchors and their cables, and twice collided with other vessels. So heavily damaged was she that she had to be rescued by two tugs. She arrived back in London on 16th November and by 2nd December she was fully repaired and ready to depart, arriving in Sydney on 13th February 1878. *The Sydney Morning Herald* of the 18th noted her arrival.

Among the splendid fleet of vessels sailing out of the port of London, and more especially to the colonies, the clipper *Cutty Sark* is one of the foremost, particularly as regards speed. While employed in the China trade she placed her name on more than one occasion in the premier rank, and she still would appear to be keeping up her prestige, judging from her passage just completed from the Channel, and this, too, not under the most happy circumstances of wind. She has arrived in first-class order… With respect to her present passage, Captain Tiptaft, who retains command of this fine craft, reports as follows…[,…] left the dock again on the 2nd of December, landed pilot at Dartmouth on the 5th and took a final departure from the Lizard on the 6th. From there to latitude 37 S had variable winds, principally between N. and the S.E. The N.E. trades were favourable, and the Island of Bonavista

TABLE 11 *Cutty Sark*'s tea voyages

LEFT LONDON	ARRIVED		DAYS	DAYS IN CHINA	TEA LOADED (pounds/ kilogrammes)	DEPARTED	ARRIVED LONDON	DAYS	TOTAL VOYAGE	NOTE	DAYS BEFORE NEXT VOYAGE
15/02/1870	Shanghai	31/05/1870	105	25	1,305,812 592,306	25/06/1870	13/10/1870	110	240		23
05/11/1870	Shanghai	02/02/1871	89	212	1,315,000 596,474	02/09/1871	21/12/1871	110	411	arrived early / made trips to Bangkok, Hong Kong and Fuzhou	44
03/02/1872	Shanghai	28/05/1872	115	20	1,303,000 591,031	17/06/1872	19/10/1872	124	259	homeward - lost rudder off South Africa	38
26/11/1872	Shanghai	12/05/1873	167	53	1,353,072 613,743	04/07/1873	03/11/1873	122	342	outward via Melbourne/ Sydney	31
04/12/1873	Hankou	19/05/1874	166	36	1,270,651 576,358	24/06/1874	21/10/1874	119	321	outward via Sydney	20
10/11/1874	Hankou	14/04/1875	155	68	1,347,699 611,306	21/06/1875	22/10/1875	123	346	outward via Sydney	34
25/11/1875	Hankou	23/04/1876	150	47	1,375,364 623,855	09/06/1876	26/09/1876	109	306	outward via Sydney	25
21/10/1876	Hankou	18/03/1877	148	80	1,334,000 605,092	02/06/1877	11/10/1877	127	355	outward via Sydney	23

(Cape Verd) was sighted on the 19th; had light variable winds from 3 N and crossed the Equator on December 28th in longitude 26 W. The S.E. trades were favourable, though high, and Trinidad was sighted on January 6th, passed the meridian of Greenwich January 13th in latitude 1 S., and ran the easting down in 46 S. with moderate winds from N.. to N.W., accompanied by a deal of thick weather and heavy rain; rounded the South Cape (Tasmania) February 13th, and from there to port had moderate S.E. winds. This vessel has made the crack passage of the season viz. 72 days.

From Sydney, she sailed on to Hankou, arriving in May, where Tiptaft could find only enough tea to fill half the ship's hold. He returned to Shanghai but was unable to find any more, so decided to sail to Nagasaki for a coal cargo, hoping to find more tea on his return. Tiptaft then fell ill and, on the same day that *Cutty Sark* returned to Shanghai, he died.

The difficulty Tiptaft had in securing a tea cargo was not because of a lack of tea being produced or delivered to the tea ports, but because of competition from steamships. From the early 1860s, steamers had competed with the clippers for tea cargoes but, possibly because so much of their hull space was devoted to coal bunkers, owners of the sailing ships, like John Willis, did not view them as a serious threat. However, as the steamers' engines became more efficient they began to make voyages just as fast as the sailing clippers.

Then, on 17th November 1869 (five days before *Cutty Sark* was launched), the Suez Canal was opened. This extraordinary feat of engineering, linking the Mediterranean with the Red Sea, cut 3,300 miles off the journey from China to London and 10–12 days off the voyage. A steamship, carrying almost twice as much tea as a sailing clipper, could now reach London in 77 days. This was impossible for sailing ships. The prevailing winds in the Red Sea are from the north-west. At the other end of the Suez Canal, the complicated wind patterns of the Mediterranean made it impractical for them to approach or depart. And the narrow, 102-mile length of the Suez Canal itself had to be traversed by a sailing ship under expensive steam-powered towage. When *Cutty Sark* first arrived in China in 1870, she was one of more than 50 clippers. In Hankou in 1877, she was one of only nine.

However, even if the steamships had not taken over, Chinese tea itself was under threat. The Chinese monopoly on its production was already broken: it was increasingly being imported from countries of the British Empire – India and Sri Lanka (Ceylon) – and British tastes were moving away from the delicate flavours of Chinese tea to robust Assam.

Never again did *Cutty Sark* carry a cargo of Chinese tea and only once more did she carry tea, but this time Indian tea (along with jute, castor oil and mail) on a voyage from Calcutta to Melbourne in 1881.

Tramping

After Captain Tiptaft's death in October 1878, *Cutty Sark* began a short career 'tramping' – travelling from port to port with whatever cargoes could be found – and continued to do so until 1883. The new captain, James Wallace, who had been the ship's first mate, took an empty *Cutty Sark* to Sydney for a coal cargo, which he carried back to Shanghai. She left, again empty, for the Philippines, where she was loaded with jute and set sail for New York.

On her return to London, Willis decided to cut down on the manpower needed for the ship by reducing the size of *Cutty Sark*'s masts and rigging. Nine and a half feet (2.9 metres) were cut off her lower masts and 7 feet (2.1 metres) off her lower yards. All other masts and yards were shortened in proportion. Gone was the skysail on her main mast; gone were her stunsails; but also gone were the wages of about four men.

With a crew of 23, *Cutty Sark* set sail on 13th May 1880 for Penarth, Wales, to load steamer coal. It was destined for the US Navy based at Yokohama, but the ship was never to reach Japan.

On board was a man who had signed on under the name of Sydney Smith, a tough and unpopular first mate so tyrannical that five seamen deserted the ship as soon as she reached Penarth. The replacements Captain Wallace was forced to sign on were far from being fine seamen. They included the Chicago-born John Francis. He had shipped as an able seaman but according to Alexander Jansen, the sailmaker on board, he was actually a cook and steward. All his shipmates agreed that he did not know the work of an able seaman. This attracted the particular wrath of First Mate

Fig. 38 Singapore. *Cutty Sark*'s cargo of Welsh coal, originally destined for the US Navy fleet in Japan, was unloaded at this port in September 1880 following the death of Able Seaman Francis and the suicide of Captain Wallace.

Singapore. Boat Quay.

Sailing *Cutty Sark*

On a particularly calm day in the 1880s, Captain Woodget took a remarkable photograph of *Cutty Sark* with almost all her sails set. She may have had another nine fore-and-aft sails in reserve: the staysails of the topmasts and topgallant masts on the three masts and the main royal staysail.

At that time she would have looked a very modern sailing ship, with her topsails divided into upper and lower. Although ships had carried such an arrangement since the 1850s it was still not common, even on the fast clipper ships. Its advantage was that it needed fewer men to handle the topsails, but many owners still preferred a single large one. (When in harbour, the crews of ships with double topsails lowered the upper-topsail yard close to the lower one, for purely aesthetic reasons. After the 1950s restoration of *Cutty Sark*, the yard was not lowered this way, attracting letters to *The Times*.)

An impressive amount of sail was set on the day that Woodget took the photograph, but it was somewhat less than *Cutty Sark* was originally designed to carry. The sails were smaller than in 1869, probably by at least 3 feet 3 inches (1 metre) in length and depth; the skysail on the main mast was gone and so too were the triangular stunsails that could be stretched from booms on the main and topsail yards. In the 1870s she could have spread over 32,300 square feet (3,000 square metres) of canvas, although it is unlikely that all the sails would ever be in use at the same time. Setting sails was a precise art.

When entering or leaving port, *Cutty Sark* might set no sail at all or perhaps only a lower topsail. London, Shanghai and Hankou are all ports on rivers too narrow for a sailing ship to navigate. Steam paddle tugs guided to and from the sea. It was only when a sailing ship reached open water that any substantial amount of sail would be set.

The fore and aft sails – particularly the jibs at the bow and the spanker at the stern – were often the first to be set and the last to be taken in. Pressure on the sails forward pushes a ship's bow downwind; pressure on the aft sails pushes the bow into the wind. By carefully balancing the sails, the ship holds her course. In good conditions, the usual sequence of unfurling sails was to begin with the lower topsails, followed by the upper topsails, the topgallants, and finally the courses – the main and lowest sail on each

mast. Only if the winds were very light would the royals be set.

The crew's primary role was to adjust the sails' and the yards' controlling ropes to ensure that the sails were kept taut, or slacked off to enable the ship to cross the wind and alter the course. Although useful in manoeuvring the ship across the wind, the ship's rudder was primarily for fine-tuning the course.

If the winds picked up and storms were approaching, the master had to decide how much sail to take in. What distinguished *Cutty Sark*'s greatest masters was their willingness to keep as much sail aloft as the ship could bear in the weather conditions.

The master would plot the ship's position by taking sightings of the sun at noon and other celestial bodies and referring to published tables. Deep sea navigation had been transformed in the previous decade by the work of Lieutenant Matthew Fontaine Maury of the US Navy. Sidelined in the Depot of Charts and Instruments, he discovered a wealth of detail about wind conditions in the ships' logs that had been deposited. Working with a team, he analysed this data and published a series of charts summarising the winds in the world's oceans. It had been known for centuries that the north-easterly winds above the equator and the south-easterly winds were separated by bands of calm, or windless, weather – the doldrums. What Maury discovered was that these bands varied greatly in width, which changed over the seasons. The analysis of logs revealed the existence of a narrow band of westerly wind near the most easterly part of Brazil where it bulges out into the Atlantic. This was of immense help to a sailing ship coming from Britain. Leaving England, they would sail south-west for Brazil, rather than hugging the coast of Africa. Once the sailing ships neared Brazil, they would head south-eastwards for the Cape of Good Hope. Then, if they were headed for China, they would cross the Indian Ocean towards Java; if headed for Australia, the strongest winds in the world, the Roaring Forties, would help them on their way – a part of the voyage known as 'running the easting down'.

Fig. 39 *Cutty Sark*, by Captain Richard Woodget (master, 1885–95), 1888. His apprentices must have taken him out in one of the ship's boats, on a becalmed day, to capture this picture.

GUIDE TO SAILS

1	Fore course	Nearly always set. Very useful in rough seas.
2	Fore lower topsail	All conditions except very rough seas.
3	Fore upper topsail	All conditions except very rough seas.
4	Fore topgallant	All conditions except rough seas.
5	Fore royal	Light weather sail.
6	Main course	Set when the wind is from the side (abeam) or when the ship is sailing as close to the wind as possible.
7	Main lower topsail	All conditions except very rough seas.
8	Main upper topsail	All conditions except very rough seas.
9	Main topgallant	All conditions except rough seas.
10	Main royal	Light weather sail.
11	Crossjack	Rarely used, except in the lightest winds because it takes wind away from the larger main course.
12	Mizzen lower topsail	All conditions except very rough seas.
13	Mizzen upper topsail	All conditions except very rough seas. Very fair weather sail.
14	Mizzen topgallant	All conditions except rough seas.
15	Mizzen royal	Light weather sail.

A	Flying jib	Light weather sail – taken in with the royals.
B	Outer jib	Used to manoeuvre in fair weather.
C	Inner jib	Used to manoeuvre in fair weather.
D	Main topgallant staysail	Set when the wind is from just behind the centre of the ship (abaft the beam) or when the ship is sailing as close to the wind as possible (close hauled).
E	Spanker	Manoeuvring sail.

Smith, who said to him several times, 'Please jump overboard', and on one occasion struck him so hard that Francis bled from his nose and ears and was confined to his bunk for two days.

The night of 10th August was a dark and dreadful one, with rain and a hard-blowing shifting wind. Francis was assigned as look-out on the anchor deck while the crew grappled with the sails. Around 8.45p.m. they were hauling aft the fore sheet when the fore lazy tack became stuck fast. The first mate called out to Francis twice to 'let go the lazy tack'. Getting no response, the entire watch sang out the same request. Francis then did let go the lazy tack, but instead of simply releasing it he let the end fly overboard. The first mate then said, "That son of a bitch has done that out of spite," and storming towards Francis he shouted: "I'll come on that fo'c's'le [head] to heave you overboard you ******, I will." To which Francis replied, "You come on this fo'c's'le to heave me over board, I've got a capstan bar waiting for you here." Smith ran forward, grabbed a broken capstan bar from the top of the windlass under the forecastle, jumped up and struck Francis on the head. The injured man fell from the forecastle to the fore hatch, where he lay in a pool of blood.

Unconscious and still bleeding from the nose and mouth, he was taken down to the 'tween deck and laid on a makeshift bed of old sails, where Captain Wallace himself dressed his wounds. The following morning Francis was moved to his bunk in the forecastle, his wet clothes removed. Smith brought his own blankets to cover him but Francis never opened his eyes again and died about 7.45 that evening.

The following day the sailmaker sewed Francis' body up in canvas and at midday he was buried at sea. Smith was now confined to his cabin but Wallace, up to this point a professional and popular captain, then started to act very strangely. He compelled a number of the men to sign a statement that Smith had acted in self-defence, yet no one saw a bar in Francis' hands and the only bar found was the one picked up by Smith, even though Francis had said to the first mate 'I've got a capstan bar waiting for you here…'. A few weeks later, a couple of days before the ship reached Anjer, the watch was getting the anchor over the bows in preparation. Captain Wallace picked up the broken capstan bar to help… and then dropped it over the side of the ship.

Around 17th August, with the ship anchored off Anjer, Smith said to John Somers, the steward (who delivered meals to him in his cabin confinement), 'I am going at 9 o'clock to-night.'

Somers replied: 'Don't talk that way as I shall have to tell the Captain.'

'You needn't trouble: the Captain has arranged everything.'

And indeed, Smith escaped and boarded the American ship *Colorado*, whose master was said to be in need of such a 'man handler', and was gone.

The incident was the inspiration for Joseph Conrad's tale, *The Secret Sharer* (1910), although the mate in that story is a more sympathetic figure. The real-life Smith changed his name to John Anderson and two years later he sailed into London on board the *Mary Ann Nottebohm*. In the South West India Docks he was recognised – probably by Edward Holdford, who had been *Cutty Sark*'s carpenter in 1880 – arrested and, in August 1882, tried for the wilful murder of John Francis on the High Seas. He was cleared of murder but found guilty of manslaughter. He had said to the sailmaker on *Cutty Sark* just after Francis died: 'I killed one son of bitch before and only got five years to work with a pick axe at guano. I'll get only seven years for manslaughter and

I'll be a young fellow even then…'. His prediction was accurate: the sentence was seven years' penal servitude.

After Smith's escape from *Cutty Sark* in August 1880, the crew were enraged by their captain's complicity and, according to Basil Lubbock, refused to work. Captain Wallace issued arms to his loyal officers and put the four leaders of the crew in irons. This left the sailing of the ship to himself and the second mate, the sailmaker, the carpenter, the cook and four apprentices. But for three days the ship was becalmed.

Wallace must have realised that, at the very least, when they reached Yokohama he would have his master's certificate suspended for helping Smith escape. The forcing of his petty officers to sign a statement would surely come out. He would also have to explain why he had disposed of the capstan bar. His whole career was heading towards disgrace. At 4.00a.m. on 9th September 1880, he was walking backwards and forwards in front of the helmsman, Frederick Clark. A few moments later, Clark heard a splash. Wallace was gone and was never seen again.

With the help of the best navigator among the apprentices, Charles Sankey, *Cutty Sark* turned back to Anjer and a telegram was sent to John Willis in London. An order came back to proceed to Singapore, for which they needed the help of a Dutch pilot.

In Singapore, where an inquiry into the events leading up to Captain Wallace's suicide was held, the coal cargo which had been destined for Yokohama was unloaded, and, as the hold was being emptied (into the bunkers of SS *Glencoe*, one of the tea steamers which had pushed *Cutty Sark* out of the tea trade), the new captain arrived. This was William Bruce, formerly the first mate of Willis' *Hallowe'en*. The master of that ship was pleased to see him promoted out of his ship: Bruce was to prove far from a good choice.

Bruce took *Cutty Sark* in ballast to Calcutta, where she would stay for four months before a cargo could be found. Finally she departed for Melbourne with jute, castor oil, Indian tea and mail. Before she reached Australia Able Seaman William

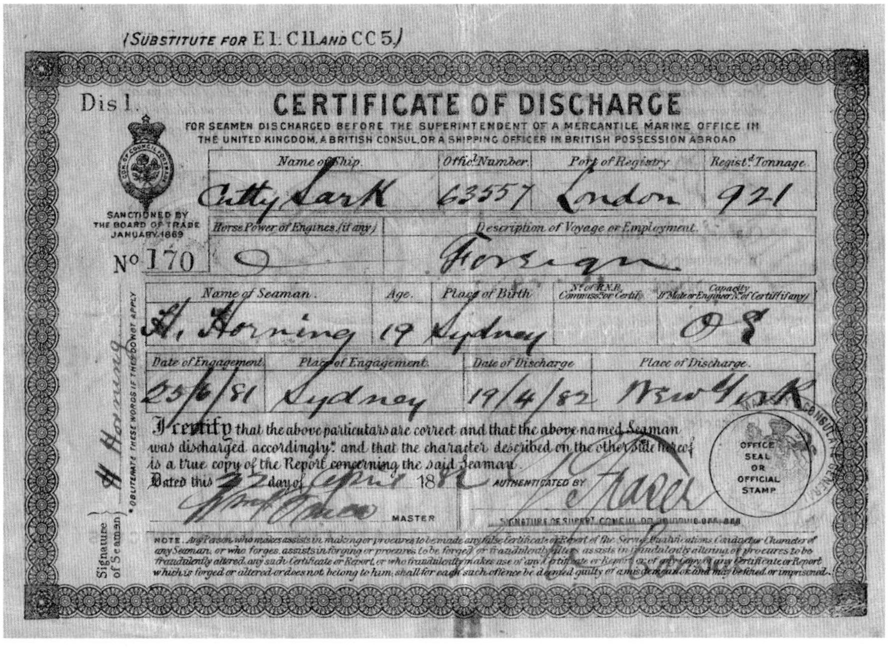

(SUBSTITUTE FOR E1. C11 AND CC5)

Dis 1.

CERTIFICATE OF DISCHARGE

FOR SEAMEN DISCHARGED BEFORE THE SUPERINTENDENT OF A MERCANTILE MARINE OFFICE IN THE UNITED KINGDOM, A BRITISH CONSUL, OR A SHIPPING OFFICER IN BRITISH POSSESSION ABROAD

SANCTIONED BY THE BOARD OF TRADE JANUARY 1869

No 170

Name of Ship.	Offic.l Number.	Port of Registry	Regist.d Tonnage.
Cutty Sark	63557	London	921

Horse Power of Engines (if any)	Description of Voyage or Employment.
O	Foreign

Name of Seaman.	Age.	Place of Birth	No. of R.N.R. Commiss.n or Certif.	Capacity If Mate or Engineer No. of Certif. (if any)
H. Horning	19	Sydney		O S

Date of Engagement.	Place of Engagement.	Date of Discharge	Place of Discharge.
25/6/81	Sydney	19/4/82	New York

I certify that the above particulars are correct and that the above named Seaman was discharged accordingly.* and that the character described on the other side hereof is a true copy of the Report concerning the said Seaman.

Dated this 22 day of April 1882 AUTHENTICATED BY

MASTER SIGNATURE OF SUPERT. CONSUL OR SHIPPING OFFICER

OFFICE SEAL OR OFFICIAL STAMP

Signature of Seaman H Horning

* OBLITERATE THESE WORDS IF THEY DO NOT APPLY

NOTE. Any Person who makes assists in making or procures to be made any false Certificate or Report of the Service Qualifications Conduct or Character of any Seaman, or who forges, assists in forging or procures to be forged, or fraudulently alters, assists in fraudulently altering or procures to be fraudulently altered, any such Certificate or Report, or who fraudulently makes use of any Certificate or Report or of any Copy of any Certificate or Report which is forged or altered or does not belong to him, shall for each such offence be deemed guilty of a misdemeanour and may be fined or imprisoned.

Fig. 40 Certificate of Discharge for Henry Horning. Ordinary Seaman Horning signed on in Sydney on 25th June 1881 and was discharged in New York on 19th April 1882. He joined the ship for the last leg of *Cutty Sark*'s eventful 12th voyage, serving under Captain Bruce.

McGregor was knocked overboard and lost. From Melbourne *Cutty Sark* sailed on to Sydney to pick up a cargo of coal. Charles Sankey later described what the crew got up to in the port:

> …just before leaving the wharf the crew was given a liberty day, which is regulation after a certain amount of time. We went in for a high old time and afterwards had some rare old shindies on board from drunken men. But that was not the worst. Some of the men had caught an infection in some of the low dives frequented on shore.

The infection was not the usual one associated with sailors: it was Asiatic cholera. A yellow flag was raised and the ship was put into quarantine. Three of the crew died and a fourth was discharged sick. Three weeks passed before *Cutty Sark* was declared infection-free but, weakened by the ordeal, the surviving crew refused to get back to work immediately. Enraged, Captain Bruce clapped three men in irons and made his way to the authorities to declare that his crew were mutinous. His plan backfired: the judge not only censured Bruce for his conduct but also ordered that only essential work should be undertaken for another fortnight.

When the ship was finally free to depart, she headed for Cebu in the Philippines for a jute cargo. This she would transport to New York, but one seaman, a German called William Blood, was left behind in a Cebu prison cell for insubordination. This was, perhaps, an indication that relations between the captain and the crew were still bad.

Basil Lubbock tells the story that en route to New York, the ship called in at Anjer to pick up alcohol. This was not cargo; it was to enable Bruce, his first mate (Rutland) and the steward to go on a drinking binge while the ship was at sea. After a near-collision, the crew intervened. After encouraging the master and mate to indulge to a state of unconsciousness, they threw the alcohol overboard.

Then, on 4th February 1882, Able Seaman Dunton was working aloft when heavy blocks fell on him, knocking him overboard. He could not be recovered. As Dunton was one of the costly seamen recruited in Sydney, there was a suspicion (pointing at Bruce and his first mate) that Dunton's death may have been not entirely accidental.

Bruce proved inadequate in even the simplest tasks. He failed to pick up sufficient provisions for the final leg of the voyage, and by the time they reached the South Atlantic all that was left was a little bread full of weevils and some tainted pork. The crew was forced to beg for food, first from a German ship, which donated some very fat smoked pork and cornmeal biscuits, and then from a Royal Navy corvette, HMS *Thalia. Cutty Sark* finally docked in New York, 697 days after she had left London.

In a pre-emptive move, Bruce and First Mate Rutland attempted to take action with the authorities against the second mate, George Rogers. Once again Bruce's strategy backfired. In the subsequent inquiry, the whole story of the voyage came out. John Willis dismissed Bruce and transferred the entire crew of *Blackadder* to *Cutty Sark*, including Captain Frederick Moore (no relation to Francis Moore, *Cutty Sark*'s second master).

Moore – described as a fine seaman, a capable ship's master and a clever navigator but whose first name is unknown – took *Cutty Sark* on her final tramping voyage. Laden with 26,816 gallons (nearly 122,000 litres) of case oil (paraffin) he set sail for Australia, but at Anjer he received an instruction to head for Semarang on

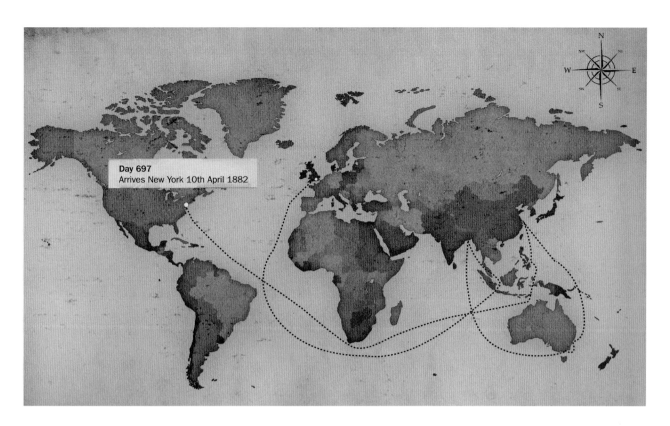

Day 697
Arrives New York 10th April 1882

the island of Java. From there, *Cutty Sark* sailed on to the Coromandel coast of India, calling at Madras (Chennai), Bimlipatnam (Bheemunipatnam) and Kakinada. The ship finally docked in London again on 2nd June 1883, unloading a cargo of 115 bales of deer horns and 4,781 bags of myrobolanes (a plum-like fruit used in dyeing).

Fig. 41 The route of the ship's 12th voyage, lasting 697 days, during which Able Seaman Francis was killed, the culprit Sydney Smith escaped, Captain Wallace committed suicide and the crew almost starved.

TABLE 12 *Cutty Sark*'s tramping voyages

DEPARTED	ON	ARRIVED	ON	DAYS AT SEA	DAYS IN PORT	DEPARTED	ARRIVED	ON	DAYS	DAYS IN PORT
London	02/12/1877	Sydney	17/02/1878	77	24	13/03/78	Shanghai	22/04/1878	40	150
Shanghai	19/09/1878	Nagasaki	26/09/1878	7	13	09/10/78	Shanghai	12/10/1878	3	80
Shanghai	31/12/1878	Sydney	20/02/1879	51	26	18/03/79	Shanghai	02/05/1879	45	41
Shanghai	12/06/1879	Manila	not known			23/09/79	New York	12/01/1880	111	33

Total voyage time 771 days

DEPARTED	ON	ARRIVED	ON	DAYS AT SEA	DAYS IN PORT	DEPARTED	ARRIVED	ON	DAYS	DAYS IN PORT
New York	14/02/1880	London	09/03/1880	24	65					
London	13/05/1880	Penarth	22/05/1880	9	13	04/06/80	Anjer	22/08/1880	79	14
Anjer	05/09/1880	Anjer	12/09/1880	7			Singapore	18/09/1880		not known
Singapore	not known	Calcutta	11/11/1880			05/03/81	Melbourne	14/05/1881	70	22
Melbourne	05/06/1881	Sydney	15/06/1881	10	17	02/07/81	Shanghai	17/08/1881	46	
Shanghai	not known	Cebu	end 10/81			06/12/81	New York	10/04/1882	125	24

Total voyage time 697

DEPARTED	ON	ARRIVED	ON	DAYS AT SEA	DAYS IN PORT	DEPARTED	ARRIVED	ON	DAYS	DAYS IN PORT
New York	04/05/1882	Semarang	20/08/1882	108	40	05/10/02	Madras	07/11/1882	33	51
Madras	28/12/1882	Bimlipatnam	08/01/1883	11	13	21/01/83	Kakinada	not known		
Kakinada	31/01/1883	London	02/06/1883							

Total voyage time 394

Fig. 42 *Cutty Sark* loading wool in Sydney, *c.* 1883–95. The ship loaded wool here eight times between 1883 and 1894.

Fig. 43 Interior of an Australian shearing shed, with wool clips in the foreground and the shearers in the background, by Charles H. Kerry, *c.* 1886, three years after *Cutty Sark* entered the wool trade.

Cutty Sark – wool clipper

Cutty Sark had called at Sydney and Melbourne several times but before 1883 the only Australian cargo of significance she had loaded was coal, destined for the steamers in Shanghai. But in 1883, and on every one of her remaining voyages under the British flag, she would load Australia's principal product: wool.

Sheep had first arrived in Australia with the first convoy of European settlers (the 'First Fleet') in 1788. Nine years later, the first Merino sheep were imported from South Africa, supplemented in 1805 by Merinos from the flock of George III. In 1808, Australian wool reached England's markets for the first time. Garraway's Coffee House in London held the first auction of Australian wool in 1821 and by the end of that decade Australia was challenging Spain and Germany as Britain's main foreign supplier of wool. In 1870, Australia, with a sheep population of nearly forty-two million, surpassed Britain to become the world's premier wool producer, and by 1892 the sheep population would expand to over one hundred million.

Many former tea clippers, including *Cutty Sark*'s old rival *Thermopylae*, were already working in the trade of transporting wool to England, joining larger vessels such as Willis' *The Tweed*. The ships would usually depart

The Masters 1870–95

1870–72
George Moodie (1831–1923)
Voyages: 3
Days at sea and in foreign ports: 910

A Scotsman from Fife, Moodie had previously served as mate on Willis' *The Tweed* and *Laurel*, before becoming master of *Lauderdale*. Willis then asked him to oversee the building of *Cutty Sark* (after which Moodie's wife officially named her), then to bring her down from Greenock to London and to be first master on her China voyages. On Moodie's third voyage on *Cutty Sark*, she lost her rudder off South Africa and Moodie argued furiously with Willis' brother Robert (who was on board), insisting on replacing it at sea rather than making for Port Elizabeth. Although he got his way, Moodie resigned as soon as they reached London and left sailing ships forever.

1872–73
Francis W. Moore (1822–unknown)
Voyages: 1
Days at sea and in foreign ports: 342

A Yorkshireman from Flamborough, Moore served on a number of Willis' ships. He had retired from commanding *Whiteadder* in 1869 to become shore superintendent for the Willis fleet, but had recently captained *Blackadder* on a single voyage. When Moodie resigned, Willis persuaded him to do the same in *Cutty Sark*, although he was aged 50 – a considerable age for a master.

1873–78
William Edward Tiptaft (1843–78)
Voyages: 6
Days at sea and in foreign ports: 1,650

Tiptaft had succeeded Moore as master of *Whiteadder*, and now (having been master of *Merse* briefly) succeeded him in *Cutty Sark*. He was a quiet, cautious man who commanded her on five successful tea voyages. Sadly, while still in the middle of the sixth (seeking a homeward tea cargo), he fell ill and died, aged just 35, at Shanghai.

1878–80
James Smith Wallace (1853–80)
Voyages: 2
Days at sea and in foreign ports: 600 (approximately)

An Aberdonian, Wallace was *Cutty Sark*'s first mate when Captain Tiptaft died in China. He took over as master but was no more successful in finding a tea cargo there for London, though he eventually loaded one of jute in the Philippines, which he delivered to New York before sailing home. He was a popular captain, an excellent seaman, a good driver of the ship, and remained in command for her next voyage. This was to Japan with Welsh coal though she never got there. After the first mate killed one of the crew and Wallace helped him escape justice, Wallace realised that this would probably ruin his own career: he committed suicide by stepping overboard in the South China Sea.

Fig. 44 Captain George Moodie

Fig. 45 Captain Frederick Moore

Fig. 46 Captain Richard Woodget

1880–82
William Bruce (1838–unknown)
Voyages: 1
Days at sea and in foreign ports: 560
(approximately)

An Aberdonian, like his predecessor, Bruce was transferred from another of Willis' tea clippers, *Hallowe'en*, owing to Wallace's suicide and the unsuitability of any of *Cutty Sark*'s officers to succeed him. Bruce proved to be a heavy drinker, an unpopular commander and an incompetent master. His single voyage in command – lasting nearly two years – has been dubbed *Cutty Sark*'s 'hell-ship' voyage by Basil Lubbock and Bruce was dismissed shortly after the ship reached her destination of New York and his mate's certificate was suspended.

1882–84
Frederick Moore (1839–unknown)
Voyages: 3
Days at sea and in foreign ports: 912

An Englishman (and no relation to Francis Moore, the second captain), Moore had worked in colliers and had even been first officer in a steamship. When instructed to join *Cutty Sark* in New York, he had only been with the Willis fleet for a comparatively short time as master of *Blackadder*. Another quiet but very capable man, he undertook one successful tramping voyage in *Cutty Sark* before taking her to Australia to join the wool fleet. Moore immediately established her as the fastest of all the sailing ships in that trade and after two profitable voyages was given command of the Willis company 'flagship', *The Tweed*.

1884–95
Richard Woodget (1845–1928)
Voyages: 10
Days at sea and in foreign ports: 2,816

Norfolk-born Woodget sailed *Cutty Sark* harder, established more records in her, and squeezed more wool into her hull than any previous master. With hobbies that included bicycling, dog-breeding and photography, he was an engaging character and well respected by his crew. Three of his sons served as apprentices on *Cutty Sark* at various times. After Willis sold her, Woodget made only one more voyage in command of a sailing ship before retiring from the sea to farm.

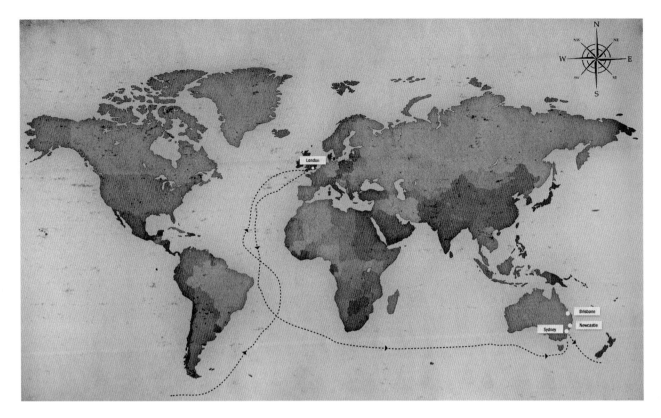

Fig. 47 On *Cutty Sark*'s outward journey to Australia, she sailed via the Cape of Good Hope but on the return leg she utilised the Roaring Forties, sailing back via Cape Horn.

from Britain in the summer and return with their bales of wool from Newcastle, New South Wales (NSW), Sydney or Brisbane for the London sales in the first few months of the new year. It was not as pleasant a cargo as one might imagine, as the poet E.J. Brady expressed clearly in his 1909 poem 'Laying on the Screw':

> You can dunnage casks o' tallow; you can handle hides an' horn;
> You can carry frozen mutton; you can lumber sacks of corn;
> But the queerest kind of cargo that you've got to haul and pull
> Is Australia's "staple product" – is her God-abandoned wool.
> For it's greasy an' it's stinkin', an' them awkward ugly bales
> Must be jammed as close as herrings in a ship afore she sails.

The screw in the title refers to the jack-screw press used for loading bales into a ship's hold. It was used in conjunction with two planks to force the bales apart so that another bale could be squeezed in.

In late 1883, Captain Moore took *Cutty Sark* down to Newcastle, NSW, loading 4,289 bales of wool. It was such a light cargo that 200 tons of ballast was needed. But whereas the ballast for tea had been only pebbles and shingle, that for wool was itself a cargo – chrome nickel.

Moore brought the ship back to London the following March in just 84 days, immediately establishing her reputation as one of the fastest clippers in the wool trade. Even though her masts, and consequently her sail area, had been cut down in 1880 to reduce the number of crew, this did not seem to affect her performance in the strong winds on the run from Australia to England (although Lubbock suggests it did affect her in light airs). And whereas she had been a competent tea clipper, so far as speed was concerned she was soon regarded as the best of the wool clippers. The route was almost certainly a key factor: *Cutty Sark* seems to have been a much better sailer in

strong winds than in light ones. Sailing back from China via the Cape of Good Hope, a ship met the doldrums – the light winds around the equator – twice, once in the South China Sea and once in the Atlantic. But sailing home from Australia she encountered the doldrums only once, in the Atlantic: for the homeward route was now via the South Pacific, round Cape Horn driven by the Roaring Forties, the constant west-to-east winds below latitude 40°S, which are consistently the world's fastest.

When the ship departed again for Australia in June 1884, the captain's wife was on board – but only as far as Dover. A crewman recalled: 'Mrs Moore accompanied us as far as Dover and I can see her now going over the side into the…boat and hear Captain Moore's gruff voice simply saying "Goodbye" and then turning round at once giving the order to square the yards.' For the crew, there may have been other delights on the voyage: it is recorded that two cases of wine and spirits were stolen by the steward, who was apparently in the habit of offering the apprentices a glass of champagne.

On the return run to London, Moore shaved four days off the previous year's time and so pleased was Willis with these fast passages that he rewarded his captain with the command of his favourite, *The Tweed*.

Willis did not look far for *Cutty Sark*'s next master. A Norfolk man, Richard Woodget, had captained Willis' 36-year-old *Coldstream* on a single but successful and surprisingly fast voyage. Willis took Woodget down to the East India Dock, pointed at *Cutty Sark* and said: 'Captain Woodget, there is your ship. My agents in Sydney are Dangar, Gedye & Co. All you have to do is drive her.'

Fig. 48 Captain Richard Woodget, master of *Cutty Sark* 1885–95, unknown artist.

Fig. 49 Advert for freight for *Cutty Sark*'s homeward journey from Australia to London. This advertisement celebrates the ship's reputation for fast passages in the wool trade.

It soon proved a shrewd choice: Woodget is widely acknowledged as the greatest of *Cutty Sark*'s masters. So successful were Woodget's passages that in 1886, particularly to celebrate *Cutty Sark* making a faster passage from Australia to London than her old rival *Thermopylae*, Willis presented the ship with a gilded weather vane in the shape of a 'cutty sark'. At the back of his mind may have been the weather vane in the form of a golden cockerel, its beak tied with a blue ribbon, which had been hoisted on the mast truck of *Thermopylae* in 1869, even before she has won a tea race (it was promptly removed by a seaman from *Taeping*, although later returned). This 'cutty sark' was thought to have been lost when the ship was severely damaged in a storm in 1916 but, incredibly, it turned up in a London saleroom in 1960 and, once money had changed hands, was reunited with the ship.

Also in 1886, in the optimistic hope of reviving her role as a tea clipper, and perhaps with the hope of setting a new sailing record for the run to China, Willis sent Woodget and *Cutty Sark* to Shanghai. *Leander* (designed by Bernard Waymouth just before he designed *Thermopylae*) and Willis' *Hallowe'en* both managed to find tea at Fuzhou, although *Hallowe'en* was wrecked at Salcombe before she could land her cargo. Woodget, by contrast, spent three and a half months in a fruitless search before abandoning the quest and heading for Australia for a more easily found wool cargo.

The following year's voyage took her back to Newcastle, NSW, where the *Newcastle Morning Herald and Miners' Advocate* of 19th November 1887 noted that:

> The ship *Cutty Sark*, which was reported off Wilson's Promontory on Saturday last, with her foretopgallant mast gone, arrived in port at

Fig. 50 The masthead vane, originally gilded, was presented to the ship by John Willis to celebrate *Cutty Sark* having made a faster passage from Australia to London than her main rival, Thermopylae. It was hoisted to the top of the main mast whenever the ship was in port.

Fig. 51 This advertisement was produced for *Cutty Sark*'s 18th voyage, leaving London for Newcastle, NSW, on 17th August 1887.

1 o'clock yesterday morning from London direct with 1,400 tons weight and measurement cargo, and 218 tons of powder and was moored in the horseshoe. The vessel's present voyage has been a lengthy one, compared with her previous performances; in fact, it is the longest ever made by her since her commencement of her career in the Anglo-Australian service. The *Cutty Sark* has justly earned the reputation of being one of the fastest sailing clippers afloat, and she and the *Thermopylae* certainly take precedence of all others so far as quick passages are concerned. Only for an unforeseen accident the *Cutty Sark* would probably have reached here twelve days ago, as her commander, Captain Woodget, fully expected to make the voyage in 78 days, whereas it lengthened out to 90, which, however, taking everything into consideration, is a very creditable performance and tends to show what the vessel is capable of even under adverse circumstances. Three years have elapsed since the vessel was last here, but the interim has been fully taken up in the trade between Sydney and London. Captain Moore, who was then in command, was appointed to take charge of *The Tweed*, belonging to the same owners, Messrs. John Willis and Sons of London, and the vacancy was filled by her present master, who was previously in another of the same lines, namely the *Coldstream*. The vessel has no passengers, and arrived in port in admirable order, notwithstanding the fact of what she has had to contend with. The vessel comes consigned to Messrs. Dangar, Gedye and Co., and upon the discharge of her inward cargo will be taken up by Messrs Dalgety and Co., Limited, to load wool for the London March sales and is announced to sail on December 10. She will be berthed alongside the cargo wharf on Monday, to discharge. The *Cutty Sark*'s last voyage from Sydney to London occupied but 72 days, whilst the voyage previous was accomplished in 73 days, two of the fastest passages recorded for a considerable time past. The best day's performance on the present voyage was 330 miles, on November 11th, followed by 292 next day, and this would have been considerably increased only for the loss of portion of her gear. Captain Woodget reports having left the Docks on August 17th, and landed the pilot off Start Point two days later. Westerly winds were experienced up to August 31st and here fresh northeast trades were fallen in within 35 degrees north, which carried the vessel to 16 degrees north. Then followed variable winds to the Equator, which was crossed on September 20th in 24.30 degrees West. The usual trades were then picked up very light, and continued to 30 degrees south, succeeded by five or six days' light variable winds, the vessel made little progress. These were followed by light westerly winds, which continued until October 22nd, when bad weather was fallen in with. On the date, when the vessel was in 39 degrees south and 45 degrees east, a terrible squall was encountered from the west-south-west, and the vessel broached to, carrying away the fore and main topmast heads, topgallant masts, and mizzen royal yard. The squall lasted several hours, and, as soon as it had abated, the crew were set to work to clear away the wreckage which was replaced by a new main topmast and main topgallant mast, the repairs occupying eight days. The foretopgallant mast, however, was not replaced, and the vessel arrives in port with that spur missing. No other damage was done in the squall. After this the vessel experienced light northerly winds and smooth water up to the 9th inst.,

Fig. 52 *Cutty Sark* (foreground) in Sydney Harbour, *c.* 1883–94, waiting for a wool cargo.

and from thence up to long. 128.30, as strong south-east gale was encountered, during which the vessel made some fast running, and this brought her off Wilson's Promontory on Saturday last, which point was kept in sight until Tuesday last at noon by calm and light airs. South-east wind then came up and brought the vessel into port. She was off the Nobbys at 9 p.m. on Thursday, but stood off until the ebb-tide made, about four hours later.

Woodget not only improved on his predecessor's sailing times, he also managed to 'screw' more bales of wool into the hold. He usually supervised the loading himself but in 1894, possibly to teach him a lesson, the stevedores of Sydney took matters into their own hands and screwed in over 5,000 bales – considerably more than Woodget had ever made them load.

Woodget also managed to show that the steamships were not all-conquering. In the early afternoon of 25th July 1889, *Cutty Sark* was approaching Sydney when she was overtaken by the P&O steamer *Britannia*. But that evening, when the steamer was sailing between $14^{1}/_{2}$ and 16 knots (17–18mph/27–30kph), *Britannia*'s second officer was amazed to see a sailing vessel gaining – so amazed that he called the captain to witness it. The log entry reads: 'Sailing ship overhauled and passed us!' They did not know it was *Cutty Sark* until they reached Sydney an hour after the clipper had anchored.

But not every voyage was so satisfying. Sailing south as far as 64°47′S (further south than the northern tip of Antarctica) to pick up the Roaring Forties, the ship frequently had to negotiate a route through towering icebergs. On the night of 22nd October 1885, sailing south from Australia, she was almost smashed to pieces in a terrific squall. In 1887 she was hit by another squall that brought down the

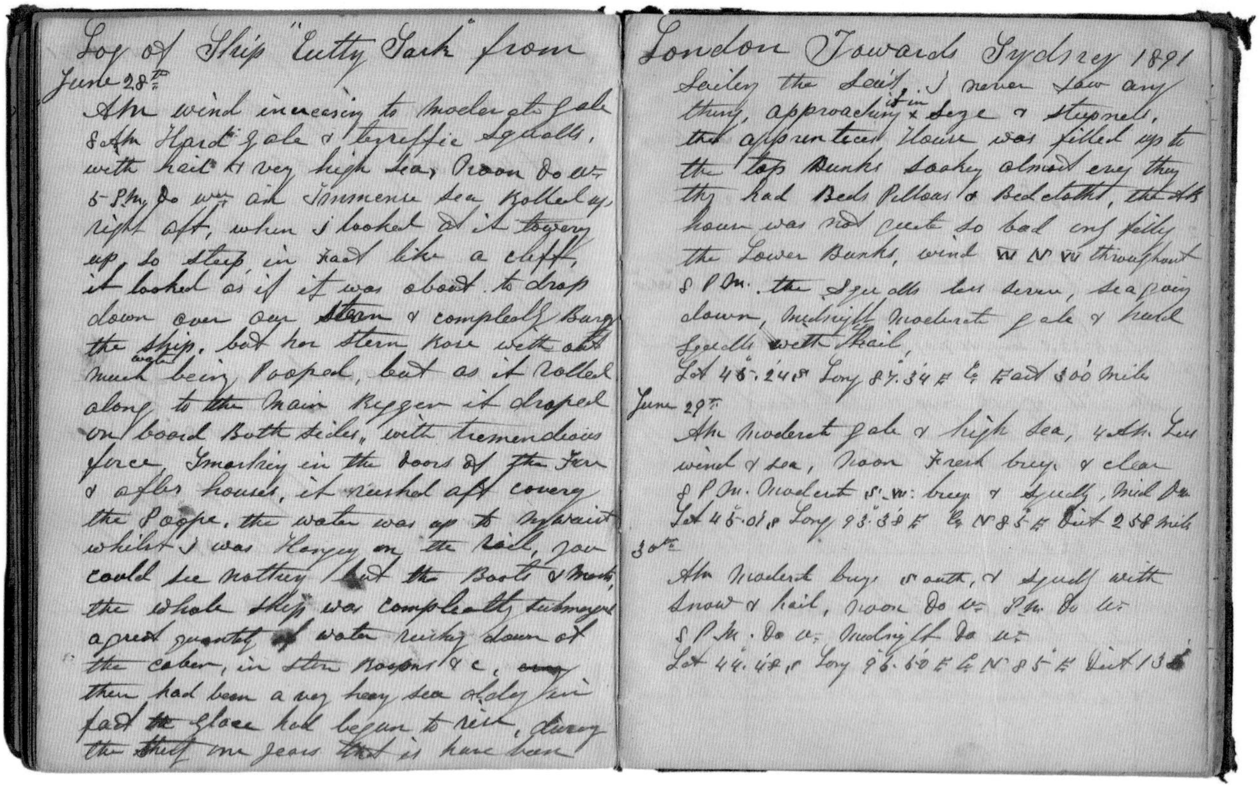

Fig. 53 Captain Woodget's log of *Cutty Sark*, 1891. This log covers the outward voyage to Sydney in which Captain Woodget describes the hard gales and fearsome squalls encountered.

fore-topgallant mast, dragging the main-topgallant mast with it. The following year, rough sea swept the 17-year-old apprentice Sidney Cook overboard and he was lost.

The most frightening incident occurred in the early evening of 28th June 1891, when the ship was at 45°24′S 87°34′E, between the Cape of Good Hope and Australia. Woodget wrote in his log:

> An immense sea rolled up right aft. When I looked at it, towering up so steep, in fact, like a cliff, it looked as if it was about to drop over our stern and completely bury the ship; but her stern rose without much water being pooped, but as it rolled along to the main rigging it dropped on board both sides with tremendous force; smashing in the door of the fore and after houses, it rushed aft covering the poop. The water was up to my waist whilst I was hanging on the rail; you could see nothing but the boats and the masts – the whole ship was completely submerged, a great quantity of water rushing down into the cabin, stern rooms, etc…. During the thirty-one years that I have been sailing the seas, I never saw anything approaching it in size and steepness. The apprentices' house was filled up to the top bunks, soaking almost everything that it had – beds, pillows, and bedclothes. The A.B.'s house was not so bad, only filling the lower bunks.

Woodget later told Basil Lubbock that the ship ran down the wall of water at an angle of 45 degrees, her bow splitting the wave with a roaring hiss. He and the helmsman lashed themselves to the wheel or they would certainly have been washed overboard. *Cutty Sark* was running under only a main-topgallant sail but still managed to travel 300 miles in 24 hours.

As the years went by, as had happened in the tea trade, cargoes were not always readily available. In 1892, the ship arrived in Sydney too late to find a cargo

Captain Woodget, photographer

Extract from Captain Woodget's private journal – 1893.

'Wednesday, 8th February. – Lat. 50° 08'S., long. 46° 41'W., course N. 50° E, distance 150 miles. Gentle S.W. breeze and fine. 6.0 a.m., foggy; 6.30 fog lifted and we found ourselves surrounded by icebergs; 8 a.m. foggy again; ice ahead, in fact there was ice all round. As soon as we cleared one berg another would be reported. You could hear the sea roaring on them and through them, the ice cracking sometimes like thunder, at other times like cannon, and often like a sharp rifle report, and yet could not see them.

At 1 p.m. the top of an iceberg was seen which one could hardly believe was ice, it looked like a streak of dark cloud. Then we could see the ice a few feet down, but we could not see the bottom. It was up at an angle of 45 degree. We were only about 1,000 feet off, so it would be 1,000 feet high, it had a circular top but we could not see the ends.

Fig. 54 Iceberg to the west of Cape Horn, 1888, by Captain Woodget.

Fig. 55 *Cutty Sark* at sea, *c.* 1887–95, by Captain Woodget, who was inspired to take up photography in 1887 by apprentice John Mayall.

Fig. 56 *Cutty Sark* at Newcastle, NSW, by Captain Woodget, *c.* 1887–92.

Fig. 57 *Cutty Sark* drying sails in Sydney, 1891, by Captain Woodget.

CUTTY SARK IN SYDNEY HARBOUR. AUGUST 1891. CAPTAIN WOODGATE.

Figs. 58 and 59 Captain Woodget's dogs on board *Cutty Sark*, photographed by the captain.

A few minutes later another was under the bows; we only cleared it by a few feet. It was about 100 feet high and flat-topped. Just as we were passing the corner there was a sharp report that made you jump, as if it was breaking in two.

Found another on the other side quite close, and a few minutes later saw the long ridge of ice almost ahead. Kept off, and then another came in sight on the other bow. We were too near it to keep away, but I felt sure that it was no part of the big one – as we were passing this point the big one came in sight, the fog cleared and we passed in between them, there being no more than 400 feet between them. When we had cleared the big one, I saw its north end and took bearings. After sailing eight miles I took other bearings and found that the east side was 19 miles long; and we could not see the end of the side we sailed along. We sailed about six miles alongside of it, water now quite smooth. Before noon the water was quite lumpy from all ways. After we cleared the passage by about three or four miles, it cleared up astern and what a sight it was! Nothing but icebergs through the passage and on the south side of the passage (for the berg was only about ½ mile long north and south, same height as the big berg). I expect it had not long broken off. There was nothing but a sea of ice astern, and another large flat-topped iceberg, which as far as you could see extended like land; it must have been 20 miles long or more.

After we were through, there was nothing but small ice from small pieces to bergs 100 feet long. Also, there was one about a mile long covered with what looked like pumice stone or lumps of tallow.'

Fig. 60 *The Great Wave*, by Donald Sinclair Swan, 1969. This painting depicts an event on 28th June 1891, when, on her outward voyage from London to Sydney, *Cutty Sark* encountered the biggest sea of her career (see page 84).

for London, although she did find one for Antwerp. This was another hard passage: the ship was surrounded by ice on the way to Cape Horn and, as she approached the English Channel, two crewmen, Clifton and Doyle, were washed off the bowsprit and lost. The following year, she again failed to secure a wool cargo for London but instead unloaded in Hull.

Nevertheless, there was some enjoyment. In Shanghai, Captain Woodget acquired a bicycle – a boneshaker on which the pedals were attached directly to the front wheel – which he learned to ride by practising on the 'tween deck. He also took up roller-skating and thanks to one of the apprentices, John Mayall, grandson of the famous portrait photographer J.J.E. Mayall, Woodget became a keen photographer himself, developing his prints on board. On at least one occasion, he brought a steam launch from England on which to cruise around Sydney Harbour.

Although the town of Anjer had been destroyed in 1883 by a tidal wave in the wake of the Krakatoa volcano eruption, it was functioning again as an anchorage by 1886. On her way to Shanghai, *Cutty Sark* anchored there and Woodget bought two monkeys (probably long-tailed macaques). The male was given the run of the ship (much to the steward's displeasure); the female was tied up on the poop. Woodget also found time to breed dogs which successfully competed in Sydney shows.

Woodget sailed on 10 voyages in *Cutty Sark*. The only man who sailed as many was the ship's cook, James Robson, who joined and left at the same time as Woodget. Robson was clearly of Far Eastern origin – he had been found as a baby in a basket in the South China Sea, rescued by a passing ship and brought up in England. He went to sea at a young age and later become the leading seaman on *The Tweed*. But this was

a role for young men, and in 1885 he opted for the probably less exhausting post of cook on *Cutty Sark*.

Robson was responsible for the food that delighted the 16-year-old apprentice Clarence Ray, whose letters, written on the way to Brisbane in 1894, give a vivid portrait of life on board and ashore (the spelling is unaltered from the original):

> SS Cutty Sark 25th June .94.
> My dear Mother,
>
> The pilot leaves tonight I expect so I am writing this short note now in case
> I get no more time. I am quite well and enjoying myself. The weather is
> beautiful but hardly any wind. We are running about 5 knots at present. I
> expect we shall be off Hastings about 6pm this evening. I hope you and all
> at home are getting on all right. I have just been hauling on the t'gallant
> halliards and therefore the writing is very bad. We have no proper watches yet
> I had to stop on deck all last night. I have been aloft as far as the main t'gallant
> yard two or 3 times.
> I must stop now our time for breakfast is nearly up.
> Don't forget to write to me
> the address will be
> ~~C. E. Ray~~
> ~~SS (sic) Cutty Sark~~
> C.E. Ray
> c/o Captain Woodget
> SS Cutty Sark
> Brisbane
> Woodget is spelt get not gate.
> Your loving son
> ~~Truly~~
> C. E. Ray

Ship Cutty Sark
Sunday 15th of July 94

My Dear Mother,

I have not commenced keeping a log or Diary yet, so I am going to write a sort of weekly letter to tell you all about the ship and how I get on. But first I must tell you how very sorry I am that I did not wish you a very many happy returns of your birthday, the 26th of June, the day I wrote the letter for the Pilot, but I only had half an hour for dinner and I had to scribble whatever came first into my head and I clean forgot about It being your birthday, but I hope you will forgive me.

We have a jolly lot of fellows in the "house", there are six of us altogether, we are divided into two watches Wilcox, Tyrrer and Nibo (the scipper's son) are in the Port and Webb Shuttleworth & I are in the Starboard Watch that is if both watches were called on deck at once we should take the starboard and all the others the port. We are under the second mate who is a very nice fellow indeed, the other are under the first mate who I suppose Auntie has told you is the Captain's son too. Wilcox and Webb have served their time in the Sark but are coming this voyage to get their 2nd mates certificate. We start work at 5.30 in the morning but that is every other morning of course because the other watch will be on deck from 4 to 8 the next morning, the dog watches from 4 to 6 and 6 till 8 at night, are so that we should not get the same watch on deck at the same time, we knock off work at 4 one day and 6 the next in our watch on deck at night we have to keep time and ring the bells the old man has got 3 dogs, scotch collies, and when we go down in the cabin to see the time they go for us which makes it rather thick. If we go to sleep in our watch on deck they make us ride the grey mare that is sit up on the upper topsail yard for the rest of the watch I have not had to do this yet but the other fellow has, twice.

Now I must tell you about the grub we get coffee at 5 o'clock every other morning coffee for breakfast and tea for tea.

Monday	
Wednesday	pea soup and pork
Friday	
Tuesday	Salt Tram Horse and bread
Thursday	
Saturday	Junk and Spuds (potatoes)
Sunday	Leu pie

Sugar and butter we get 14 ozs every week
We get a pannikin of lime juice every day at 12 o'clock.

Leu pie is my favourite dinner it is cooked altogether in a great kid, fresh meat and spuds all in soup like, underneath and dough on the top. Oh Lor, I could eat 3 whacks of it now, of course, we get any amount of dog biscuit. We shall finish the last piece of cake today for tea. We have kept it 3 weeks which I think is a long time.

… Uncle and Frank saw me aboard on Sunday night then I put my fixings right and tried to go to sleep but it missed stays, but the next night, after a hard day's work I slept like a top, you bet, but was fetched out of it in the middle to drop anchor in the Downs when the tug "Shamrock" left us. We were a long time getting down the river on account of having to stop at Gravesend to take in 70 tons of Gunpowder and dynamite. Then the next morning we heaved the anchor and set sail for the deep blue sea and back only 9 each. The old man has got a steam launch on board and of course he must start pulling the engine, boiler, coal bunker and everything else out of her to clean. I chip, repair, paint and generally do up! Unluckily he found out that I knew more about engine work than any of the other 'prentices and so he has had me helping him nearly all the time since we left London. Of course I have had to do my share of work on deck and aloft and a jolly lot more too because the queer fellow in my watch says he cannot go up unless someone goes with him so the old man he sends me worse luck, then I have to do all the work, which is generally overhauling and stopping buntlines, clew lines and leech lines and making the stay sails fast which is the worst of all especially if she is rolling at all.

We have not had any very bad weather yet except in the Bay where she rolled till her lee main yard arm nearly touched the water and shipped seas over the foc's'le head and amid ships like one o'clock, that was the first night I had oilskins and seaboots on, I was ordered up to make the mizzen t'gallant stasail fast, to do this I had to get onto the cap of the main mast, undo the gasket and ride the sail down, passing the gasket the sail and the topmast stay all this sounds very easy to talk about but when I got down I could not use my left arm for a great big bruise on the muscle - or where it ought to be - because

while I was clinging all arms and legs round the sail it blew me up against the mast which knocked all my wind out I thought of the saying "those who are born to be king won't be drownd" and stuck on.

Since then we have had fine weather, it is getting very warm I never have more than a shirt and pants on ever at night. We get any amount of flying fish, they fly aboard at night, then all we have to do is catch them, cut their heads, wings, tails and fins off, clean them and then put them on a plate with some butter over them, and give them to Jimmy to cook for our breakfast. Last night I caught thirteen.

Our first job at 5.30 in the morning is to wash the pigs and closets out. I always heard that pigs were unclean animals but now I know it for a positive fact and can prove it too.

Ah it is a hard life but you need not think that I do not like it for I am enjoying myself very much.

Last week I had to go to the wheel and learn to steer. I learnt in one dog watch I must put a round turn on now. I am always thinking of you all at home and I know I shall be jolly glad to get back and see you all again.

The pigs Ray disliked so much were penned under the anchor deck. At the other end of the main deck, just forward of the poop, were coops for chickens.

Ray was on board during *Cutty Sark*'s first visit to Brisbane, where Willis' *Blackadder* was already loading. But neither Clarence Ray nor Captain Woodget had any inkling that this voyage would be her last to Australia. The wool trade, like the tea trade in the previous decade, was increasingly being taken over by the steamers. Willis, now 75, had been a sailing-ship man all his life and showed no interest in running a fleet of steam-driven vessels. He also had no close heir to whom the family business could be passed and was gradually disposing of his fleet: by 1895 it was down to four vessels. *Cutty Sark* herself, now 25 years old, was showing signs of age herself and was in need of a major overhaul. But rather than pay for such work, on 8th July 1895, around the time of year she would normally be setting sail for Australia, Willis sold her. Woodget was given command of *Coldinghame* and, with her, he made another successful run home with wool from Brisbane. But that single voyage seems to have been enough for him: after it he retired from the sea, returning to his native Norfolk to farm.

TABLE 13
Longevity of tea trade clippers
(analysis of data in MacGregor, 1985)

Age range	Count
<5 years	31
6–10 years	33
11–15 years	38
16–20 years	42
21–25 years	36
26–30 years	30
31–35 years	31
36–40 years	18
41–45 years	7
46–50 years	1
50> years	9

TABLE 14
Fate of the sailing vessels in the tea trade
(analysis of data in MacGregor, 1985)

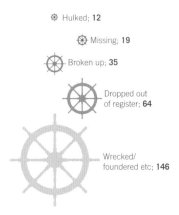

Hulked; **12**

Missing; **19**

Broken up; **35**

Dropped out of register; **64**

Wrecked/ foundered etc; **146**

By this time, of all the graceful clippers which had once worked in the China tea trade, *Cutty Sark* was one of only nine still afloat. Indeed, only a third of the tea clippers had survived for more than 25 years before being wrecked, foundered or condemned.

The era of the clipper was at an end. Although commercial deep-sea sail was to survive well into the next century, the next generation of sailing ships were four-masted steel barques with much larger carrying capacities and much less elegance – more bulk carriers than sleek greyhounds of the sea.

The year *Cutty Sark* was sold (1895) was also the year that the ex-tea clipper *Ambassador* set sail from Jacksonville, Florida, bound for Honolulu. She failed to round the Horn and put into Port Stanley in the Falkland Islands with damage so severe she was condemned. She was eventually towed to Chile to serve as a hulk. Today, a beached skeleton stripped of her planking, she lies at Estancia San Gregorio. She is the only surviving remnant of the tea clippers, except *Cutty Sark*.

TABLE 15 *Cutty Sark*'s wool voyages

LEFT LONDON	ARRIVED		DAYS	DAYS IN AUSTRALIA	WOOL BALES LOADED	DEPARTED	ARRIVED HOME	DAYS	TOTAL VOYAGE	NOTE	DAYS BEFORE NEXT VOYAGE
04/07/1883	Newcastle	10/10/1883	98	79	4,289	28/12/1883	21/03/1884	84	261		86
15/06/1884	Newcastle	05/09/1884	82	95	4,300	09/12/1884	27/02/1885	80	257		33
01/04/1885	Sydney	19/06/1885	79	121	4,465	18/10/1885	30/12/1885	73	273		49
17/02/1886	Sydney	05/12/1886	291	111	4,298	26/03/1887	17/06/1887	83	485	via Shanghai	61
17/08/1887	Newcastle	17/11/1887	92	41	4,515	28/12/1887	10/03/1888	73	206		68
17/05/1888	Sydney	05/08/1888	80	83	4,496	27/10/1888	20/01/1889	85	248		104
04/05/1889	Sydney	26/07/1889	83	99	4,577	02/11/1889	17/01/1890	76	258		117
14/05/1890	Sydney	02/08/1890	80	134	4,617	14/12/1890	17/03/1891	93	307		37
23/04/1891	Sydney	13/07/1891	81	115	4,638	05/11/1891	29/01/1892	85	281		196
12/08/1892	Newcastle	07/11/1892	87	61	4,723	07/01/1893	15/04/1893	98	246	arrived in	108

The World of *Cutty Sark*

Many aspects of cultural and artistic life that emerged during the time Cutty Sark was under sail are still familiar to us. Wagner's *Die Valkyrie* (1870,) Verdi's *Aida* (1871), Bizet's *Carmen* (1875), Tchaikovsky's *Swan Lake* (1877), Gilbert and Sullivan's *The Pirates of Penzance* (1879) and *The Mikado* (1885) all had their first performances; Whistler completed the famous portrait of his mother (1871), Van Gogh began his sunflower series (1888) and Munch revealed *The Scream* (1895). Books from the period that still influence us include *Alice Through the Looking Glass* (1871) and *The Adventures of Sherlock Holmes* (1891). Two of Britain's finest Victorian Gothic buildings – Manchester Town Hall and St Pancras Station – were completed in 1877: Tower Bridge followed in 1894. Blackpool Tower opened the same year, seven years after the Eiffel Tower in Paris. In America, Levi Strauss received a patent for riveted jeans (1873) and in 1886 Coca-Cola was invented. Also in that year , Heinz Baked Beans were launched at Fortnum & Mason's prestigious London store and a vessel almost as famous as *Cutty Sark*, the *Mary Celeste*, was found unaccountably abandoned in the Atlantic, 600 miles west of Portugal.

Cutty Sark's launch in 1869 was into a world of frenetic commercial activity, where trade was growing at over 30 per cent every decade. She flew the flag of the most prosperous country on Earth. Even though the government of Britain switched between Liberal and Conservative administrations seven times between 1868 and 1895, both were resolute supporters of the expansion of British Empire. Between the 1870s and the 1890s, this empire – already the largest ever seen – expanded into Africa, and despite occasional defeats by Zulus, Sudanese and Boers, reached its zenith before *Cutty Sark* left British ownership in 1895. The ship's home port of London was throughout the period the richest and most populous city in the world, even though terrorised by Fenian bombing (1881–85) and later by Jack the Ripper (1888).

Abroad, Prussia humiliated France in their war of 1870–71 and, through a combination of arms and diplomacy, forged a united Germany. But France recovered remarkably quickly to become Britain's principal colonial rival in Africa. So intense was the rivalry that towards the end of the century, preparations were being made in Britain to fight off a French invasion.

Meanwhile, on the other side of the Atlantic, the transcontinental railroad was finally completed in 1869. Yet the country was not completely pacified: seven years later General Custer and his men were killed at the Battle of Little Big Horn.

When, in 1870, *Cutty Sark* first arrived in Shanghai, the Qing dynasty's Tongzhi emperor ruled the Celestial Empire from within the Forbidden City, in the centre of Beijing, as he had done since 1861, when at the age of six he had succeeded his father. He is best remembered for the

Fig. 64 Completion of the first transcontinental railroad on 10th May 1869 at Promontory Point, Utah, when the Central Pacific Railroad coming from Sacramento, met the Union Pacific Railroad building out from Chicago. The two railroads had started the project six years earlier, in 1863.

Fig. 65 Guangxu, (1871–1908), Emperor of China from 1875 to 1908.

Fig. 66 The first performance of Carmen at the Opéra Comique in Paris, March 1875.

'Tongzhi Restoration'. This was an attempt to strengthen China's resistance to internal dissent and foreign intervention through limited modernisation but adhering to the country's traditions. Although the movement bears his name, its architect was his mother, the dowager empress Cixi. After the emperor's death from smallpox in 1875, it was Cixi who arranged for her nephew to become the next ruler, reigning as the Guangxu emperor.

In the same year as the Guangxu emperor's accession, Augustus Margary, a British diplomat and explorer, was murdered in the remote south-west province of Yunnan. Like the incidents that provoked the Opium Wars in previous decades, this was used as an excuse by the British to extort silver from the Chinese government as compensation, and to force the opening of more ports to international trade.

This was also the year in which the rains failed in northern China. Crop failures ensued, leading to a three-year famine between 1876 and 1879 in which over nine million people starved to death. The south of the country did not escape its share of natural disasters of floods, earthquakes and plagues. For tens of thousands, emigration was the only option. For those who went as indentured labourers to the sugar plantations and guano mines of South America, their conditions were little better than slavery.

Only five years before *Cutty Sark* first reached Australia in 1873, the *Hougoumont* had arrived in Western Australia – the last ship to transport convicts from Britain. The great influx of settlers enticed by the gold rush of the 1840s had lessened but there was still a large number of settlers arriving each year, some being deserters from ships like *Cutty Sark*.

In the late nineteenth century, Australia was not a commonwealth but six separate colonies. They were in some respects relatively liberal societies: labour parties were formed and were contesting elections, and the cause of women's suffrage made greater advances than in Britain. But the land of the original native population was being appropriated for European settlers: the Half Caste Act of 1886 allowed the forced removal of children from Aboriginal families, and considerable prejudice against Chinese workers (attracted, like Europeans,

Fig. 67 The 92nd Gordon Highlanders in retreat at the Battle of Majuba Hill, 26th–27th February, during the First Boer War.

Fig. 68 The murders of Jack the Ripper held London in fear in 1888.

by the discoveries of gold deposits) led to legislation to reduce their numbers. When Australia's long economic boom came to an end in the 1890s, a number of major strikes took place but each failed to achieve improvements in pay and conditions. Ironically, the Great London Dock Strike of 1889 was successful largely owing to the contribution of £30,000 sent by Australians to the strike fund (more than 60 per cent of the total collected).

When *Cutty Sark* was renamed *Ferreira* in 1895, she flew the flag of Portugal, at that time a constitutional monarchy under King Carlos I of the House of Braganza, the ruling Portuguese dynasty since 1640. Unfortunately, the decades of stability and prosperity the country had until then enjoyed were coming to an end. Portugal entered a sustained period of financial crisis, originating in the costs of her colonial ventures and a programme of massive public works. Rather than prompting reform, a failed coup in 1906 led King Carlos to support the appointment of a repressive and dictatorial government. In 1908, as he and his son rode through the streets of Lisbon in an open carriage, they were assassinated. Although a successor, Manuel II, was crowned, constitutional monarchy was

doomed and in 1910 the Republicans staged a successful coup. One of the Republicans' grievances was Portugal's acquiescence to Britain's demands, made 20 years earlier, to withdraw their troops from what are now Zaire and Zimbabwe, which would have established a Portuguese colonial 'belt' right across southern Africa, from Angola to Mozambique.

However, by this time European imperial rivalries were brewing even greater storms, the avoidability of two incidents of 1912 symbolising both the hubris of the era and its potential risks: one was the loss of the *Titanic*, the other that of Captain Scott's small party in their failed race to beat the much better-prepared Amundsen expedition to the South Pole. Both events, in different degrees, featured tragically unnecessary death, courage and folly – consequences of attitudes and habits that brought far greater general catastrophe two years later, in their contribution to the outbreak of the First World War. Astonishingly, *Cutty Sark* survived it: several empires and millions of people did not.

Under the Portuguese flag

Ferreira

Scrawled across *Cutty Sark*'s Certificate of British Registry (Fig. 21) are the words:

> Certificate cancelled & Registry closed 22nd July 1895 on Sale of the
> Vessel to Foreigners (Portuguese Subject). Advice from owner.

But the owner who advised the Registry of the sale was not John Willis but John Richards of '37 Wroughton Road, Balham… Gentleman'. The address is of a modest Victorian terraced house, still standing. The 1891 Census notes that Richards, his wife and children were sharing the house with a bank clerk, his wife and his sister. Richards' own occupation is given as 'merchant's clerk', amended in the 1901 Census to 'merchantile clerk'. By the time of the 1911 Census, Richards had left trading affairs and had become an 'engineer's clerk' for a firm of electrical engineers. *Cutty Sark*, purchased when he was no more than 30, was not a stepping stone to building up his own fleet – why did he buy her? It is an unsolved mystery.

In fact, 16 days after he had bought *Cutty Sark* from Willis he sold her to the Lisbon-based company Joaquim Antunes Ferreira & Ca. for £1,250. It renamed her *Ferreira* and she arrived in Lisbon for the first time on 28th October 1895.

The following year, the ship began to follow a regular triangular route from Lisbon to Portugal's African colonies, then across the Atlantic to Brazil, New Orleans or Barbados. She was still occasionally visited by those who remembered her clipper days – and around 1903, in an unnamed foreign port, her bell was allegedly stolen by an officer who had once served on board. The Portuguese crew then stole the bell of the nearest ship, the barque *Shakespeare*. The original bell was returned nearly 30 years later when the ship came back into British ownership, the culprit taking *Shakespeare*'s bell in exchange.

In the 27 years that she flew the Portuguese flag, *Ferreira* sailed hundreds of thousands of miles without mishap, but there were two occasions when the ship came close to being wrecked.

The first was when she was caught by the Great Hurricane of 1906, which struck Pensacola, Florida, in the early hours of 27th September, killing 134 people and damaging over 5,000 houses. *Ferreira* was moored at Muscogee Wharf alongside a large Swedish barque, *Alfhild*. Both were torn loose from their moorings by the storm and crashed into the pier, destroying it. *Alfhild* was swept past *Ferreira* but her progress was stopped when she embedded her bow in the old clipper ship.

At the end of the year *Ferreira* was towed to Mobile for repairs and, although she soon returned to Pensacola, it would be four months before she was able to leave. She was supposed to take a timber cargo down to Rio de Janeiro, but just eight days after sailing she ran ashore on the Cosgrove Shoal near Key West and lost her rudder.

In 1907 the number of old tea clippers afloat was reduced by another one with the sinking of *Thermopylae*. She had left the wool trade much earlier than *Cutty Sark*, was sold to Canadian owners in the early 1890s and was used to trade between the west coast of Canada and the ports of south-east Asia. She was then sold to the Portuguese navy, arriving in Lisbon on 29th May 1897. Renamed *Pedro Nunes* (after the sixteenth-century mathematician and cosmographer), it was planned to convert

Previous pages:
Fig. 69 *Ferreira* under tow after losing her main and mizzen masts, 1916. Captain da Sousa ordered them to be cut away to save the ship from capsizing.

Fig. 70 *Ferreira*, ex-*Cutty Sark*, at Birkenhead, 1914. She arrived in from Angola, carrying whale bone and oil.

Ports of call

Fig. 71 The entrance to the East India Docks, nineteenth century.

Fig. 72 Shanghai, China, c. 1880.

Fig. 73 Hong Kong, 1870s.

Fig. 74 Cutty Sark alongside Brilliant and Yalleroi in Sydney, 1883–95.

Fig. 75 Hull docks, by Francis Frith c. 1885.

Cutty Sark was a highly specialised vessel, designed not only to transport valuable cargoes at great speed but also to cross the sandbars at the mouths of the great rivers of China. She was built for long voyages to the tea ports and, consequently, called at relatively few places during her early years. Departing from London for the East, she might anchor briefly off Anjer, Java (Sunda Strait), for mail and telegrams, and then sail to Shanghai, or perhaps go up to Hankou under tow. She never called at Guangzhou, the traditional tea port of China, and only once visited Fuzhou and Hong Kong: not to collect tea from the former but pine poles (for which Fujian/Fukien was equally famous) and to discharge rice loaded in Bangkok at the latter. When she began to sail to China via Australia, Sydney was always the port of departure on the final leg. As a wool clipper from 1883, Sydney was again her principal port, even though she began in this trade by loading at Newcastle, also in New South Wales (NSW).

It was in the brief period between finishing as a tea clipper and starting in the wool trade that she visited more ports in the East than ever before or after while flying the

British flag. Searching for cargoes between 1878 and 1883, she tramped the South China Sea, calling at Singapore, the Philippines and then across the Indian Ocean to Calcutta. Later she would travel from New York to Java and on to a number of relatively small ports on the east coast of India, loading strange and exotic cargoes.

Cutty Sark called at only one port in continental Europe – Antwerp – to unload wool. She never returned to Scotland, the country where she was built. Indeed, other than London, Penarth and Hull were the only UK ports where she ever berthed while working under British registry.

Ironically, she called at more British ports in her time as *Ferreira*, registered and based at Lisbon: Birkenhead, Newport, Swansea, London and Falmouth. But this was later in her career – her early Portuguese voyages confined her to the Atlantic and the south-east coast of Africa. She never returned to the South China Sea or the Pacific, but within the Atlantic, she called at virtually every major harbour. These included the ports in the Portuguese colonies of Angola and Mozambique, Portuguese-speaking Brazil, and the mid-Atlantic 'province' of the Azores,

and also Barbados and the seaports of the American Gulf coast. Not all such calls were voluntary, to load or unload cargo; Mobile and Cape Town were both visited for urgent repairs.

The ship was still crossing the Atlantic until almost the very end of her working life: her last ocean voyage took her from Lisbon out to the Azores, across to Pensacola in Florida, (presumably to pick up timber felled from the abundant pine forests) and then on to London. Her final commercial journey in 1922, not as *Ferreira* but now as *Maria do Amparo*, perhaps reflected her condition as a vessel in very poor repair: it was just a modest voyage from Lisbon to the small ports on the north coast of Spain.

Fig. 76 Lisbon, *c.* 1900.

Fig. 77 Pernambuco, *c.* 1850.

Fig. 78 Ships on the Hooghly, Calcutta (now Kolkata),
Francis Frith & Co., *c.* 1860.

Fig. 79 Antwerp docks, *c.* 1890.

Fig. 80 New York Harbour, *c.* 1870.

Fig. 81 Lourenço Marques (now known as Maputo), *c.* 1900.

Fig. 82 *Ferreira* aground at Muscogee
Wharf, Pensacola, 1906. The ship was
caught in the Great Hurricane of 1906.

her into a sail-training vessel but this proved uneconomic and instead she became a coal hulk. By 1907 she was no longer fit for even this role, so she was taken out to the mouth of the River Tagus, where, watched by Maria Amélia, the last Queen Consort of Portugal (who was there primarily to present new colours to the fleet), she was scuttled by torpedo.

Ferreira, however, was still a very active working ship. In 1914 and 1915, she made her first visits back to Britain, docking at Birkenhead, part of the Port of Liverpool. What she brought on her first voyage is not known but on the second she unloaded whale oil, whale bone and fish guano from Namibe (then known as Mossamedes) in Angola, returning there with coal, bricks and empty oil drums. The following year, not many days after leaving Lisbon for Namibe, she lost a rudder for the third time. Fortunately her captain, Frederic Vincenzo da Sousa, managed to rig up a jury rudder and reach his destination without diverting for repairs, rather like Captain Moodie over 40 years earlier. The rudder on the ship today is the replacement fitted at Namibe.

Ferreira was almost sunk during the First World War, not by enemy action, but by the combination of an unintended consequence of Portugal's entry into the war and appalling weather. The ship arrived in Maputo (then known as Lourenço Marques) in Mozambique in October 1915. Portugal had just entered the war and the authorities in the port now attempted to transfer *Ferreira*'s entire crew to the Portuguese navy. Captain da Sousa managed to reduce the demand to nine reservists, leaving him with six apprentices, a cook and two foreign sailors. Eventually he managed to recruit a number of non-seafaring – but keen – locals and a couple of fishermen, making the crew up to 18. It was too few for a ship of this size but it was all he could muster.

It had taken da Sousa months to assemble this crew and the ship did not sail until late April 1916. She was laden with coal, bound for Namibe. On 1st May 1916, off the South African coast between Port Elizabeth and East London (close to where, as *Cutty Sark*, she had lost her rudder in 1872) *Ferreira* ran into heavy weather. This worsened until the winds were reaching Force 10. The new seamen were, understandably, terrified and little use in such conditions. Then the ship rolled right over to port, with the ends of the lower yardarms in the water. She stayed like that because 15 to 20 tons of her coal cargo had not been loaded properly and had shifted. With the aid of a single hurricane lantern, the apprentices spent the whole day shifting the coal to get the ship back on an even keel. They succeeded but the weather did not improve and, on 3rd May, she was again listing to port. Captain da Sousa thought it too risky to attempt to make for Port Elizabeth, so all he could do was to send his apprentices back into the hold once more and to hope that the weather would improve. But it did not and, again and again, the coal shifted. Finally it shifted so much that da Sousa knew there was no possibility of levelling her. His only chance of saving the ship was to cut away the masts and rigging. Over the next few days more and more was pitched over the side until all that remained was the foremast and fore-topmast.

By 10th May, the wind finally subsided and, after nine days of wondering if his ship would sink, Captain da Sousa finally felt that, if he could find a ship to tow him, he could reach Cape Town. He managed to make contact with the SS *Kia Ora*, a passenger and cargo steamer, and went aboard to ask for help. Unfortunately, *Kia Ora* was bound for Sydney, not Cape Town, and her captain was worried about German submarines in the area. He advised da Sousa to scuttle *Ferreira*. But the Portuguese captain had come through too much for that. He returned to his vessel. After two more days they were drifting towards Cape Aghulas, and almost certain shipwreck, when another steamer came into view. She took *Ferreira* under tow into Table Bay, arriving on 14th May.

Fig. 83 Portuguese crew on board
Ferreira, c. 1921.

Cargoes

Fig. 84 Bill of lading for *Cutty Sark*, for a consignment of beer from London to Newcastle, NSW, 1883.

Cutty Sark's fame rests on the fast bulk transport of two cargoes – tea and wool. Yet it should not be overlooked that a third bulk commodity also played a significant role in her career. This was coal, and during her period under the British flag, the ship carried around 10,000 tons of it, far greater than the total amount of tea she ever carried. It came mostly from the Australian coalfields around Sydney and Newcastle, NSW, although it was Welsh coal loaded at Penarth that she carried on her 'hell-ship' voyage in 1880. Ironically, all the coal was destined for use in steamships, the vessels that would eventually drive her out of both the tea and wool trades.

In contrast, there was never a bulk freight in *Cutty Sark* when she sailed from London. The hold would instead be filled with an enormous variety of goods and products, often described in the shipping press as 'general cargo'. When the ship began to call at Sydney on her way to China, the *Sydney Morning Herald* would give a more fulsome breakdown. The cargo she unloaded in 1878 typified the range:

643 kegs of nails, 981 bars and bundles of iron, 97 bales of paper, 387 bundles of wire, 310 casks and cases of wine and spirits, 16 rolls of lead, 12 cases of galvanised iron, 187 boxes of tin plates, 300 boxes of candles, 21 cases of type, 340 packages of oilstones, 20 bundles of twine, 449 packages of drapery, 37 coils of rope, 307 packages of unspecified hardware, and (amazingly) 67 anchors, 27 chains, 80 bundles of oakum (tarred rope fibres), 55 cases of vestas (matches), 22 hogsheads (over 1,100 gallons/5,250 litres) of oil and over 11,000 other packages.

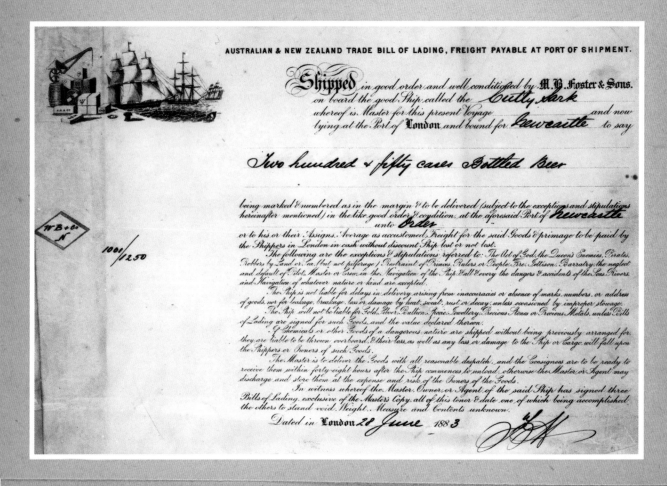

Fig. 85 *Ferreira* discharging cocoa beans in London.

On other voyages, the ship carried pianos and other musical instruments, vast quantities of beer, marmalade, tobacco, medicinal drugs, machinery, boots and shoes, and even hops. In the 1880s and 1890s, on her way down the Thames, she would call in at Gravesend to load around 80 tons of gunpowder, destined for the Australian mines. Even though steamers had taken the homeward cargoes away from the sailing ships, they did not prise the outward freights away too: *Cutty Sark* continued to take these general loads to Australia right to the end of her career under the British flag in 1895.

On at least one occasion *Cutty Sark* also carried a few passengers, though this was unusual since she had no separate accommodation for them. However, the ship's income register for 1873 records £60 received from Messrs Osborne and Ware for 'cabin passage money' on a voyage between Sydney and Shanghai.

Under Portuguese ownership the ship again transported large quantities of coal, most notably from Maputo and which, in 1916, almost caused her to be abandoned because of bad loading. During this period she also carried a wide range of other bulk products, including whale bone, whale oil, guano, pitch-pine, empty oil drums and cocoa beans. One of her last commercial cargoes was scrap iron. There is no clear evidence that she ever carried passengers during her years as *Ferreira*, but a description of her in 1913 suggests that there had once been portholes on her 'tween deck towards the stern: perhaps, for a brief period, she transported emigrants to the Portuguese colonies.

Fig. 86 *Ferreira* ex-*Cutty Sark*, in Cape Town, dismasted, *c.* 1916.

Captain da Sousa's log, as translated in Lubbock's *The Log of the Cutty Sark*, identifies the steamer that rescued *Ferriera* as the Blue Funnel Line's *Indraghiri*. Launched in Glasgow in 1912, this vessel had joined the 'Blue-Flue' fleet in 1915 and was, in fact, then renamed *Eurylochus*. Her own fate was to be sunk in 1941 off Sierra Leone by the German auxiliary cruiser *Kormoran*.

The insured value of *Ferreira* was only £700 – but the estimate to repair the damage from the storm and the loss of her masts and rigging was £2,250. Not only that, the war had created a shortage of suitable wood for replacement masts and yards. Therefore the owners decided to re-rig her, not as a ship but as a barquentine,

a vessel with square sails on the foremast but fore-and-aft sails on the main and mizzen masts. Not only did this require fewer yards, it also needed fewer men to work the vessel than required on a full-rigged ship.

Nevertheless, *Ferreira* spent the remainder of 1916 and all of 1917 in Table Bay. Finally, in January 1918, she was towed out of the dock... and promptly collided with the quayside, damaging both her stem and her figurehead. But she was finally back at sea and 1918 was largely spent sailing up the western coast of Africa, calling at Namibe, the island of Sao Tomé and the Ghanaian capital, Accra. However, on her way back to Lisbon, when she called at Ponta Delgada on the Azores island of São

Miguel on 16th January 1919, her captain discovered that *Ferreira* had been sold in the previous month to another Portuguese ship-owner, João Pires Correia.

Ferreira made her first visit to London in 24 years on 4th June 1919, then on to Swansea. She was next seen on the Thames early in November 1921, having made the crossing from Pensacola in 50 days. It was a measure of her enduring fame that the newspaper *The Daily Mirror* ran a photographic feature on her under the headline 'World famous clipper 'Cutty Sark', still at work'. She left London again for Lisbon on 12th January 1922 but, after losing sails and her mizzen boom in a storm, she took shelter in Falmouth on the 30th. Here she dragged her anchors and managed to damage her own jib-boom as well as the forecastle of another vessel, and it was not until 30th March that she set off again for Lisbon.

At the end of the previous year, João Pires Correia had decided to put the ship up for sale. His London agents, Tatham, Bromage & Co., notified *Lloyd's List* in December 1921 that they were open to offers but it was not until June 1922 that she was bought. The purchaser was another Lisbon-based concern, the Companhia de Navegaçao de Portugal. It renamed her *Maria do Amparo* ('Mary that shelters' – a reference to the Virgin Mary), although she seems to have made only two voyages under its ownership, from Lisbon to Gijon on the north coast of Spain and then on to nearby Santander. These were the old clipper's last independent passages under sail.

Fig. 87 Stern view of *Ferreira*.

Fig. 88 *Ferreira* ex-*Cutty Sark*, in Union Dock, Limehouse, 1921.

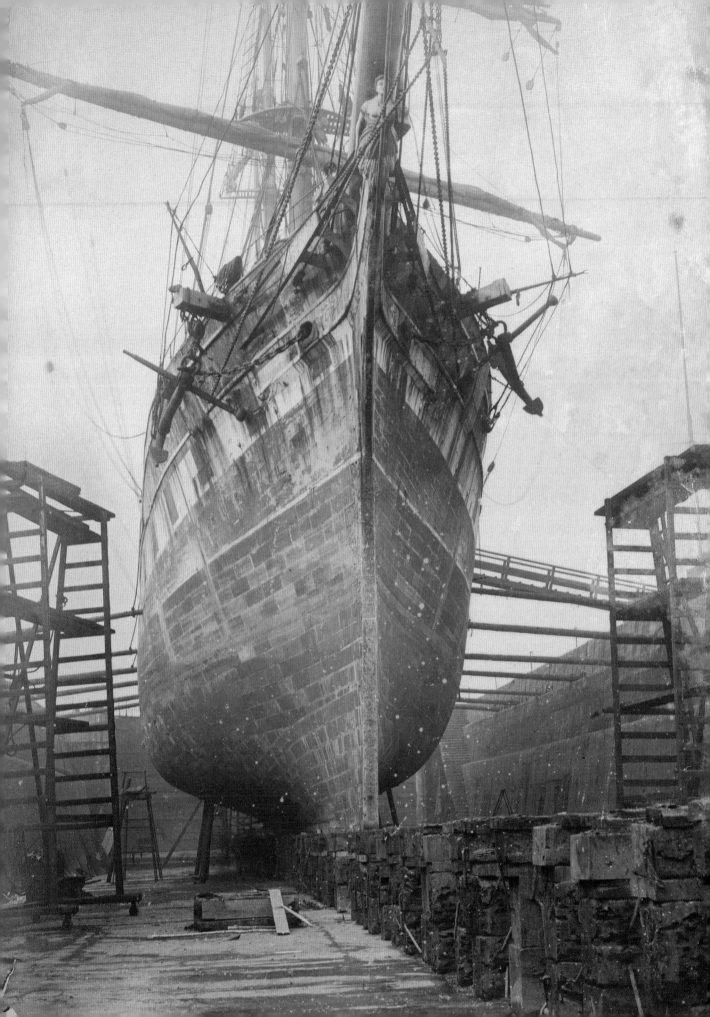

TABLE 16   Voyages of *Ferreira*
(source: Platt, Waite and Sexton, 2009)

DEPARTED	ON	ARRIVED	ON	AT	ON
Gravesend	05/09/1895	Porto	11/10/1895		
Porto		Lisbon	28/10/1895		
Lisbon	12/02/1896	Luanda, Angola	05/04/1896		
Namibe, Angola	29/08/1896	Luanda	03/09/1896		
Luanda	22/09/1896	New Orleans	06/12/1896		
New Orleans	28/12/1896	Lisbon	07/02/1897		
Lisbon	20/05/1897	Lourenço Marques Mozambique	29/07/1897		
Lourenço Marques	09/11/1897	Barbados			
Barbados		New Orleans	26/01/1898		
New Orleans	28/02/1898	Cadiz	14/04/1898		
Cadiz	30/05/1898	Santos		Rio de Janeiro	09/08/1898
Rio de Janeiro	08/09/1898	New Orleans	04/11/1898		
New Orleans	25/11/1898	Lisbon	11/01/1899		
Lisbon	09/06/1899	Benguela, Angola	03/10/1899		
Benguela		New Orleans	20/01/1900		
New Orleans	21/02/1900	Lisbon	05/04/1900		
Lisbon	02/07/1900	Lourenço Marques	06/09/1900		
Lourenço Marques	22/01/1901	Beira, Angola	14/02/1901	Bartholomew Dias (Angola?)	27/05/1901
Bartholomew Dias		Lisbon	30/07/1901		
Lisbon	12/12/1901	Lourenço Marques	11/02/1902		
Lourenço Marques	28/05/1902	New Orleans	16/08/1902		
New Orleans	11/09/1902	Lisbon	23/10/1902		
Lisbon	13/12/1902	Porto	18/12/1902		
Porto		Leixoes	11/03/1903		
Leixoes	16/03/1903	Cardiff	21/03/1903		
Cardiff	04/05/1903	Lourenço Marques	12/07/1903		
Lourenço Marques	11/09/1903	Pernambuco, Brazil	23/10/1903		
Pernambuco	25/11/1903	Porto	11/01/1904		
Porto	29/02/1904	Cardiff	28/03/1904		
Cardiff	13/05/1904	Luanda	07/07/1904		
Luanda	22/08/1904	Barbados	26/09/1904		
Barbados	28/10/1904	New Orleans	15/11/1904		
New Orleans	06/12/1904	Lisbon	14/01/1906		
Lisbon	09/09/1905	Luanda	13/10/1905		
Luanda	21/11/1905	Benguela			
Benguela		New Orleans	05/02/1906		
New Orleans	04/03/1906	Lisbon	18/04/1906		
Lisbon	30/06/1906	Pensacola	06/08/1906		
Mobile	05/01/1907	Pensacola	07/01/1907		
Pensacola	25/03/1907	Rio de Janeiro	17/09/1907		
Rio de Janeiro	29/10/1907	Leixoes	17/12/1907		
Leixoes		Porto	19/12/1907		
Porto	17/04/1908	Lisbon			
Lisbon	24/05/1908	Lourenço Marques	02/08/1908		
Lourenço Marques	31/08/1908	Lisbon	31/10/1908		
Lisbon	05/01/1909	New Orleans	12/02/1909		
New Orleans	02/03/1909	Lisbon	21/04/1909		

DEPARTED	ON	ARRIVED	ON	AT	ON
Lisbon	10/07/1909	Luanda			
Loanda	08/11/1909	Barbados	06/12/1909		
Barbados	20/12/1909	New Orleans	04/01/1910		
New Orleans	15/02/1910	Porto	07/04/1910		
Porto	08/05/1910	New Orleans	13/06/1910		
New Orleans	28/06/1910			Leixoes	31/07/1910
Leixoes		Porto	07/08/1910		
Porto	02/09/1910	Lisbon			
Lisbon	21/12/1910	Namibe	17/02/1911		
Benguela		Luanda	16/04/1911		
Luanda	28/06/1911	San Tome			
				Lisbon	17/10/1911
Lisbon	25/02/1912	Rio de Janeiro	07/04/1912		
Rio de Janeiro	11/05/1912	New Orleans	29/06/1912		
New Orleans	24/07/1912	Lisbon	29/08/1912		
Lisbon	22/11/1912	Rio de Janeiro	18/12/1912		
Rio de Janeiro	15/03/1913	New Orleans	08/05/1913		
New Orleans	05/06/1913	Lisbon	27/07/1913		
Lisbon	19/10/1913	Namibe	08/01/1914		
Namibe	18/03/1914	Liverpool	18/05/1914		
Liverpool	18/07/1914	Namibe	30/09/1914		
Namibe		Liverpool	22/01/1915		
Liverpool	23/04/1915	Newport	25/04/1915		
Newport	12/05/1915	Lisbon			
Lisbon	15/06/1915	Namibe	14/09/1915		
Namibe	12/02/1916	Lourenço Marques	06/04/1916		
Lourenço Marques	23/04/1916	Cape Town (under tow)	15/05/1916		
Cape Town	10/01/1918	Namibe	21/01/1918		
		Sao Thomé	21/06/1918		
Sao Thomé	27/08/1918	Accra	08/09/1918		
Accra		San Miguel, Azores	16/01/1919		
San Miguel, Azores	12/04/1919	Le Havre	14/05/1919		
Le Havre		Gravesend	04/06/1919		
London	02/07/1919	Swansea	11/07/1919		
				Lisbon	16/12/1919
				Lisbon	22/07/1920
				Lisbon	17/11/1920
				Lisbon	13/02/1921
				Lisbon	16/05/1921
Lisbon	09/06/1921	Terceira, Azores			
Terceira, Azores		Pensacola	18/08/1921		
Pensacola	14/09/1921	London	09/11/1921		
London	21/12/1921	Falmouth	30/01/1922		
Falmouth	30/03/1922	Lisbon	14/04/1922		

As *Maria do Amparo*

DEPARTED	ON	ARRIVED	ON	AT	ON
Lisbon	21/06/1922	Gijon	04/07/1922		
Gijon	03/08/1922	Santander	06/08/1922		

The changing fabric of the ship

Fig. 89 Moving teak, c. 1900. Teak was used for the upper planking and main deck of *Cutty Sark*.

Cutty Sark's hull – a combination of Indian teak and American rock elm on a framework of Scottish wrought iron – has proved incredibly durable, and has lasted far longer than the 30 years usually expected for a ship of her period. Collisions, of course, caused damage – such as when she hit two other ships after dragging her anchors off the Kent coast in 1877 – which resulted in the replacement of some of the upper teak planks. But apart from these, there are few instances of planks being replaced for reasons of deterioration during the ship's working life under the British flag. This may partly have been due to the regular replacement, every couple of years, of the protective Muntz metal sheathing of her lower hull.

The ship changed only slightly in appearance during her years in the Willis fleet, most obviously with the addition of a second deckhouse in 1872 and the cutting down of her masts and yards in 1880 (with the loss of her skysail and stunsails). Even less-noticeable modifications were small: the most significant seem to have been the addition of two extra panting beams in the bow (to supplement the five the surveyors insisted on during the ship's construction, to stop the planking moving in and out in rough sea) and the replacement, after 10 years, of the red-pine 'tween deck with one of pitch pine.

More profound changes took place during the ship's years in Portuguese ownership. Again, most were the result of damage rather than decay and included two new rudders, the replacement of all her spars except the lower foremast after her dismasting in 1916, and re-rigging as a barquentine. The 'winged' anchor deck was simplified to a square-edged one. The saloon accommodation was also modified to create a second companionway immediately forward of the ship's wheel, the master then occupying the second mate's cabin and possible knocking through into the steward's cabin.

When *Cutty Sark* returned to British waters, her restoration in Falmouth concentrated largely on re-rigging her as a ship, re-laying the decks and fitting companionways into the hatches. Despite her shabby appearance when she first arrived, the condition of her planks was judged to be excellent. It was still so 16 years later when she was transferred to the Incorporated Thames Nautical Training College. However, the college replaced Captain Dowman's 'tween deck with a near-continuous deck between the bulkheads, closing the hatchways down to the hold. To give more light in the 'tween deck space, 36 portholes were cut through the hull planks, and in places through the diagonal iron bracing. These were covered up again during the 1950s' restoration but the holes in the diagonal bracing are still visible.

Cutty Sark's removal from water was seen as essential to the survival of the ship's original fabric. Nevertheless, she underwent considerable restoration. This included replacing the masts and yards and re-rigging the ship more accurately than Captain Dowman had been able to achieve. New deckhouses were installed and the companionways were replaced in teak and extended down through hatches cut in the 'tween deck to a new deck in the lower hold, which had never existed when the ship was a cargo-carrier. The main deck was relaid, but with teak covering Dowman's pine planking.

It was during these works that the iron framework was seen to be severely wasted in places. However, it was judged that if the rusted metal was chipped back and repainted this would be sufficient to maintain a vessel that would never go back to sea. But the condition of the ironwork continued to deteriorate and, during the 1970s, 47 intermediary frames were inserted into the hull between the existing frames to give her additional strength. These remain in place.

The priority of the 2006–12 conservation project was to retain as much of the fabric as possible from the ship's working life, which was defined as the period from 1869 to 1922. It also sought to clarify the ship's original appearance by removing the 1950s' lower deck (installed to create more exhibition space) and replacing it with a steel platform. The fine teak companionways installed in the hatchways in the 1950s, which, with the patina of age, had taken on the appearance of original features were also removed and replaced – the forward one with a more obviously modern stairway and the aft with a lift, to improve access to the ship for all.

As part of the plan to expose and treat the ironwork, the officers' accommodation was completely dismantled. The saloon's fine maple panelling was assumed to be original, but when it was removed, it was discovered that it had been modified to fit: it had come from another vessel, possibly during the construction of the ship.

Cutty Sark is, like every other historic working structure, a composite of fabric accumulated over the years. Essentially, the upper part of the vessel – the deckhouses, fixtures and fittings, and the rigging – is largely mid-twentieth century (with the notable exceptions of the steering gear and lower forward mast); but the hull is almost entirely original. The planks and the frames, shaped to create one of the fastest sailing ships, are almost all those that sailed the South China Sea on those tea voyages long ago. They are the same elements that were fitted and fastened by Scott & Linton's workforce in the Woodyard in Dumbarton in 1869.

Fig. 90 Stamp in *Cutty Sark*'s ironwork, revealing the source of manufacture – the Monklands ironworks just south of Airdrie, Scotland.

Fig. 91 American rock elm (*Ulmus thomasii*), used for the lower hull planks on *Cutty Sark*.

Saved for the nation

I f *Ferreira* had not been damaged on her way from London to Lisbon in 1922, and
never called in at Falmouth, she might have sailed for a few more years under the
Portuguese flag. Had things gone that way, lack of maintenance would soon have
made her uneconomic to repair and she would most probably have been broken up.
However, during her two-month stay in the Cornish port she was spotted by a retired
sea captain, Wilfred Dowman. Despite her battered appearance, a black-and-white
colour scheme and the rig of a barquentine, he recognised her as the vessel that in
1895 had surged past him – like she had the *Britannia* in 1889 (see page 83) – when he
had been a 16-year-old apprentice on board the sailing ship *Hawksdale*. He knew *Cutty
Sark* was a very special ship and was determined to save her for the nation. Dowman
pursued her back to Portugal and bought her (by then she had been renamed *Maria
do Amparo*) for very much more than her commercial value (her owners realising
that she was of historical interest to the British). For many years it was believed that
Dowman paid £3,750 but in 2017 the National Maritime Museum acquired the
original documents relating to the purchase and her return to Britain. These reveal
that the Dowmans paid £3,500. It is not a huge difference, but a demonstration that
new discoveries are still to be made about the ship's history.

Dowman had been born in 1879, became a ship's boy at 12, an apprentice
at 18 and the master of a steamship at 25. Unfortunately, he lost his position five
and a half years later when his employers reduced the size of their fleet. However,
in 1912 he signed on as first mate of the four-masted barque, *Port Jackson*, a cadet
ship training young gentlemen for careers at the sea. Along with the 24 cadets (and

Figs 96 & 97 Letter from Captain
Dowman to Captain Woodget
(master of *Cutty Sark,* 1885–95),
dated 30th September 1922. At
the time of writing, the ship was
under tow from Santander, having
just been purchased by Dowman:
'I expect her about Sunday night
or early Monday morning and shall
not rest peacefully until I see her
actually in Falmouth harbour.'

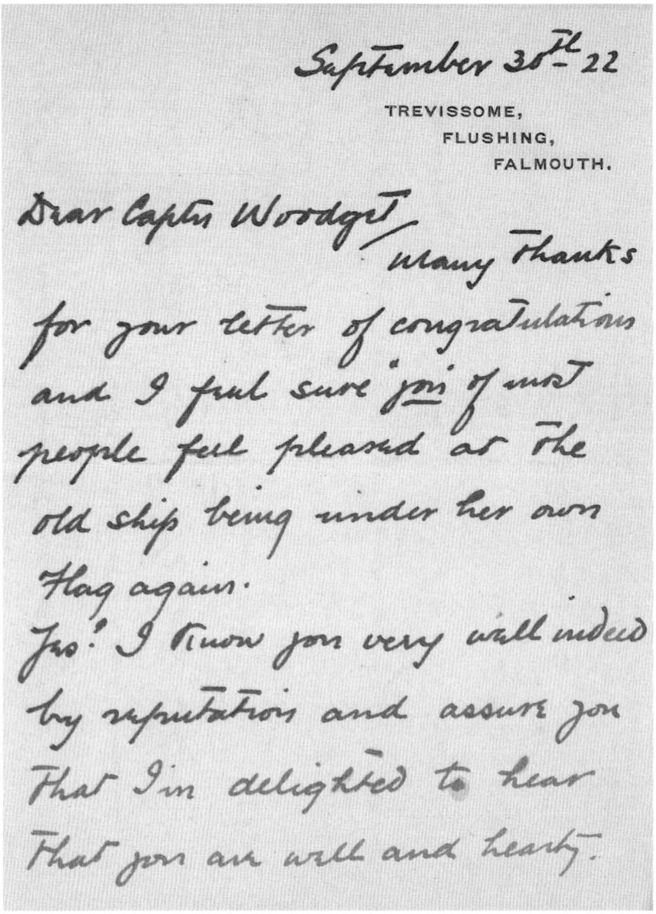

September 30th 22

TREVISSOME,
FLUSHING,
FALMOUTH.

Dear Captn Woodget,

Many thanks for your letter of congratulations and I feel sure you & most people feel pleased at the old ship being under her own Flag again.

Yes! I know you very well indeed by reputation and assure you That I'm delighted to hear That you are well and hearty.

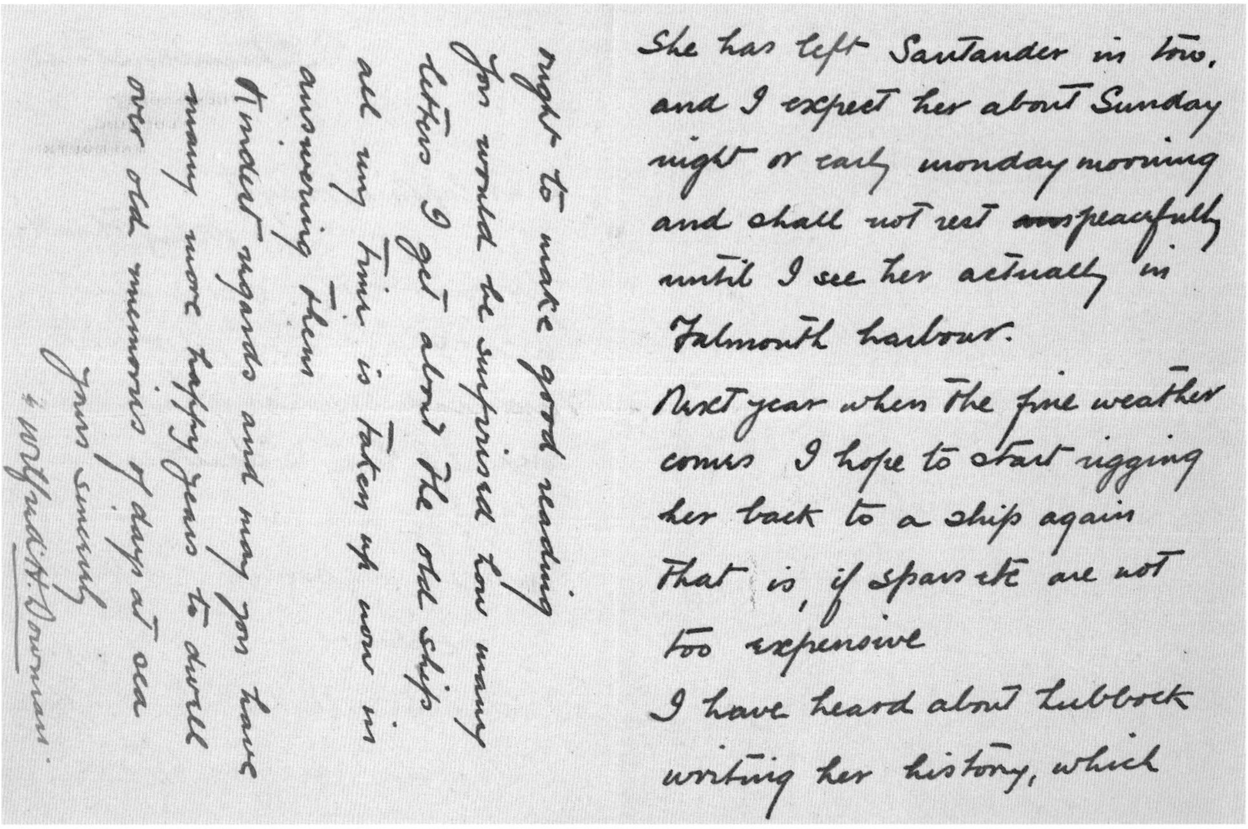

She has left Santander in tow, and I expect her about Sunday night or early monday morning and shall not rest peacefully until I see her actually in Falmouth harbour.

Next year when the fine weather comes I hope to start rigging her back to a ship again That is, if spars etc are not too expensive

I have heard about Lubbock writing her history, which

night to make good reading. You would be surprised how many letters I get about the old ship all my Time is taken up now in answering them

I indeed regards and may you have many more happy years to dwell over old memories of days at sea

yours sincerely
* W.[illegible] [H.] Dowman.

34 crew) for the voyage to Sydney, were two passengers – sisters from the wealthy textile-manufacturing family, the Courtaulds.

Catharine was the younger of the two, an artist and a suffragette, and during this voyage, she and Wilfred fell in love, although Dowman was already married. The First World War intervened (during which time Dowman served in the Royal Naval Reserve) but in mid-1918 his wife began divorce proceedings. It is a measure of the relationship between Wilfred and Catharine that she changed her name to Dowman by deed-poll three months before these proceedings began. Wilfred was demobilised in January 1919 and retired from the sea. His marriage was dissolved on 1st November 1920 and 11 days later he and Catharine married.

The couple lived at Trevissome House, at Flushing, which faces Falmouth across the Penryn River. They owned the topsail schooner *Lady of Avenel*, which was used to train cadets for the merchant service, or Merchant Navy. However, this was a small vessel – a restored *Cutty Sark* would offer far more accommodation, as well as a much

greater challenge for the cadets. As a retired sea captain, Dowman could not have afforded to buy and restore the ship: it was Catharine's money that enabled them to save *Cutty Sark*. Although the ship was re-registered in Wilfred's name alone, at least as much credit belongs to Catharine.

Nevertheless, despite her Courtauld inheritance, the Dowmans made considerable sacrifices to acquire and ready the old clipper, including selling off a farm on their estate.

The ship was towed all the way from Portugal, reaching Falmouth on 2nd October 1922. Re-registered as *Cutty Sark*, she was moored off the foreshore of Trefussis Fields at Flushing. Dowman then attempted to restore the ship to her appearance in 1870, although he did not have access to as much historical information as later restorers. Most of the work was undertaken at the Ponsharden Shipyard,

Fig. 100 Captain Woodget at the wheel, 1924, 28 years after he commanded the vessel. *Cutty Sark* was the Committee Vessel at the Fowey Regatta and Woodget was one of a number of special guests invited to accompany her from Falmouth.

on the Falmouth side of the Penryn River, a yard in which Dowman had an interest. It was a considerable boon to the local economy.

The return of *Cutty Sark* was not just a local issue: it was also widely reported in the national press. *The Observer* of 24th September 1922, under the headline 'The Cutty Sark home again', began its article: 'A shipping transaction of national interest has just been carried through.' So common was knowledge of the ship's return that it came up in conversation at a luncheon held by the London wine merchants Berry Brothers & Rudd the following year. The company's guest was the well-known Scottish artist James McBey (1883–1959), and it discussed with him its plans to launch a scotch whisky for the American market, as soon as Prohibition ended (although this only occurred in 1933, much later than they predicted). But what to call the whisky? The topical name 'Cutty Sark' was suggested and during the meal McBey sketched out the design for a label. This was immediately taken up by Berry Brothers & Rudd and (although, due to a printer's error, the cream paper became the distinctive yellow) one of the world's best-known brands was created.

By 1924, restoration of the ship was complete. Dowman may have nurtured a vision to sail her to Australia and back but it was not to be. Only once did *Cutty Sark* venture out of Falmouth during Dowman's time. In August of 1924, she was taken under tow to Fowey to be Committee Vessel for the regatta there. The man who took the helm for part of the journey was her old, last and greatest, master, Captain Woodget, who came down to Falmouth for the occasion.

In Falmouth, *Cutty Sark* was a cadet-training establishment, with ex-Royal Navy Warrant Officer James Gilbert engaged as the superintendent and chief cadet instructor. Other employees of Dowman helped with the maintenance of the ship. As a result, dozens of boys, from a wide variety of backgrounds, were given an education

Remembering *Cutty Sark* in Falmouth
Memories from the Cutty Sark Trust's oral history archive

Extracts from an interview with David Mudd, by Simon Schofield – 19th November 2003.

'My grandfather, Captain Edward Rooney, was a square-rig skipper as well as a steam skipper. He became a Lloyd's surveyor at Falmouth. In connection with that he got to know the seafaring fraternity, particularly Wilfred Dowman. And Wilfred Dowman thought the one person who could really bring [*Cutty Sark*] safely back to Britain was my grandfather. So he was dispatched to pick up this rather tatty, grotty old barquentine-rigged coffin ship, as he called her. As he looked aloft, he saw the Portuguese flag. I won't say what he said but it would have been a very appropriate nautical oath, like "get rid of that rag". Down fluttered the Portuguese ensign and in complete contradiction of etiquette, the rules of the sea and nationality, he broke out the Red Ensign, so that she sailed into Falmouth for the last time under the "red duster".

By an amazing coincidence, 16 years later, in 1938, when she left Falmouth my own father, who was a Trinity House pilot, took her out. There were crowds, but she had only been in Falmouth for 16 years and big sailing ships – *Pamir*, *Viking* and, *Passat* – were still calling in Falmouth in 1949 and 1950: so therefore, to Falmouth, it was perhaps not such a great event when it happened as it would seem with hindsight. It was just a well-loved ship, a well-loved feature going out of port. I think that, sadly, *Cutty Sark* is no longer regarded as part of Falmouth, except in one particular way. The work that went into her from 1922 onwards really brought out the finest craftsmanship of the shipwrights and the chippies and the boat-building industry in Falmouth. It is probably that which helped shield the recession when it finally broke in the 1930s. People had rekindled old skills [and] qualities of craftsmanship, so there was a living legacy there. I would say that one of the reasons that Falmouth, [specifically] one of our local enterprises, Pendennis [Shipyard], is dealing so well in the luxury yacht class is because *Cutty Sark* rekindled workmanship among skilled workers.'

**Extracts from an interview with Gordon Martin,
by Simon Schofield – 2nd November 2003.**

'It is difficult to say when I first can remember seeing her. It must have been [when I was] four or five years old. She was moored head [to the] west in the harbour, and a beautiful sight with the *Foudroyant*, another old naval 'wooden wall' captured from the French. And of course one was woken up in this area after the first of May each morning with the gun of the Falmouth or Royal Cornwall Yacht Club firing and the bugle on the Foudroyant, and the boys on the *Cutty Sark* hoisting the flag. *Cutty Sark* always was part-and-parcel of Falmouth harbour. I loved her: I looked at her many times and when I got old enough and began to be a naughty boy, sometimes coming home late from school, Father used to say to me: "Right, you're aboard the *Cutty*. You pick up Captain Gilbert tomorrow." Captain Gilbert was put in charge of *Cutty Sark* on her moorings for Captain Dowman. He looked after the young cadets on there. Now I can't ever say that I was a cadet but, on such times at weekends when I've been a bit of a rascal, Father would send me out there, and on Saturday morning I rowed Captain Gilbert aboard the *Cutty Sark* and I stayed there until Monday morning. And far and away from [teaching] anything, he used to go aft and sit on the poop and perhaps read a book and set me to do what I had to do.

Sometimes we had 12 boys: some of them were undergraduates, some of them were "scurfers", "sailorfares" from St Mawes who never had much money. Captain Dowman looked on them with a little bit of fondness and said, "Right, my lad, come aboard". And some of the boys paid their way because *Cutty Sark* was mostly for young cadets that were going into the Merchant Navy, whereas the *Foudroyant* astern of her was manned by all-uniform naval [cadets]. And she was for pre-entry into the [Royal] Navy. We intermingled with her: some of their boys came with us sometimes, sometimes ours went over there. We had the advantage of having three tall masts, whereas Foudroyant had a little broomstick and [that] didn't allow much for doing aloft work.

You were allowed to wear shoes on the deck provided you made them yourself. And they were usually made of four-strand sennit. Great long piece, and then you sewed it all together and you sewed a bit of canvas on the top; and very comfortable they were too. Captain Gilbert liked them because they helped to clean the deck.

The boatmen used to do fairly well from the Quay and from the Prince of Wales Pier, even from Greenbank and Flushing. They used to row them [out to *Cutty Sark*] and charge them for coming aboard; and of course, when they came aboard, then we were allowed in the centre castle to make a cup of tea. During the time of visitors coming aboard, especially in the summer, boys were disbanded and they could show them around and sometimes got a little tip!

[James Gilbert would] say to me: "Right, we've visitors coming aboard today, we'll clear away and just do knots, bends and hitches", whereby we had several lengths of rope put out with tails on them, so like I'd tell them how to do the different knots and bends and hitches that went with it, which I was very deft at.

[When *Cutty Sark* left in 1938] I think upon Pendennis Head there were hundreds of people watching her go out. Not so when the *Foudroyant* went away: nobody, I don't think anybody, knew she went! But when *Cutty* went, it was like cutting off your leg. It was a big shame.'

Fig. 102 Certificate of Discharge for Henry Gibbins, *Cutty Sark* cadet, 1924. The certificate is signed by James Gilbert, the chief cadet instructor on board the training ship *Cutty Sark*.

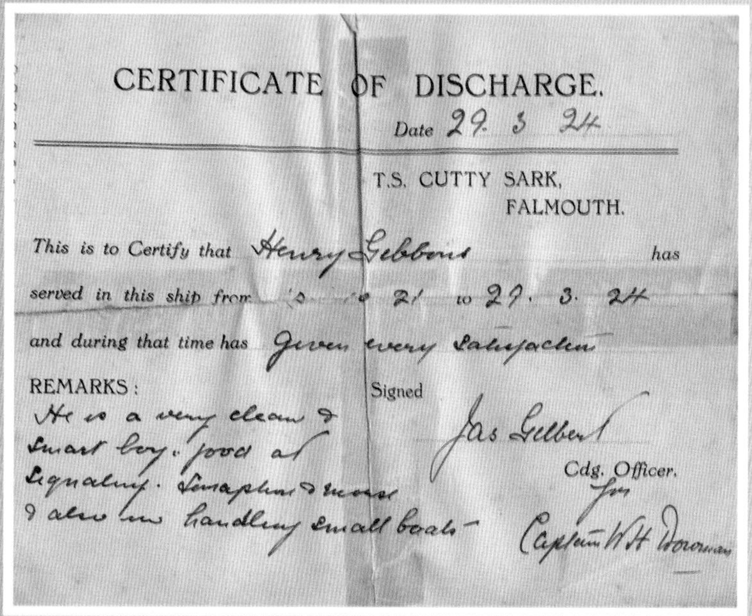

CERTIFICATE OF DISCHARGE.

Date 29. 3 24

T.S. CUTTY SARK,
FALMOUTH.

This is to Certify that *Henry Gibbins* has served in this ship from *'s 21* to *29. 3. 24* and during that time has *given every satisfaction*

REMARKS: *He is a very clean & smart boy. good at Signalling. Semaphore & morse I also in handling small boats*

Signed *Jas Gilbert*

Cdg. Officer.
for *Captain W.H. Dowman*

to start their careers in the merchant service. *Cutty Sark* was also a visitor attraction in Falmouth (although she was only accessible by rowing boat).

Fig. 103 *Cutty Sark* used as a training ship for boys.

She was, however, not the only historic ship in Falmouth being used as a training vessel. Both the frigate *Foudroyant* (now in Hartlepool and restored under her original name of *Trincomalee*) and the 74-gun *Implacable* (which would later play an off-stage role in the *Cutty Sark*'s own survival) were there during part of *Cutty Sark*'s Falmouth years, although both these ships were used to train young men for the Royal Navy, not the merchant service.

Dowman was a genial and generous man, famed for his hospitality and for the parties he hosted at Trevissome House, although he apparently always retained an air of command and strictness. He did much to popularise yachting in Falmouth and was one of the first to introduce the *Sunbeam* class to the town. He and Catharine owned separate craft and were keen competitors in the weekly races. Their summers were usually spent in Cornwall and winters at Portofino, in Italy, with the family's schooner, *Mermerus*, sailing down to the Mediterranean to join them for the season. The Dowmans were described as the 'very epitome of gentlefolk', but Wilfred's health was poor. Attempting to improve it, in 1936 he travelled alone to the West Indies, but during the homeward journey he died very suddenly of a cerebral haemorrhage. He had only just reached the age of 57.

Back in Falmouth, there was no one to take over the ship. It is said that Catharine offered *Cutty Sark* to Falmouth Council with enough money to provide for three years' maintenance, but it declined to accept her. And with expensive harbour dues to be paid, the fate of *Cutty Sark* was once more uncertain.

Cutty Sark at Greenhithe, 1938–53

The Worshipful Company of Shipwrights expressed an interest in *Cutty Sark* becoming its headquarters on the Thames but this came to nothing, even though plans for her conversion were drawn up. However, another institution further downstream saw an opportunity to add a practical vessel to its establishment. The Incorporated Thames Nautical Training College at Greenhithe in Kent was the successor to the Thames Marine Officer Training School, which had been established in 1862 with the loan from the Admiralty of two warships in succession. The first was the 50-gun frigate HMS *Worcester*; shortly afterwards, when she was broken up, the 86-gun two-decker HMS *Frederick William* replaced her (and was duly renamed *Worcester*). The cadets lived on board these ships but *Cutty Sark* would be a welcome addition to the establishment as a much handier ship for teaching sail drill.

Catharine Dowman 'sold' the ship to the college for 10 shillings – and then made a donation of £5,000 for the vessel's upkeep. On 15th June 1938, *Cutty Sark* left Falmouth and made her very last sea voyage, albeit under tow, round the south coast to her new Kent home on the south bank of the River Thames. It is said that a couple of headsails, lower topsails and a spanker were made for this voyage, so this might also be counted as her last voyage under sail. At some points she was allegedly out-sailing the tug.

With the outbreak of the Second World War, *Cutty Sark*'s topmasts and topgallant masts were lowered and her upper yards struck to reduce her size and thus her potential as a target for German bombers. She was also converted to an emergency shelter for the college cadets in case of a gas or bomb attack. Her decks were made gas-proof (as it would have been impossible to seal all the gun-ports on *Worcester*). Sandbags were filled with ballast from her hold, decontamination showers were installed, and boarding nets and ladders were placed over her sides for fast embarking and disembarking.

Fig. 104 Signing the documents transferring ownership of *Cutty Sark* from Mrs Dowman to the Incorporated Thames Nautical Training College, 21st May 1938.

Fig. 105 *Worcester* cadets crowded on the stern of *Cutty Sark*.

Following pages:
Fig. 106 *Cutty Sark* arriving at Greenhithe, 1938. The cadets welcome her from *Worcester II*, the main training ship used by the Incorporated Thames Nautical Training College.

CUTTY SARK: THE LAST OF THE TEA CLIPPERS

These preparations proved unnecessary. The government soon decided to evacuate all training ships and the college moved to Foots Cray Place in south-east London. Ironically, the new site incurred substantial bomb damage whereas *Cutty Sark* survived the war unscathed. However, the ship suffered terribly from the lack of regular maintenance. She was also in a vulnerable position on the Thames and 1952 was a particularly bad year for her. In January, a fully laden tanker of 800 tons ran foul of her bow – *Cutty Sark*'s 40-foot (12-metre) jib-boom immediately caught the fo'c's'le rails of the *Worcester* and snapped, carrying away all the fittings, as well as the arm of the figurehead. Then, in November, a lighter scraped along her starboard side, ripping off a large quantity of her protective Muntz metal sheathing.

Unfortunately, the college's priorities now lay elsewhere. In January 1946 it had taken possession of the third *Worcester* from the Admiralty, the former HMS *Exmouth*. Launched in 1905, she had been the Royal Navy's first purpose-built training vessel, although she had spent the war as a depot ship. The college's resources were now ploughed into converting her into a modern training vessel. Now sail-training was no longer considered important and *Cutty Sark* was no longer needed.

Fig. 107 *Cutty Sark* alongside *Worcester II, c.* 1938–39. Both ships are dressed overall for Prize Day at the Incorporated Thames Nautical Training College.

Remembering HMS *Worcester* and *Cutty Sark* in Greenhithe

Memories from the Cutty Sark Trust's oral history archive

Extracts from an interview with Barbara Bullen – a Greenhithe schoolgirl in 1945 – by Simon Schofield, 27th September 2004.

'It was the end of the war, the summer of '45. I can't remember the exact date but it must have been June because it was a hot sunny day. We were just beginning to get some freedom after being stuck in concrete shelters for what seemed like forever. So to come out into the sunshine… We had to walk [to the riverside]: it was about a mile and a half away, Swanscombe School to Greenhithe Pier. It's called a promenade but it was very derelict really. There's a small footpath, a green tunnel-like footpath. As you come up to Ingress Abbey you walk up a slope and there suddenly it all opens up. There was a beautiful blue sky and we were able to run down the bank onto the promenade and there was the big black Worcester ship, quite stark-looking. Behind that was the *Cutty Sark*, and she was beautiful. She looked like a...I don't know, a fairy? Something along those lines, so elegant with all the flags flying because she didn't have to be hidden anymore from the aeroplanes. There we could see sailors lined up with white bands round their navy-blue caps and we were marshalled into little rowing boats about 10 or so at a time and rowed to the back of the *Worcester* onto the *Cutty Sark*. We had been learning about the Plimsoll Line, and we were told to look for that but I can't remember doing it.

There were rope ladders hanging down and sailors leaning over waiting to pull us up. I don't think anybody fell but we were all very excited: we must have made a lot of noise! Then when we got up on the deck we were able to ramble and roam around a little bit and they spread out some food on the…I don't know what they are called… slats that cover the deck to the holds. It was absolutely marvellous to have cake; we probably had lemonade; I don't remember what else but we must have been there an hour or more. Some of the boys wanted to climb the rigging but I think they were dissuaded from that! I didn't want to go down into the ship because it looked very dark and black. So we stood on the deck and the sun shone and there was a light breeze and the ship rocked gently and it was the most amazing experience that I've never, ever forgotten.'

Remembering HMS *Worcester* and *Cutty Sark* in Greenhithe cont.

Extracts from an interview with Malcolm Borland – ex-*Worcester* cadet – by Jessica Lewis, 10th June 2011.

'Of course she had gone through the war and been neglected and she really wasn't safe for the cadets to do much aboard, but when on the day you were Officer of the Watch or Mate of the Deck on *Worcester*, one of your duties was to go round and light the anchor lights on *Cutty Sark* and put them out again in the morning; and one did go across for things like that. But at spring tides on the ebb, there are very strong tides at the *Worcester* and it was not easy sometimes to row round to the *Cutty Sark*: slack water was the time to do it because it was a three- to four-knot tide.'

Extracts from an interview with Gerry Smith – ex-*Worcester* cadet – by Simon Schofield, 22nd March 2005.

'No one lived on board [*Cutty Sark*]. She was commonly supposed to be haunted – [by] a mad Chinese cook. [*Worcester*] was a culture shock. The first term was hell, the second term wasn't too bad and by the third term I had just about found my feet. The food was atrocious. We all slept in hammocks [on the *Worcester*]. And I think we all roused out at about half past six or seven o'clock in the morning and you had to trice your hammock up and carry them along the deck and put them in the hammock nettings, where they were stored over during the day, and then up to the showers. I think we swept [and] cleaned up decks first. We went up and did some physical exercises on the upper deck, and then breakfast, and

then into class for classroom studies. That lasted all day really, with a break for lunch. The studies were mixed: part of them were school work and part were seamanship and we did a lot of boat work. We did anything connected with nautical things: wire splicing, knots and splices. We had some splendid old Petty Officers on board. Then of course there were school staff, with the teachers. We did a lot of games. If it was too wet to go ashore we used to play deck hockey, which was great fun, and there were plenty of sports facilities ashore. There was rugby, cricket, tennis and running. It was fun, I enjoyed it. You occasionally had what was called a free walk on Sunday afternoons but there was nowhere really to walk. It was too far to walk into Gravesend and there was nothing in Greenhithe. Fraternisation was frowned upon. In fact, in the summer time, some of the girls from Greenhithe would hire themselves some rowing boats, especially if the tide was slack, and row out to the ship and peer through the lower deck windows at the cadets in their hammocks; and quite often we would get turned out to turn the fire hoses on them to drive them away!'

Extracts from an interview with Brian Beale – ex-Worcester cadet – by Simon Schofield, 8th March 2004.

'One of the outstanding images I have of going on board [*Cutty Sark*] was the nostalgic, musty smell of the decks and tarred hemp, and the blocks and the height of the decks, and particularly the actual

length of some of the apprentices' bunks. Now on the *Worcester* we probably had about 80 square feet of space for each cadet: that was with our sea chest and hammock space, and that wasn't particularly spacious by any means. But when you went on the *Cutty Sark* and you realised what sort of conditions people had to sail in, in those days; and as I say the bunks were about 5 feet long, which made you wonder how anybody ever slept at the time. The cabins were extremely small and we used to go there for cleaning parties and also for some seamanship.

[The day the ship was transferred to the Cutty Sark Preservation Society] was a day of high emotion because we all realised by then that the *Cutty Sark* was a very famous ship and that the whole nation had become interested in this project to preserve it. We had practised for some months to meet the Duke of Edinburgh and present him with this Guard of Honour. During that day there were a lot of visitors on the ship and the whole ship's company turned out for the Duke. From what I can remember, the foreshore was absolutely lined with the public all waving flags, as it had been known locally that the Duke was going to come along to take over the deeds, and it was almost like a coronation-day really.'

Fig. 109 *Cutty Sark* alongside *Worcester III*, 1953. In January 1946, the college had taken possession of the third *Worcester* for training cadets.

Cutty Sark restored

The college's first thought was to offer *Cutty Sark* to the National Maritime Museum at nearby Greenwich, but the museum had neither the authority nor the resources to take her over. Its director, Frank Carr, would nevertheless play the most significant role in ensuring that the ship was saved.

Cutty Sark's future may have looked bleak but her survival was in some degree helped by the loss of another historic vessel: HMS *Implacable*, originally the French-built 74-gun *Duguay-Trouin* of 1800, had fought at the Battle of Trafalgar in 1805 and was captured shortly afterwards. Renamed *Implacable* as a ship of the Royal Navy, she survived into the 1900s as a training vessel, by which time she was the last surviving '74' (British or French) – which, as a type, was the mainstay of the battle fleets of the Napoleonic period. At one time she had been moored at Falmouth, close to *Cutty Sark*, and underwent several restorations in the 1920s and 1930s. Despite these, by the late 1940s she was again in very poor condition. Nevertheless, recognising the ship's significance, the London County Council (LCC) offered a place at Greenwich to *Implacable*, but her restoration costs were thought to be too great to be borne by the government in post-war Britain. On 2nd December 1949, after her figurehead and stern decorations were removed (and preserved in the National Maritime Museum), *Implacable* was scuttled off the Isle of Wight, jointly flying French and British colours. Frank Carr later recalled: 'I was there and I wept.'

Carr was determined that a similar fate should not befall *Cutty Sark*. He reminded the London County Council (LCC) that it had offered the Greenwich site of the former Ship Hotel (flattened by wartime bombing) for *Implacable* and he now persuaded it to make this same site available for *Cutty Sark* instead. He even cajoled the LCC into paying for the ship to be towed to Millwall Docks in February 1951 for a survey and a coat of paint. *Cutty Sark* was then anchored off Deptford as part of the

Fig. 110 HRH The Duke of Edinburgh (far right) receives the transfer papers for *Cutty Sark* on behalf of the Cutty Sark Preservation Society.

Festival of Britain, partly to gauge the public interest in her as an attraction. Crucially, Carr had also engaged the enthusiasm and support of HRH The Duke of Edinburgh. This led to the creation of the Cutty Sark Steering Committee, which investigated the feasibility of preserving the ship. When it concluded that preservation was entirely practicable if the resources could be found, the Cutty Sark Preservation Society was established with HRH the Duke as its patron. Registered in October 1952, the society aimed to raise £250,000 by public subscription and succeeded in doing so. This was the sum needed not only to restore the ship but also to create a new dry-dock or dry berth for her on the Greenwich waterfront.

On 28th May 1953, HRH The Duke of Edinburgh came downriver and boarded *Cutty Sark* to accept the Bill of Sale transferring her ownership to the Cutty Sark Preservation Society. However, it was not until 18th February of the following year that two tugs towed *Cutty Sark* from Greenhithe to the South Import Dock in the East India Docks.

Several positions in what is now Cutty Sark Gardens were considered. The one eventually selected involved the demolition of 13 back-to-back homes and the resettlement of the families who occupied them. Given the housing shortage in post-war Britain, this was a task achieved with laudable diplomatic skill.

Work on the ship's new dry berth began on 22nd February 1954 and three months later the Duke of Edinburgh started the driving of the last pile and laid the foundation stone. It read:

THIS STONE WAS LAID ON 3RD JUNE 1954 BY

HIS ROYAL HIGHNESS

THE DUKE OF EDINBURGH

PATRON OF THE CUTTY SARK PRESERVATION SOCIETY

IT ACKNOWLEDGES THE GENEROUS PUBLIC SUBSCRIPTIONS

FROM ALL OVER THE WORLD WHICH ENABLED THIS BERTH

TO BE CONSTRUCTED ON LAND MADE AVAILABLE

BY THE LONDON COUNTY COUNCIL

The berth was essentially a concrete box, 260 feet (79 metres) in length with a maximum width of 30 feet (9 metres) and 31 feet (9.5 metres) below ground level. Internally it was 253 feet (77 metres) long with a depth of 19 feet 7 inches (6 metres). Along the centre-line lay a low, 205-foot (62.5-metre) concrete plinth on which the ship's keel would sit. Built by Sir Robert McAlpine & Sons, the dock cost £90,000 – well under the original estimate of £140,000.

Not only did the Cutty Sark Preservation Society wish to preserve the last of the tea clippers, it also wanted to preserve *Cutty Sark* as a permanent memorial to the merchant service – and particularly the more than 44,000 merchant seamen lost in the two world wars. The modernist sculptor Maurice Lambert (1901–64) – at the time as famous as Henry Moore, Ben Nicholson and Barbara Hepworth – was commissioned to design a memorial wreath, very loosely based on the Star of India on the ship's stern, but incorporating the national flowers of the home nations.

Cast in concrete, it formed part of the short, southern face of the dock wall, above the foundation stone laid by the Duke of Edinburgh. It was flanked by two more memorials. The one on the right read:

IN MEMORY OF THOSE
WHOSE SERVICE IN
THE MERCHANT NAVY
HELPED TO ENLARGE
THE LIVELIHOOD OF
BRITAIN AND PROTECT
THE FREEDOM OF THE
BRITISH COMMONWEALTH
OF NATIONS.

And on the left:

HERE TO COMMEMORATE
AN ERA THE CUTTY SARK
HAS BEEN PRESERVED AS
A TRIBUTE TO THE SHIPS
AND MEN OF THE MERCHANT
NAVY IN THE DAYS OF SAIL.

This second plaque ends with the couplet:

They mark our passage as a race of men

Earth will not see such ships as these again

These are the final two lines from the poem *Ships* (with the penultimate word 'these' substituted for 'those' in the original, published in *Salt-Water Poems and Ballads*, 1912), by John Masefield, who was the Poet Laureate at the time (he held the post from 1930 to 1967).

The original sculpture is today concealed by changes made in the 2006–12 conservation project, but the design has been reproduced in the centre of the dock's new floor as part of the new interpretation scheme.

In the excavation of the dock, a narrow temporary channel was cut from its northern end to the river. Because of the nearness of the roof of the Greenwich foot tunnel this had to be slightly curved and the end of Greenwich pier dismantled to accommodate the ship's entry. The date selected for the first attempt to float the ship into the dock was 10th December 1954 – the start of three days of spring tides. Yet, even though conditions were not ideal and she had less than 1 foot 6 inches (about 45 centimetres) of water under her keel, she was manoeuvred into position on that first try, and, as the tide fell, she came to rest less than 3 inches (8 centimetres) from perfectly square on the central concrete plinth.

The natural ebb of the tide was sufficient to drain the dock dry. The entrance was quickly sealed with bags of cement before the next tide, and concreted, the channel filled in and the river wall rebuilt: *Cutty Sark* was now landlocked. The restoration could begin.

The ship had been altered in a few minor ways from the time she was launched, both when under the British and Portuguese flags, and again during her years in Falmouth and Greenhithe. It was now decided to restore her to her appearance as a tea clipper around 1872 – a date chosen because this was when the aft deckhouse had been installed. The ship was also re-rigged more accurately than Captain Dowman could achieve with the limited knowledge at his disposal. New information came to light from descendants of John Willis and Hercules Linton, particularly about the decoration of the vessel. A descendent of Willis even came forward with the original Star of India emblem

from the ship's stern, which must have been removed when *Cutty Sark* was sold in 1895.

Some compromises were made: a number of portholes cut at Greenhithe on the 'tween deck aft of the bulkhead were retained for ventilation and the Portuguese companionway at the stern, giving access to the officers' accommodation, was also kept for the ease of visitor flow (it is thought that during the Portuguese period, the master used what had been designated as the second mate's cabin).

As the ship was being restored, the Cutty Sark Preservation Society accepted a donation of the world's largest collection of merchant-ship figureheads. They came from an avid collector called Sydney Cumbers (1875–1959). Despite an eye patch, which gave him a piratical appearance and the nickname 'Long John Silver' or 'Captain Silver', Cumbers had no maritime background: the eye patch was the result of a childhood accident with a toy gun. He was, in fact, a successful businessman in the printers' ink trade. For many years he had displayed his collection in 'The Look-Out' on the seafront at Gravesend, leased from the Clarendon Hotel. Hearing of *Cutty Sark*'s restoration, Cumbers decided that this would be a fitting venue for the collection's display. It is dedicated to the 'Little Ships of Dunkirk,' which had saved so many lives in the wartime evacuation of the British Expeditionary Force and its allies in 1940.

Part of the collection is a roll-call of the great and good of Victorian Britain, with representations in wood of such famous figures as Disraeli, Gladstone, General Gordon and Florence Nightingale. But many of the ships from which the figureheads came have never been identified, and were probably salvaged from wrecks. Their veiled history makes them all the more fitting as a memorial to all those who have served in the merchant service.

Cutty Sark was opened by Her Majesty The Queen on 25th June 1957, three and a half years after being docked in Greenwich. Such was the importance of the event that it was shown live on television, with commentary by Richard Dimbleby, the most distinguished broadcaster of the day.

Shortly afterwards, the 'cutty sark' masthead vane, lost when the topmast was cut away in the May storm of 1916, was reunited with the ship (see page 81). It had somehow been rescued when the ship was de-masted in 1916 and presented to a Cape Town collector (although of Africana rather than maritime memorabilia). On his death, some of his artefacts were sold, including the vane. A photograph was sent to Captain Woodget in Norfolk, who verified its authenticity, though it also came with a letter that confirmed its provenance, signed in 1916 by the Portuguese Consul at Cape Town. Purchased by the Cutty Sark Trust, the vane is now on display on board the ship.

Fig. 115 Sydney Cumbers, also known as 'Captain Long John Silver', unknown artist, 1930s.

Fig. 116 Figureheads and their dedication plaque at 'The Look-Out' in Gravesend, *c*. 1945–53. Sydney Cumbers dedicated his collection to the men of the merchant service and the 'Little Ships of Dunkirk'.

THE SILVER COLLECTION

DEDICATED
TO THE
MERCHANT SEAMEN OF BRITAIN
AND
THE MEN OF THE LITTLE SHIPS
WHO WENT TO
DUNKIRK.

Lifebelt

This was on *Cutty Sark* during the period she was a training ship at Greenhithe.

THE
OPIUM WAR

Up to 1842, China exported its [...]
Guangdong and Macao, taking p[...]
in silver. To recoup some of this [...]
British smuggled opium into Chi[...]
Chinese authorities resisted, the[...]
two wars (1839-1842 and 1856[...]
seizing Hong Kong and forcing o[...]
be opened up to foreign trade.

Over the next 49 years, nearly fifteen million visitors came aboard the ship, but many more millions enjoyed the view of her from the piazza in which she stands – Cutty Sark Gardens. Her status as a London icon and as one of the most famous ships in the world was further strengthened from 1981 when she became a landmark on the route of the annual London Marathon, first run in that year.

Encouraged by the success of *Cutty Sark*'s restoration, the Maritime Trust was established, which incorporated the Cutty Sark Preservation Society, to acquire a significant number of other historic vessels around the country, most notably the research vessel *Discovery*, the steam coaster *Robin*, the schooner *Kathleen & May* and the steam drifter *Lydia Eva*. The surpluses generated by *Cutty Sark* from admissions contributed substantially to the restoration of these vessels. But as a consequence, there was little left in reserve when major works were needed on *Cutty Sark* herself.

When *Cutty Sark* was restored in the 1950s it was believed that she was now preserved forever. However, the effect of the London air had not been taken into consideration. Within a decade, all the ship's Muntz metal sheathing was so badly corroded that it had to be replaced with plates of Alumbro, an aluminium-bearing brass, which does not contain the high zinc content of Muntz metal. The method of supporting the ship in the dock – a system of props and shores – was standard practice for holding a vessel for a few months while she was repaired, but after several decades it began to distort the shape of the hull, which was her most significant attribute. The main deck was frequently repaired but it continued to leak badly and rainwater seeped down to the bottom of the hold, where the water caused the floors – the lowest part of the frames – to corrode away (entirely in some places, to tissue thinness in others).

In the 1970s, the weakness of the iron structure became critical and a number of steel frames were inserted between the original iron ones in order to strengthen the hull. This gave the ship stability for another 20 years but a survey in the mid-1990s estimated that more than 60 per cent of fastenings holding the planking to the iron framework had failed and the condition of the iron framework was extremely weak. The surveyors predicted that, unless she was strengthened substantially within the next 10 years, her counter would drop, sending a shockwave through the structure, leaving a pile of iron and timber in the dock. It was clear that *Cutty Sark* was, once again, in need of very major works if she was to survive.

Remembering the restoration of *Cutty Sark* in the 1950s
Memories from the Cutty Sark Trust's oral history archive

Extracts from an interview with Bryan Pearson – who was on the tug Kenia, which brought *Cutty Sark* to her Greenwich dock – by Simon Schofield, 12th January 2004.

'I was told I had to be a bit smart for that particular day – clean shirt! So I had to go and buy one. We just chugged round to where the *Cutty Sark* was lying. Captain William Simmons said what we've got to do. Now I must admit I did wonder, because it was not long after the war and I did believe that we were towing it to be scrapped. We're going back to 1954 now and she looked, to be perfectly honest, she looked a hulk and there were so many of those hulks up and down this river.

We brought her round and the other two tugs did the actual manoeuvring side of [positioning] the ship, [and] backed her round. Getting it in wasn't too bad because you had two great big tugs there, which were quite capable of towing liners around. One tug would have done her but being as delicate as she was [they were cautious]. They brought her head up past it [the dock entrance] and put her [in] stern first. We had the press on board and they took all the photographs.

I don't really think at that particular time that there were any tears in anybody's eyes, or glee. We were just doing a job. But every time I come past in the train, I always say to my grandchild, I do feel proud that I have done something.

You've got to be dead from the neck up not to appreciate her when you see her. I mean the way she is, she is so beautiful and there's nothing like a nice sailing ship.'

Extracts from an interview with John Dodge – apprentice carpenter with Green & Silley Weir – by Jessica Lewis, 29th September 2010.

'Everybody knew that it had come in: "Ooh, the *Cutty Sark*'s coming" – but it wasn't so well publicised in those days and "What's the *Cutty Sark*?", "Oh, it's an old sailing ship"; and then of course we used to work in different docks with different jobs and I did happen to see this sad-looking hulk in Millwall Dock.

I can't remember when she came in, but I went into the drawing office at the end of 1953 and the whole drawings for the project came into our office from the Greater London Council. And I thought, what's the GLC doing with drawings of ships – because the GLC were not (how shall I say) very efficient about anything? They were very good drawings so the [Green & Silley Weir] drawing office didn't have any input into it – they'd already been done. I went off to sea at the end of 1954, came back in May '57, and one of the first jobs was the *Cutty Sark*; and I did work in the woodwork shop at Blackwall yard and then we came up and fitted bits in, and did this and did that, and it was panic for the Queen to come on in June,

We did the gingerbread on the stern and the steering wheel; we worked on the saloon and the captain's cabin, we made the buckets, the fire buckets and things like that. We made the windlass, which we got working.

I actually made the [glass carriers in the saloon and] some fancy cornice pieces. I fitted them all up with a little shelf.

A lot [of the restoration workforce] came from the other side of the river; but no doubt there were a few that lived this side of the river – Bermondsey and places like that – because there was a lot of work

at Surrey Docks, which is on this side of the river [and] we used to work at Surrey Docks quite often. Wherever the job was, you had to travel across the river either way, or walk through the [Greenwich foot] tunnel, because nobody had cars or anything like that. We used to have to walk through that tunnel carrying the tools, which weighed 70 pounds.

There were hundreds of [workmen from Green & Silley Weir] working in the yard, and on site – all trades. Every morning you would come in and there would be something flying from the top of the mast – usually a pair of ladies' knickers .

– that had been put there overnight by the young naval officers from the [Royal Naval] College; and Lou the gaffer rigger - who came from Mauritius if I remember rightly – he used to phone the college and complain, but he would send somebody up there to take it down. But just a few days before the ship opened we came in and the ship was dressed overall from end to end with toilet paper. So, Lou phoned the Naval College and asked to speak to the commander of the watch. He came on the phone and [Lou] said "Would you take a look out of your window at my ship? It's dressed overall, and I'm not sending my men up there to get it down." And the officer of the watch said, "Don't touch anything, I'll be over." And he came over, and he marched all these young naval officers over and he lined them up on the quay, and we're all leaning on the bulwarks. He walked up and down and he ranted and raved at all these young naval officers and he says, "Right, up there, and clear every bit off"; and they says, well, "Permission to change into our overalls sir"; "Permission denied", he says. "You go up in your uniforms": so they went up in their uniforms and came back covered in Stockholm tar and grease and muck and everything. They didn't do it again!'

Fig. 118 Starboard view of *Cutty Sark* undergoing restoration, 1957.

Saving the ship for the twenty-first century

Fig. 119 The ironwork, exposed following the removal of the hull planks at the stern, revealed extensive corrosion in 2007.

The Conservation Project 2006–12

Philosophies about conservation have seemingly been debated for millennia. In his biography of Theseus, Plutarch wrote:

The ship wherein Theseus and the youth of Athens returned [from Crete] … was preserved by the Athenians down even to the time of Demetrius Phalereus [around 300BC], for they took away the old planks as they decayed putting in new and stronger timber in their place, insomuch that this ship became a standing example among the philosophers, for the logical question as to things that grow; one side holding that the ship remained the same, and the other contending that it was not the same.

(From Plutarch, *Lives. Volume One.* Translated by J. Dryden. Little Brown: Boston, 1910, p.21.)

In the first half of the twentieth century, there was relatively little compunction about replacing defective parts with new. The aim of both the 1920s' and 1950s' restorations was to recreate the appearance of the ship at a particular moment. Even when the 2006–12 project began, there were several critics who advocated this approach, pointing out, correctly, that it was the most economical. However, in conservation circles the philosophy for preserving historic structures had shifted significantly. Instead of seeking to restore to a particular moment, the priority became

Fig. 120 Removing the hull planks for conservation, and to expose the ironwork, 2007.

to treat the structure's original fabric in such a way that it would be safeguarded from further deterioration or damage for many years to come.

This was the ethos adopted by the Cutty Sark Trust for the 2006–12 conservation project. 'Original fabric' was defined as any material – wood, metal, fixture or fitting – that was on the ship between 1869 and 1922: that is, during *Cutty Sark*'s working life as a sailing ship. Damaged timber would be consolidated, primarily with glues, not cut out and replaced unless the condition of the wood gave no alternative. Corroded iron would be treated to halt the rusting process, not removed and substituted with more modern, durable materials. The result would be a ship still composed almost entirely of the same planks and frames that had sailed the South China Sea. But this approach would make it an expensive project. It was made even more so by the complication of composite construction: treatments that are effective for wood do not work on metal, and vice versa. Ultimately the entire project would cost more than £50 million.

Thanks to a very large grant from the Heritage Lottery Fund and contributions from a number of other supporters, funding was found for the largest ship conservation

project ever undertaken. The ship was closed to the public at the beginning of November 2006 and subsequently slowly dismantled. First the masts were taken down, then the deckhouses craned off, the panelling of the saloon painstakingly removed, the figureheads displayed in the lower hold wrapped, boxed and put into storage, and all the office accommodation on board stripped out. Then began the careful work of unbolting each plank and putting it in a bespoke cradle, to ensure it retained its shape, before taking it away for conservation treatment. Week by week, more and more of the ship's framework was revealed.

Then, in the early hours of Monday 21st May 2007, a fire broke out. Flames quickly spread, burning through all three of the ship's decks and destroying the canopy built over it to protect the works. Firemen later reported that, at one point, the heart of the fire reached a heat of about 1,000°C. At this temperature the framework, particularly the plates under the main and 'tween decks, began to distort.

It was prompt action by the London Fire Brigade that brought the blaze under control: by 9.00a.m. the fire was out. But in the short time it had raged, all three decks were completely destroyed. However, the deck in the lower hold was only inserted in the 1950s: there was never one there when the ship was at sea. The main deck, a composite affair that leaked continually, was due to be torn out and replaced anyway. The 'tween deck, on the other hand, was a more serious loss, at least financially. It had been installed in 1938, and so was not strictly part of the original fabric of the ship, but the project had not planned to replace it. A number of hull planks were also badly

The conservation project – views from the inside

Richard Doughty
Director of the Cutty Sark Trust 2001–2014

I joined the Trust in 2001, shortly after an unsuccessful attempt had been made to raise funds to restore the ship. My ambition was not only to preserve as much of the fabric that makes up *Cutty Sark* but also to reinvigorate the business and turn her back into a 'must-see' London destination. She had been up there with all the city's major sights in the late 1950s, 60s and 70s, but she had lost her way: the ship had a tired feeling of an unloved tourist attraction and her audiences had fallen by 71 per cent in little over a decade. Even the organisation was antiquated. I wanted to breathe fresh life into it, to move it along to something that would make it stand out and play to *Cutty Sark*'s significance as one of the great maritime icons not just of London but of the world. I suppose the aspiration was to make her worthy of the sum of her parts.

I recognised that there are certain things that a successful visitor attraction needs and the ship lacked. When I joined, the shop was nothing more than a desk across the aft end of the 'tween deck, behind which

all the merchandise was kept, and warders wearing Merchant Navy-style uniforms gave a very old-fashioned appearance to the ship. I wanted an up-to-date retail facility, improved provision for formal and informal learning, and I even aspired to a catering offer of some sort. Surely, of all places, you should be able to enjoy a cup of tea on board *Cutty Sark*? But my vision was wider than that, I wanted to enliven the way we told the ship's stories, to do more than just allow the ship to speak for herself. And by doing all those things, visitor attendance would be significantly increased.

That was the essence of my vision for the ship. I certainly didn't have a notion of raising her in those early days. Initially my focus was on gaining a foothold in Cutty Sark Gardens for a building to house interpretation and all the facilities the ship needed. But as Greenwich Council had just spent £2 million resurfacing the whole of the Gardens this was not going to be an option. In the end though, the Council became one of our greatest supporters, and the Leader joined the board of trustees.

But before that, there was the fire. On that dreadful May morning, I heard my hall telephone ring at about 4.30a.m. It was a researcher for the *Today* radio programme, who said: 'I'd like to get your reaction Mr Doughty to the fire on board *Cutty Sark*.' My first thought was that it was a hoax call, but I took his name and number and promised to call him back. I then picked up my rather

antiquated mobile phone and, leaning out the window to get a signal, I found a whole series of calls had been made to me. The first message was from a senior fire officer saying that I needed to get down to Greenwich as quickly as possible because the ship was 'alight from stem to stern'. Even now when I use that expression I remember how I felt at that moment: having already worked for several years on the project to get it up and running, the prospect of that all going literally up in smoke was harrowing. I jumped into my clothes, and my wife Jayne drove me to the station and I caught the first train to London. From that moment, the phone never stopped ringing. I gave my first live interview to James Naughtie on the *Today* radio programme fearing the worst. I changed trains twice, finally getting off at New Cross, a couple of miles from Greenwich, only to discover I didn't have my wallet – or a train ticket or any cash. I had to talk my way through the ticket barrier and then flag down a taxi and explain to the driver that I didn't have any money but my ship was burning down and I needed to get to her. The cabbie kindly took me to the bottom of Deptford Creek Road anyway, where the police had cordoned off the road. I had to run the last quarter of a mile towards a pall of black smoke hanging over where I knew the ship was. There was that very evocative smell of Stockholm tar – it was the smell that you got not so much on the deck but in the hold where our riggers' workshop had been before the project. I thought then we'd lost the ship. But as soon as I reached the ship I realised that other people thought that a three-masted ship had burned down, so badly that you could see right through her from the port side to the starboard. But I knew of course, we'd taken down the masts and we'd

**The conservation project –
views from the inside**

removed a large number of planks as part of the early stages of the project. So shock was immediately replaced with hope. I took two steps onto the burning 'tween deck – because no one stopped me – looked down the line of frames and thought: this is a mess but it is retrievable. And the public response was very moving and quite extraordinary. How we managed to achieve this level of support still amazes me and reinforces in my mind how special *Cutty Sark* is.

The fire was, strangely, not the lowest point in the project for me, although standing down the professional team and asking the workforce for voluntary redundancies in the immediate aftermath was amongst the lowest. The real low came a year later after the full extent of the strengthening works required to save the ship became clear. These pushed the cost of the project up £5 million almost overnight. At the very same moment a major prospective funder reneged on a multi-million pound pledge. This killer combination undermined the Heritage Lottery's confidence in our ability to secure match-funding and they suspended our grant until we could satisfy them we had a viable way forward.

An extraordinary meeting of the Trust was called and one of the trustees, Michael Edwards, asked to talk to me out of the meeting. He said: 'I don't want to speak out of turn but would £1 million restore the viability of the project?' What prompted him? My belief is that it was mainly because he realised that if we did go into administration, there was a real risk *Cutty Sark* would be sold to the highest bidder and could well have left the country. Mike was the saviour of the ship at that moment.

Others, too, made a substantial contribution – Nicky Edmiston not only

made the first significant gift to help us with the fire recovery, he also introduced us to Alisher Usmanov, who proved to be a very generous funder. And of course HRH The Duke of Edinburgh was a great support even before this project was a glint in anyone's eye. The events he hosted at Buckingham Palace, Frogmore House and St James's Palace enabled us to cultivate our prospects and inspire them to donate to the project. Thanks to his backing, our small trust with a permanent staff of just four employees was able to punch well above its weight.

Lord Sterling in particular had an immense impact on the project. He came in quietly but opened a number of very important doors. Not just in the corridors of power but with his close friends like Sammy Ofer, who became our principal private patron. Equally important, Lord Sterling assembled a team of very experienced people to oversee the construction elements of the project and get them back on track. Given the extreme reactions from some quarters about raising the ship, he wanted to satisfy himself that the project stacked up, so went through the discipline of checking and double checking everything, to make sure this was something worthy, regardless of the money.

Perhaps strangely, my most memorable moments were not about the fire or the raising of the ship – once we had Lord Sterling on side I never doubted for a minute that we would not conserve or lift the ship. Nor did I doubt that our solution would prove to be very popular. But there was sheer

elation when I took the phone call in 2005, on Burns' Night strangely enough, from Ellen Dempster, our Heritage Lottery Fund Case Officer and heard that we were going to be given a £13 million grant – and they went on to become by far the greatest contributors to the project, meeting half the cost of the entire project.

Another magic moment was after I made a presentation at Buckingham Palace and a hardened industrialist half-lifted himself from his wheelchair and said, 'Well done, Richard, you can count me in for a quarter of a million pounds!' This enthusiastic response seemed to be the confirmation that we would be able to raise the match funding for the ship.

I am enormously proud of what we have achieved. This isn't one person's triumph: this is the culmination of a lot of people investing more than they had been asked to give. We saved the ship from almost certain destruction because she had no future without a unique and bold new vision. But this is the recurring story of *Cutty Sark* – she has been consistently reinvented by each new generation. She has gone from being a tea clipper to wool clipper to cargo vessel to sail training to museum ship and now a major visitor attraction at the heart of a World Heritage Site, an integral part of Royal Museums Greenwich. We have been privileged to have been given a once-in-a-lifetime opportunity to see *Cutty Sark* safely on to the next stage of her journey

Interviewed 27th August 2013

scorched, but not one was lost. Similarly, although some of the iron framework buckled, particularly the cross-bracing under the decks (which took the most intense heat of the fire), nowhere was the damage so severe that it had to be cut out. In all, probably no more than 5 per cent of the original fabric from the ship's working life was lost.

However, the site became a hazardous area, as the fire had released lead into the atmosphere. It was also a crime scene until the cause of the blaze could be established. After an investigation lasting over a year, the police report was not conclusive but, by a process of elimination, suggested that the probable cause was an industrial dust-extractor, which had been left on over the weekend and had overheated.

Fig. 123 *Cutty Sark's* lower hold the day after the fire in 2007. Six months into the project, a major fire broke out on board and destroyed the deck here, on the 'tween deck and the main deck.

Fig. 124 Hull plank alongside, 2008. *Cutty Sark's* composite construction required the complete disassembly of the vessel to enable each structural element to be conserved.

Following pages:
Fig. 125 The hull raised more than 10 feet (3 metres) above her original position in the dock, 2011.

Fig. 126 *Cutty Sark's* hull has been sheathed with brass plates, the closest modern approximation to the original Muntz metal cladding, 2012.

The conservation project – views from the inside

Christopher Nash
Lead architect at Grimshaw

This was a dream project for me. It came at a point in my career when I wanted a change from huge projects like Zurich Airport and airport master-plans. But I've always had a personal interest in sailing. As a boy, my reading of choice was about ships and I'd visited *Cutty Sark* several times. I was a student in Bristol so, through the SS *Great Britain*, I knew something about Victorian maritime history and understood the place of *Cutty Sark* in the overall scene. As a sailor, I felt I could bring more enthusiasm and insight to the *Cutty Sark* project than without this experience. I also had a family connection: my grandfather was born in Greenwich and was apprenticed as a carpenter to a Thames-barge builder in Barking Creek. Carpenters frequently become foremen on building sites because they have to think how things go together and ultimately that's what an architect does: work out how it all goes together.

When we were engaged to work on the project, it was clear we needed a radical idea to make the ship exciting and accessible, as well as make sure she was conserved, and to accommodate the displays and her management needs. At that time the ship hull seemed to be half-full of offices, a shop and a ticketing deck. All this had to be cleared out for a proper appreciation of her. For a long time we thought about a separate building near the ship but, even if this had been possible, it would not have gained the *Cutty Sark* much: it still needed a radical idea to transform it into a modern visitor attraction.

Early on, I went down into the dock and under the ship. Not only was it a great sculptural experience to see her this way, but I also realised that I hadn't really appreciated how important the engineering and the hull shape were to the success and importance of *Cutty Sark* as a fast sailing vessel. Perhaps in the back of my mind was the experience of walking under the blue whale at the Natural History Museum. Again it's a very common experience for sailors to look at their boats from below in a boatyard but it's not common for most people, and it would be the best opportunity for them to appreciate the ship's shape. This was the beginning of the radical idea, which was also an opportunity to relieve the stresses on the ship's original fabric.

If we were to get people under *Cutty Sark* there were two ways of doing it: we could either make the dry berth bigger or raise the ship within it. With the river so close, making the dock bigger was never going to be practical, so the second option seemed more promising. The first advantage of lifting the ship was that people would not have to go so far to get below the hull. At this stage we didn't know whether it would be possible but, once engineers looked at it, within a couple of weeks we were all confident it was indeed a practical idea. And as the design developed, we realised that this was an opportunity to relieve the stresses on *Cutty Sark*'s original fabric once and for all. I knew we were able to design the support structure with minimal visual intrusion, although ensuring the compression members tucked behind the original curved beams in the 'tween deck without reducing the already-

low headroom was particularly challenging. And the complexity at the junction outboard, where the forces are resolved, was also quite difficult; but that is the kind of challenge that we, as architects, enjoy.

The feeling was that we could not just raise *Cutty Sark* without protecting visitors from the elements in some way, so we began to think about a canopy around the hull. The first design was what I call a 'crinkly-glass sea', the ship sitting in what looks like a sea of fractured glass, with open sides. But heritage organisations opposed this very strongly and we developed a number of options leading to a glass-bubble canopy that received planning approval. After the resurrection of the project following the fire, it was the Austrian glass company, Seele, who interpreted the 'bubble' with a cost-saving proposal for a framed glass structure and, working with them, we developed a sophisticated solution – a continuous geodesic dome, stretched long and thin, in which the ship appears to sit. It's a great piece of engineering, on which we worked hard to improve its elegance.

It was not only the design of the canopy that was controversial. Some people even opposed the idea of lifting *Cutty Sark* at all. I was very surprised by this view because, to my mind, once it was raised you could see more of the ship. It was as if the accident of history in the 1950s, which put *Cutty Sark* at a particular level in an artificial berth, had become a historical thing itself. To my mind, this opposition displayed a bit of 'Disney-thinking': perhaps they wanted a few jolly jack tars sitting around on bollards to make it more of a *Pirates of the Caribbean* set.

It's not in the blood of my generation of architects to work like this. Even though there are commercial pressures for these

attractions, and previous generations might have worked this way, we have moved away from replicas and pastiche. We wanted to design the new parts in a contemporary manner, which we think we do well, so that they are distinguishable from the original structure and fabric. In fact, we would like to have been even more radical, such as using frameless glass structures, but there were constraints of programme and budget.

I'm sure quite a lot more time went unrecorded but 'official' records show we spent 19,760 hours on the project – the equivalent of one person working for 12 years' full-time. But it was a team effort, with much done by a lot of good people:

I will mention Simon Beames, the design architect in the early conceptual stages, and Den Farnworth, the project architect in the realisation of the building. It was a long project, with many memorable moments. Looking back, if you ask me to pick just one, it was when all the scaffolding was taken away from the newly raised ship: it looked like she was floating on air out of the ground. We had realised the radical idea.

Interviewed 15th July 2013

The project was now seriously delayed but, since so little of the ship had been lost, there was never any question over its continuation. Donations poured in from all over the world. The Heritage Lottery Fund stepped forward once more, as did the Department of Culture, Media and Sport, Greenwich Council and a number of commercial and private donors.

Extensive experiments had already been made with electrolysis to remove chlorides from the iron structure, but it was found that more effective results could be achieved through grit-blasting and treatment with a sophisticated paint system, somewhat similar to that used on another iconic wrought iron Victorian structure, the Forth Rail Bridge. A new system for supporting the ship was also developed: instead of props and shores, a new triangular framework would be installed connecting the sides of the ship, the keel and the upper edges of the dock. This would involve raising the ship, which had the added bonus of opening up the bottom of the dock where visitors could have better and more exciting views of the hull than ever before.

In preparation for the lifting of the ship, the new internal framework was completed and some of the hull planking reinstated to give the ship a little additional rigidity. Then on 29th March 2011, 24 jacks began their work, raising the ship just 6 inches (15 centimetres). This allowed the engineers to check that the hull structure was responding to the lift as predicted, and to allow the welding in of the bottom keel plate – an important component of the new support system.

With everyone satisfied with the success of these operations, the second phase of the process was started on 4th May: by the 6th, *Cutty Sark* had been raised more than 10 feet (3 metres) above her original position.

The remaining planks were then refastened, the new main and 'tween decks laid, the deckhouses reinstated, the masts returned and rigged, and finally the sheathing replaced. Instead of Muntz metal, the new plates were of brass, 70 per cent copper and 30 per cent zinc. They give the same appearance as yellow metal but are much more readily available. During the replacement of the original Muntz in the 1960s, the plates were overlapped (like tiles on a roof) to prevent rainwater seeping in. Now the underwater hull was protected by a canopy, which allowed the plates to be reinstated in the correct, underlapping, manner.

Cutty Sark was opened to the public once again by HM The Queen on 25th April 2012, almost 55 years after she had first performed this task.

The conservation project – views from the inside

Jim Solomon
Lead conservation consultant at BuroHappold, engineers

When you work on historic structures each one is different, but the philosophy is the same: you are trying to keep as much of the historic fabric as possible, despite the fact that all these changes are happening to the structure. It's a case of managing the process, understanding what is significant while at the same time changing or modifying its use to make it successful, profitable and interesting.

When we first came on the job, the Cutty Sark Trust had been investigating whether it would be possible to treat the iron corrosion without the need to remove the planks. Extensive electrolysis trials had been undertaken, in collaboration with Portsmouth University and the Hampshire County Museum Service, which suggested it might be possible for the ship to be electrolysed with the planks in situ. The idea being considered at this stage was simply to immerse the ship in electrolyte, or at least the lower half where the corrosion was at its worst.

We conducted some further trials with the involvement of the *Cutty Sark* conservation workforce and interrogated the results carefully. We found that the method certainly worked but it was very expensive to execute, because the process has to be carried out incrementally, in small tanks, which are very difficult to make watertight. Electrolysis is normally used on quite small artefacts, say a cannon from the sea or a musket. But when you have big structures it is much more complex.

Fig. 128 Jim Solomon, Conservation Consultant.

Fig. 129 Additional steelwork was introduced to support the ship's fragile lower structure.

The conservation project – views from the inside

We employed a paint specialist, principally to advise us on what coatings to use on electrolysed surfaces. Interestingly, he argued that electrolysis was not the way to go because in doing so you are saturating the joints and you are getting a surface that is no better that you would get with grit blasting. So we took a large plate from the bulwarks and undertook surface preparation trials. After that, we trialled various paint coatings and we came up with the specification that was eventually used on the ship.

This was a much better strategy, both in terms of effectiveness and cost. It was a long process and we had to convince the English Heritage Conservation Officer and others, but we took the right steps in getting from electrolysis to surface preparation and paint. Finding the treatment for the ironworks was the most challenging part of the project – it's the conservation of the ironwork that will determine the life of the ship, so it was very important that we got that right – but it was also the most interesting and rewarding.

Once the Cutty Sark Trust accepted this alternative approach it opened up the possibility of introducing an internal framework supported by an external framework, because essentially by taking the planks off we were dismantling the ship. If we hadn't taken this route I don't think we could ever have implemented the framework support we've now got. And we were able to treat the planks and the wrought iron frame of the ship properly.

In terms of the ironwork, very little was lost – most of it would have been corrosion and packed rust. In terms of the planks, out of a total of 541 only four were in such poor condition that they could not go back onto the ship. Another 29 were removed to make way for the new steel works.

When we took the planks off, what concerned us most of all was the degree of iron corrosion, particularly at the stern. Some of the lower parts of the ribs were completely wasted. We realised we would have to introduce quite a lot of additional strengthening work in order to lift the ship, particularly as the bow and stern are cantilevered. Again, we would never have found this corrosion if we had not taken all the planks off.

We did a great deal of testing of the ironwork after the fire and in terms of the

Fig. 130 *Cutty Sark* prior to being lifted, March 2011.

Fig. 131 The ship and canopy in final stages of the 2006–12 conservation project.

material properties it had no effect at all, unsurprisingly. The expansion of the riveted joints could have over-stressed them but there was no evidence for this. The biggest problem was the distortion of the horizontal plates by the heat below. We managed to straighten some, but the client, Richard Doughty, decided not to straighten others because they tell a story. The main problem we had was with laying the decks because we had to cut and carve the timbers over the buckled plates. But if the fire had been three or four months earlier, when there were more planks and other material on the ship, you would have got tremendous distortion and the ship would likely have been irrecoverable.

Our concern with raising the ship was the robustness of the vessel and the ability to lift without undue damage. We considered options like supporting the keel on columns, but these would affect the appearance of the ship. The structural analysis was extremely challenging. It was two steps forward and one step back at times. When you have an existing structure which has been in poor condition and you introduce new structure, you can get a very good approximation of the new stiffness produced but it's not an exact science by any means – there's a lot of engineering judgement involved. But when we lifted the ship, there was no lag in the stern or deflection in the bow. We expected to see at least a few rivets to sheer, but she just lifted up slowly and evenly.

The best moment for me though – the turning point – was getting the paint on the ironwork. Up to that point we had been working for many months on a dilapidated ship in poor condition, timbers falling apart and corrosion everywhere, but when we started to get the white paint on we felt there was light at the end of the tunnel.

If it's maintained properly you will get at least another 50 or 60 years out of it, but it's terribly important to get to the places you can't see and check the condition of the ship regularly. That's what is going to govern the life of the ship. It was interesting working on the ship and I learnt a great deal. But I am not sure I'd do another!

Interviewed 30th July 2013

Cutty Sark since 2012 – views from the inside

Louise Macfarlane
Curator, *Cutty Sark*

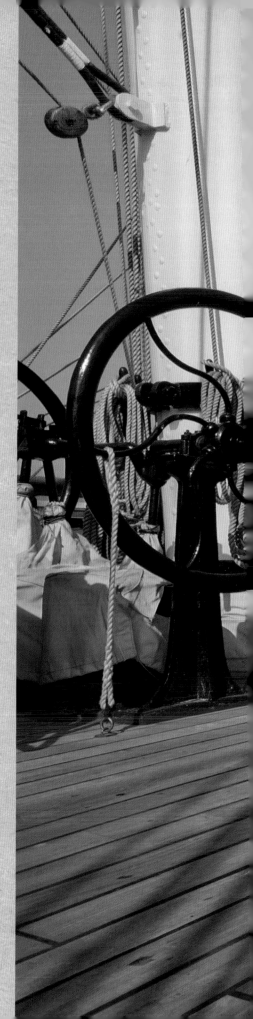

Once this Victorian ship battled the world's seas to secure her all-important profits, and again today *Cutty Sark* must compete on a world stage to ensure her survival. For those of us responsible for her, we must be both thoughtful and innovative about how we preserve her structure and share her story. *Cutty Sark*'s survival is dependent upon how widely we can spread the celebration and enjoyment of this unique vessel. Without visitors there is no *Cutty Sark*. There is much to be done but thankfully, there is also much to be proud of since 2012.

She has been visited by almost two million people and has reached a grand total of 17 million visitors since first opening in Greenwich in 1957.

In January 2014, the Michael Edwards Studio Theatre opened in the Lower Hold. What was once the ship's main cargo space can now be transformed into an eclectic and unique after-hours performing arts area.

On 10th December 2014, the ship celebrated 60 years in her dry dock in Greenwich. The ship – which was built to last for 30 years – served as a working ship for 52 years and as a cadet training ship for almost 30, and has spent longer in Greenwich than anywhere else. To mark the occasion, *Cutty Sark* hosted a tea party under the ship's hull for visitors to share their memories, old and recent, of the ship and her time in the borough. Hosting a vibrant programme of events, particularly in the space under the ship – from operas to silent discos – now forms an important part of the ship's activities. In fact, since 2012, we have hosted more than 200 events, raising the ship's profile and funds to ensure her ongoing survival.

Cutty Sark's learning programme welcomes thousands of visitors to the ship every year. Toddler Time, where our youngest visitors enjoy stories and arts and crafts, has been a particular hit with the local community. More than 2,000 young visitors and their carers have taken part since it began in January 2015. British Sign Language and Audio Described Tours of the ship form a vital part of our offer for auditory and visually impaired visitors. Aspects of the ship's interpretation, such as tactile models and maps, have been especially designed to enhance and improve access for all visitors.

In August 2015, *Cutty Sark* joined the National Maritime Museum, Queen's House and Royal Observatory to become one of Royal Museums Greenwich's (RMG) four sites. Providing access to a wide range of experts and expertise, the ship can now add 'largest object in a national collection' to her many identities.

The 22nd November 2019 marks 150 years since the ship was launched in Dumbarton. The conservation project of 2006–2012 made tremendous strides in ensuring the ship's survival. But the work is never complete. In coming years, many areas of the ship will require further, extensive care and attention. If there is anything that we have learnt over the past three centuries, however, it is that *Cutty Sark* is a survivor. Her remarkable story continues to attract worldwide recognition and admiration. It is down to us all to ensure that she will be here to tell her story of the next 150 years.

Afterword

If ever a ship could be called 'lucky' then surely *Cutty Sark* can be so described. After less than a decade in the tea-carrying role for which she was built, she found new roles as a wool clipper, a general cargo vessel (twice), a sail-training ship (twice) and a tourist attraction (twice).

Britain's maritime heritage has been considerably enriched by the number of historically significant vessels that have been recognised as worth preservation and – after often heroic work to achieve that – are now available for the public to enjoy. They include great warships, such as *Victory*, *Trincomalee*, *Unicorn* and *Belfast*; fishing vessels, like *Lydia Eva* and the Fifie *Reaper*; technological pioneers, such as *Great Britain* and *Turbinia*; and beautiful leisure craft, such as the Victorian steamboats of Lake Windermere.

Among these vessels, one might argue that *Cutty Sark* holds an important but not a unique place. She is not the only composite vessel: HMS *Gannet* and *City of Adelaide* were also built using this technique. She is not the only clipper ship; again, *City of Adelaide* is of the type – built in Sunderland in 1864, although not an 'extreme' clipper for the tea trade, but one for transporting emigrants to Australia (at the time of writing, ambitious plans, not dissimilar to *Cutty Sark*'s display in Greenwich, to place her at the heart of a seaport village in Adelaide are underway). Nor is *Cutty Sark* the final word in the sailing-ship story: in British waters there is the barque *Glenlee*, one of the steel-hulled bulk carriers whose four-masted cousins carried on deep-water transport long after *Cutty Sark*'s final voyage.

Yet, more than any other of these other ships, it is *Cutty Sark* that has caught the imagination of a wide public. She inspired not only a whisky brand but also Francis Chichester, whose circumnavigation of the globe in 1966–67, in the yacht *Gipsy Moth IV*, followed the clipper route to Australia and back (sponsored, appropriately, by the International Wool Secretariat). Chichester was subsequently knighted in Greenwich. *Cutty Sark* also inspired the career choice of Stephen Payne. It was his visits to the clipper, beginning at the age of seven, that led him to a career in naval architecture, in which he went on to design Cunard's *Queen Mary 2*. Grimshaw, the architectural practice that would later work on the 2006–12 conservation project, took inspiration from the ship for its long-span structures, such as the *Western Morning News*' offices in Plymouth and the Oxford Ice Rink (which is known locally as 'Cutty Sark'). Images of her are used widely to evoke or symbolise the great age of sail, even adorning London buses to convey the idea of speed. Public houses called 'Cutty Sark' are found in all the places that have a strong association with the ship – Dumbarton, Falmouth, Greenwich and Cape Town – but also some less likely spots, such as Ljubljana in Slovenia. On composite postcards of London, her image is usually found alongside Tower Bridge and the Houses of Parliament, and she is one of only a handful of London attractions whose name is reflected in that of a station. She has had an aircraft named after her, a pop band and has even been mentioned in a Simpsons' cartoon.

Equally, if not more important, is the inspiration she has given to thousands of painters and model-makers. *Cutty Sark* at sea has been the subject of probably more paintings than any other vessel, even though her sailing career ended in 1922. Along with countless amateurs, various eminent marine painters have depicted her – including John Everett (1876–1949), Montague Dawson (1895–1973) and Geoff Hunt (1948–). And it is difficult to imagine a vessel more modelled than this clipper.

The days when every boy spent his leisure time with glue and small pots of paint may be past, but even today there are at least nine kit models of *Cutty Sark* available, ranging in price from £15 to over £1,000.

This small sailing ship, built in a forgotten yard, launched almost at the end of the great clipper age, and which worked for only a few years in the trade for which she was built, is more than just a survivor. She is the icon of an era of the most elegant sailing ships, with their knife-like hulls and over-canvassed yards. As such, she is held in affection around the globe as an enrichment to our lives.

Fig. 132 *Cutty Sark and a brig*, by John Everett, 1921.

Timeline of *Cutty Sark*'s survival

1869 September

Work on the construction of *Cutty Sark* is suspended when Scott & Linton becomes insolvent.

1872 15 August

Cutty Sark's rudder is torn off in an Indian Ocean storm. Henry Henderson, the ship's carpenter, constructs a temporary rudder and the ship reaches home on 19th October.

1877 8–16 November

One of 60 ships sheltering in the Downs (off Deal, Kent), *Cutty Sark* has her anchor cables parted by hurricane-force winds. Helpless, she collides with a number of other vessels. Captain Tiptaft eventually signals for assistance and two tugs tow her to safety on the 16th.

1885 22 October

Cutty Sark hit by a terrific squall south of Sydney. In freezing temperatures, she broaches-to and the lee side of the deck fills with water. The port lifeboat is swept away and the dinghy smashed. Several sails are reduced to shreds.

1891 28 June

An immense sea rolls up from astern: *Cutty Sark* rides it but it breaks over both her sides, smashing in the doors of both deckhouses and completely submerging the ship. Captain Woodget and his helmsman are lashed to the wheel or would have been washed overboard. Yet the ship survives the biggest sea of her career.

1906 27 September

Now called *Ferreira*, the ship is tied up at a quay in Pensacola, Florida, when she is caught by the Great Hurricane and severely damaged. Many in the shipping world believe she has been wrecked.

1907 2 April

After undergoing repairs at Mobile, *Ferreira* was finally ready to transport lumber to Rio de Janeiro. However, she was grounded at Cosgrove Shoal and lost her rudder.

1915 25 June

Ferreira loses her rudder, 10 days after leaving Lisbon. A jury rudder is fitted which takes her on to Angola.

1916 7 May

A badly loaded coal cargo shifts and forces the crew to cut away all the masts and rigging, except the lower foremast. Advised to abandon ship, Captain da Sousa refuses, eventually secures a tow and arrives in Table Bay on 14th May. The ship makes a lengthy stay there for repairs, which also keeps her out of the Atlantic and out of danger from First World War U-boats.

1922   January

Now a poorly maintained barquentine, *Ferreira* is caught in a channel gale and puts into Falmouth for repairs. She is recognised there by Captain Wilfred Dowman as the old *Cutty Sark*: later in the year, he succeeds in purchasing and restoring her. The last surviving extreme clipper ship is saved for the nation.

1938

Two years after Dowman's death, a new home is found for *Cutty Sark* at Greenhithe, on the River Thames, as part of the Incorporated Thames Nautical Training College.

1952

The Cutty Sark Preservation Society is formed, thanks to the efforts of Frank Carr, second Director of the National Maritime Museum, and HRH The Duke of Edinburgh, to create a permanent home for *Cutty Sark* at Greenwich. After being moved into a purpose-built dry dock there in 1954 and extensive restoration, HM The Queen opens her to the public in 1957.

1996

Surveyors report that, because of the fragile condition of her ironwork, *Cutty Sark* will be a dangerous structure in 10 years and likely to collapse.

1999

A plan to restore the ship fails to gain support from the Heritage Lottery Fund. The Cutty Sark Trust is formed to develop a conservation solution.

2006

The project to strengthen the ship and conserve her fabric begins, primarily financed by a grant of £13 million from the Heritage Lottery Fund.

2007   21 May

A fire breaks out in the lower hold of the ship, destroying three decks, buckling ironwork and charring planks. The Heritage Lottery Fund provides an additional grant of £10 million and contributions pour in from around the world.

2012   25 April

With the conservation project completed, *Cutty Sark*'s future is secured for another 50 years and HM The Queen reopens the ship to the public.

2015   1 August

Cutty Sark formally joins Royal Museums Greenwich. She is now one of four sites (joining the National Maritime Museum, Queen's House and Royal Observatory) of a national museum.

2019   22 November

Cutty Sark celebrates 150 years since her launch in Dumbarton. Still thriving as a visitor attraction, many challenges lie ahead to ensure her continued survival.

Appendix A: The contract specification with a note on colour

The original specification for the vessel that would be launched as *Cutty Sark* is held by Dumbarton Public Library.

SPECIFICATION OF A COMPOSITE SAILING SHIP OF ABOUT 1,300 TONS BUILDERS' MEASUREMENT

No.1 Dimensions
Deck for measurement of Tonnage
Length 210 ft
Beam Extreme 36 ft
Depth of Hold 20 ft 9 in
Length of Quarter Deck 45 ft in Main Deck and 4 ft high

Registered Tonnage about 900 Tons under Main Deck and not to exceed 950 tons New National Measurement.

No.2 Hull Description. The vessel to be ship rigged with Main and Lower Decks laid with a raised Quarter Deck aft 45 ft long and 4 ft high and level with the main rail and Liverpool house fitted on centre 30 ft long with a break 4 ft long on fore part for Captain, Officers and a few passengers as may be arranged for.

Approval of plans to be submitted by builders. Anchor Deck forward, Forecastle fitted below for crew. Small House to be fitted in wake of Foremast for Galley, Petty Officers, etc.

Vessel to be built under special survey and classed at Lloyds for 16 years. Special Survey fees to be paid by owners.

No.3 Keel. To be of American Rock Elm in long lengths 16 ½" x 15" and to be scarfed and fastened in accordance with Lloyds' requirements and all through bolts to be of yellow metal.

No.4 Stem. To be of Teak 15" x 15" in one piece and bolted with yellow metal through bolts in accordance with Lloyds' requirements

No.5 Sternpost. To be of Teak 16 ½" x 15" of one piece and through bolted with yellow metal bolts to Lloyds' requirements.

No.6 Frames. To be of angle iron 3 ¾" x 4 ½" x ⁹⁄₁₆" in one length from keel to Gunwale and of full size and proportions for a vessel of size and tonnage and classified to Lloyds' requirements.

No.7 Reverse Frames. To be of angle iron 3" x 3" x ⁷⁄₁₆" and to be run from the bottom up to the lower and main decks alternately as per Lloyds' rules.

No.8 Floors. To be 24" deep in centre x ⁹⁄₁₆" running well up the bilge, wash plates of iron to be properly fitted and riveted to angle iron in bilges in body of ship.

No.9 Centre Keelson. To be box framed side plates 16" x ⁹⁄₁₆", top plate 10 ½" x 9/16" having angle irons on lower side 3 ¾" x 4 ½" x ⁹⁄₁₆" and on upper sides 3" x 3" x ⁷⁄₁₆" to be perforated where required and made to act as ventilators.

No.10 Bilge Keelsons. To be in number and size as required by Lloyds and to be two angle irons riveted together with a bulb iron bar between.

No.11 Bilge Plates. To be 24" wide by ⁵⁄₈" tapering to 12" as per Lloyds' requirements.

No.12 Keel Plate. To be 30" x ¹³⁄₁₆" running up to the ends of the two above 'tween deck Beams and fastened to the Keel with yellow metal through bolts and galvanised screw bolts in accordance with Lloyds' requirements.

No.13 Stringers. Main Deck 30 ½" x ⁵⁄₁₆" and fitted home to outside plating and riveted to angle irons 4" x 4" x ½". Iron gutter way to be 16" wide. Hold Beam Stringers to be 25 ½" x ⁵⁄₈" in accordance with Lloyds.

No.14 Ceiling. To be of red pine. Laid in hatchways 6 ft long with rings to lift, 2 ¾" thick upper turn of the Bilge. Remainder 2 ½".

No.15 Diagonal Ties. On frames to be plate 9" x ⁵⁄₈" placed as required for classification. Ties on Main Deck Beams to be 13 ½" x ⁵⁄₈" placed as required. Ties on Tween Deck Beams 15 ½" x ⁵⁄₈" and all in size and requirements of Lloyds.

No.16 Beams. Main Deck beams to be bulbed T iron 9 x 6 ¾" x ⁵⁄₁₆". Hold Beams to be bulbed T iron 10" x 7" x 5/8" to be secured to the sides of the vessel by the ends of the beam being turned down forming a solid knee and riveted to the frames.

No.17 Stanchions. Hold and Tween Deck stanchions to be of round iron and larger than ⁵⁄₄" larger than Lloyds' rules. To have double stanchions at fore and main hatches with bars between for ladders.

No.18 Bulkheads. To have watertight iron bulkheads of ³⁄₈" plate iron at each end of vessel up to Main Deck level and strengthened by angle iron spaced 2 ½" apart. Foremast Bulkhead to be far enough aft to give space in forecastle for 22 men.

No.19 Sheer strake. To be formed of plate iron 35 ½" x ⁵⁄₈".

No.20 Planking. Garboard strake to be 11" thick x 12" wide of American Rock Elm 6" thick up to ⅛th depth of hold from stringer plate, from thence to plank sheer 4 ¾". The whole outside planking of the vessel to be of Teak except the bottom which is to be of Rock Elm as before specified, the whole bottom and ship outside to be smoothly planed.

No.21 Fastenings. The whole of the outside planking to be bolted to the frames with yellow metal screw bolts of approved size by Lloyds, and the most approved method adopted for preventing oxidation of frames, more especially in bottom by surrounding the bolts and nuts with washers in wake of frames or as may be otherwise approved.

No.22 Bulwarks. To be of plate iron ⁵⁄₁₆" thick to extend 4 ft above stringer plate according to tracing. Stanchions to be of iron H framed with rivets in each palm and to the 1 ½" in diameter. Six ports of large and approved size and made to unship if required, to be cut in each side to allow the escape of water, to have rings, etc. to lift or lash, to have hinges fitted inside so as to give a smooth appearance outside and the frame to be solid with the hinge.

No.23 Main Rail. To be Teak 4" x 12" to have large pin rail in wake of rigging to be in line with break of poop.

No.24 Top Gallant Rail. To be Teak 6 ½" x 3 ½" to be or oval form on top. Bulwark to be panelled inside in ornamental Teak work.

No.25 Main Deck. To be of Teak 3 ½" x 5", to be well secured to beams by galvanised screw bolts, to be free from sap, rot or shakes and to be fair and evenly laid, the Decks to be caulked and payed with pitch and resin.

No.26 Raised Quarter Deck (*Poop*). To be of the same material and size as the Main Deck and the sides of raised deck to be adapted for store rooms with entrance as may be arranged on. Roof of Liverpool house to be 2 ½" x 5" Teak, house to be formed of strong angle Iron framing 3 ½" x 3", one upright angle iron on every beam with knee plates top and bottom.

The sides of the house to be neatly divided into windows with strong glass plate. Brass scuttles each berth and a Teak skylight on top, front of break of deck to be plated with iron. Companion of Teak half dome entrance in for part.

No.27 Sweat Boards. To be fitted under Main deck stringer in tween Deck with moveable boards to convey off any sweat from cargo into sides.

No.28 Rudder. To be of English Oak. Main piece from counter upward to be 16 ¼" diameter and to be of approved curve and size to be submitted to owner.

No.29 Braces. To be of hard Brass of size and shape as per rules.

No.30 Windlass. To be Emerson & Walker or Harfield's Patent as purchaser may decide on. Owner to pay the difference of price from a Common Windlass.

No.31 Cathead. To be of Teak with four patent Roller Sheaves, steel pins and patent strappers.

No.32 Steering Gear. To have Pickup's and Buchannan's Patent or right and left hand screw apparatus and to have spare iron tiller fitted on after part of rudder head with bolts so arranged in case of accident to screw. (Present one made by Paul of Dumbarton.)

No.33 Anchor Deck (Monkey Foc'sle). To have small Anchor Deck. Forward as far aft as windlass with lockers for paint, etc. to be planked with 2 ½" pine and to be same height as main rail with washboards 18" high bolted down on after part leading aft from centre so as to prevent water going on main deck and to topgallant bulwarks round forecastle to have moveable shutter to allow water to run off.

No.34 Deck House. To be iron framed and plated with Teak and panelled. Galley to be fitted at after end and to be properly lined in wake of cooking range with sheet iron. Floor to be neatly tiled with coloured tiles. Funnel to be of galvanised iron. Fore end of house to be fitted for Carpenter, Sailmaker, Boatswain, Apprentice, etc. and of a size as may be required.

No.35 Cabin. To be fitted to plans approved by owners, and saloon to be of different kinds of hard wood neatly panelled or else enamelled white and gold as may be approved of. Captain's cabin to be fitted up with drawers, Chronometer Case, Chart Racks, etc. and also Officers' Cabin.

No.36 Hatches. To be three in number of a size as may be agreed on. Coamings to be formed of iron 18" high. Hatches to be planked with 1 ¹⁄₁₈" tongue and grooved pine. Carlings to be of oak, to have hatch bars, cleats, etc. complete. Top of coamings outside and on lower part inside to have half round iron riveted to them. After hatch to have a Teak Booby hatch on top of iron coamings.

No.37 Capstan. To be placed in front of break of Deck, to be brass mounted to have racks for bars, etc. also to have one in forecastle.

No.38 Main Stay Plates. To be riveted to upper deck beams to be 2 ft wide and of such length as to take two beams. Diagonal rods to be carried from thence to lower deck beams so as to distribute the strain.

No.39 Lower Deck. To be of yellow pine 3" x 6" laid throughout with iron or teak coamings and to be 6ft 9" high Deck to Deck.

No.40 Forecastle (Foc'sle). To be fitted up bellow with Teak companion side lights and ventilators and scuppers for running off water, water closets, etc.,

No.41 Hawse Pipes. To be two in number of No.1 Cold blast, to have large thick lips and to be bolted into Teak Chocks. Pipes to have a fair and direct lead to windlass.

No.42 Chain Lockers. To be 2 ½" red pine firmly bolted to angle-iron framing and to be of sufficient size to contain chain.

No.43 Mooring Pipes. To be four in number on Main Deck with large inside flange riveted to Bulwarks and finished flush with outside

No.44 Mooring Bitts. Four pairs to be placed on Main Deck, two in front of Foremast and two in front of Quarter Deck, to be large size, say 14" x 9", and to be bolted through stringer plate, to be round headed with tops to unscrew to act as ventilators, also to have two smaller bitts on Poop aft.

No.45 Boat Skids. To be 7" square supported on iron stanchions finished with Teak, and to be placed where most convenient.

No.46 Boat Davits. To be of sufficient size and number, and one pair on each side, and to be fitted with patent blocks and falls complete, one with four fold patent blocks and the other with three fold patent blocks with mats and grips for each boat and chafing poles to Davit.

No.47 Chain Plates. To be riveted to upper edge of sheer strake and with a flat palm and four ³⁄₈" rivets. Rods to be 1 ³⁄₈" in diameter.

No.48 Dead Eyes. To be in number and size as required for rigging and to be lignum vitae.

No.49 Fife Rails. To be fitted with square stanchions of Teak, abaft the main mast and fore mast with six sheaves in each and a Teak rail running between them, stout iron hoops with eyes in them round lower part of masts and pin hoops above, all galvanised.

No.50 Water Tanks. Ten in number to contain 400 gallons each, to be placed where most convenient.

No.51 Pumps. To be of Redpath's patent of sufficient size for ship with bilge pumps fitted and spare upper and lower boxes to each pump and separate sounding pipe between pumps.

No.52 Boats. To be four in number according to scale of Board of Trade, viz. two life boats, one Cutter and Gig. Captain's Gig to be of Teak and fitted with Mast and Sails. The other boats to have Teak top strakes, all boats to stand on chocks or have skids and to be placed as may be required. To be copper fastened and to have rowlocks, yokes with rudder for each and a set of ash oars, boathook and bucket for each and gratings for each boat where required.

No.53 Compasses. Three binnacles to be found, viz. Steering Binnacle and Compass, Standard in front of Poop with Board of Trade Compass, Azimuth on Skids between Boats, one suspended Cabin Compass, two spare cards, two spare Agates and two spare pivots to each compass with deviation card to be found, and two spare brass compasses all to be properly adjusted by swinging the vessel.

No.54 Brass Work. All the Bitt ends, cabin door locks and hinges, and door slides, mounting for capstan with plate and ship's name. Helmets for compasses, Teak hand-rail in front of poop stairway and Brass perforated plates on steps of stairs, Ship's bell 50 lbs. with name engraved, skylight hinges, Quadrants and guard side light frames to be of brass, small bell for Quarter Deck.

No.55 Plans, etc. The Builder to furnish model and Plans for approval, according to which the ship is to be built in strict terms, Deck plans and midship section showing Keelsons, Beams, Stringers, Decks and Stanchions with Bulwarks, rails, etc. Rigging Plan and profile.

No.56   Rigging. All blocks to have lignum vitae sheaves, steel pins, and the principal blocks Patent Roller Bushes on Brace and Halliard Blocks, all the deadeyes, Hearts and Bull's Eyes to be Lignum Vitae. Iron for binding to be best scrap Yorkshire. Sheerpoles to be served. Rigging to be or iron wire, Newall's best charcoal galvanised; standing rigging to be served and parcelled overall. Standing rigging and stays fore and main 5" remainder in proportion, size of rigging stays, etc. to be first approved by owners.

No.57   Lower Masts & Yards, etc. Fore and Main masts and Bowsprit to be of iron, Mizzen Mast to be Vancouvers *[actually 5–⁶/₁₆" thick iron plate]*, Top Masts of Vancouvers, remainder of Spars to be pitch pine or black spruce, spars to be in size as agreed on. All iron masts and steel yards to be made on the most approved plan and in no case less than the size and requirements of Liverpool Underwriters' Rules.

No.58   Yellow Metal Sheathing. Vessel to be sheathed from Keel to 18 ft water mark on top of paper and tar sheathing to be to be smoothly put on, sheets to be 22, 24, 26 oz. metal.

No.59   Cargo Winches. Double purchase to be found at fore and main hatches, foremost winch to have chain lifter attached.

No.60   Scuppers. Upper Main Deck, four on each side, to be large and oval, to be formed by turning angle-irons up with piece of angle – iron above and level with stringer plate, all to be made quite tight, no scuppers to be cut through stringer plate.

No.61   Cementing. Vessel to be cemented to the level of limber holes amidships thence to the top of the bilges so as to cover bolt heads. Frames and floors to be well filled. all to meet Board of Trade requirements.

No.62   Painting. Three coats or red iron paint from Keel to Gunwale and rail outside and inside woodwork to be properly painted. Bulwarks to be finished suitable colours, Masts and Spars white last coat zinc. Twixt decks white, Beams white, Deck unpainted.

No.63   Sails. A double suit of sails of best extra all long flax canvas (except Royals, Mainstay sails, Skysail, Mizzen Staysail, flying jibs of which there is one of each) with one set of studding sails, Boat covers and mast covers as per list herewith.

No.64   Sundries. Four hen coops of Teak 8 ft long. Pig houses covered with teak to be found and fitted with all requisites necessary and placed where required. Racks for arms to be fitted, one four pounder gun to be found and fitted with carriage, Breech ropes and fixings, ladders for hold and Twix Deck and for Peaks and skids. Handsome stairway with perforated brass steps. Teak hand rails, Belaying pins and rigging winches at fore and main rigging. Spare tiller to be found, Gratings aft and covers for steering gear in Teak. The Block Sheaves, Hearts, Deadeyes and Bull's eyes to be of Lignum Vitae, the pins steel. The bindings inside fore and main deadeyes 9" in diameter, remainder in proportion. A figurehead by Allan with suitable carving about the stern and to correspond with the name of the ship.

No.65   Anchors. As required by Lloyds, all Trotman's and Admiralty tested.

No.66   Cables. Two chain cables, one Stream cable as per Lloyds and Admiralty proof Test, one Towline 120 fathoms 9", three warps 90 fathoms each 8, 6 and 5 inch. Owners to have option of ordering anchors. Cables and all other chains from Brown and Lennox or other approved makers and, if any differences of prices between them and others as supplied on the Clyde, to be paid for by the owners.

No.67   Sails. 1 Flying Jib, 3 Standing Jibs, 2 Fore Topmast Staysails, 2 Fore Sails, 2 Upper Fore Topsails, 2 Lower Topsails, 2 Topgallant Sails, 1 Royal (Fore), 2 Main Sails, 1 Royal (Main), 2 Upper Main topsails, 2 Lower Main topsails, 2 Main Top Gallant sails, 1 Main Skysail, 1 Main Topmast Staysail, 1 Main Spencer, 1 Mizzen Cross Jack, 1 Mizzen Top Gallant Sail, 2 Upper Mizzen Topsails, 2 Lower Mizzen Topsails, 2 Spankers, 1 Mizzen Topmast Staysail, 1 Mizzen Top Gallant Staysail, 3 Topmast Studding Sails, 3 Top Gallant Studding Sails, 2 Lower Studding Sails, 2 Wind Sails, 1 Main Top Gallant Staysail, set of boat sails, spars and gear complete as specified. A Quarter Deck Awning to after hatch with stanchions complete with wire ridge rope, 2 setting pins, 6 palms assorted, 24 sail needles assorted, 6 sail hooks and 4 iron rubbers.

No.68   Carpenter's and Boatswain's Stores. 1 Hand Copper Pump, 3 Pump Spars, 3 Lower Boxes, 1 Brake Burgee Spare, 1 Pair rigging screws, 2 Laundering Rods. Full set of Studding sail Booms and Yards with Blocks and Gear complete as specified, all studding sail booms to be under the yards; side ladders with two brass headed stanchions with ropes complete on both sides. Hold ladders, forecastle and half-deck ladder, ditto as before provided. 1 Teak accommodation ladder with Crane complete. 1 Booby Hatch of Teak for Half-deck as specified. 2 sets of tarpaulins for each hatch. 6 handspikes. Capstan Bars (Complete sets to each Capstan in Racks). 1 Pitch Pot and ladle, 12 chain hooks, 1 Grindstone and trough, 6 Tar Brushes, 1 set of ash oars for each boat. 7 Double Luff Tackle Blocks. 7 Single Blocks. 24 Spare Sheaves and pins, 12 spare blocks assorted, chain stoppers as before provided, 2 shank painters, 1 spunyarn winch (iron), 1 Double purchase block, 1 single purchase block, 2 cat blocks, 2 Top Blocks, 1 Purchase Gin and chain, 1 Ballast Chain, 1 Purchase Gaff, 1 Anchor Fish-hook, 1 Boat hook to each boat, 2 Watch Tackle blocks, 2 snatch blocks iron bound, 9 Ballast shovels, 2 Marline spikes, 6 Serving Mallets, 1 iron long 6 lb gun with carriage complete; 4 pair chain can hooks, 2 pairs timber grips, 1 pair puncheon slings. Hen coops as may be required. 4 cork fenders, boat chocks complete. 1 Double purchase winch to be fitted with Gipsey ends for taking cable. 1 iron capstan on Main Deck and one for forecastle as specified. Pig Houses with iron bars as before described. 1 dozen assorted connecting shackles 60 ft (lineal) soft wood deck deal, 30 ft lineal Elman Redwood, 12 scrapers, 4 iron Crow Bars, 2 iron slices, 2 flat files, 12 Hooks and Thimbles assorted, 2 Buoys and Ropes, 2 Life Buoys as specified of Cork, 2 spare shackles for Anchors, 2 Doz. Assorted Forelocks, 2 Doz. Washers for Boats, Fids for Masts as specified patent with lifting screws, 1 cwt. of assorted nails, 1 Head Pump, 1 Stern Pump, Fire Engine with Leather hose.

No.69   Spare Spars. 1 Spare Spar for Lower Yard or Topmast (Vancouver); 1 Spar for Lower Topsail Yard or Jibboom; 1 Spar for Lower Topgallant Yard; 6 Spars for Lower Studding Sail Booms

No.70   Cooper's Stores. 4 Water Casks (100 gallons each), 4 Breakers (20 gallons each), 2 Harness Casks Teak with Brass Hoops, 12 Buckets Teak with brass hoops in Teak stands, 1 Water can, 1 Wash Deck Tub, 5 Mess Kids, 2 Water Funnels, 2 Draw Buckets, 6 Bread Boxes, 1 Cask for flour, 1 Steep Tub, 2 Cook's Buckets, 2 Cabin Buckets.

No.71   Ship Chandler's Stores. 1 Barometer, 4 Hour Glasses, 1 Spy Glass, 2 Half Hour glasses, 1 Log Reel, 1 Deep Sea Lead, 1 Deep Sea Lead Line and Reel, 2 Hand Leads and Lines, 2 Lead Log Boards, 1 Harpoon, 1 Pair Grains, ½ Hide Pump Leather, 2 Brass Signal Lantern, 1 Forecastle Globe Lantern, 18 Fishing Hooks, 3 Fishing Lines, 1 Spare Log Line, 1 Brass Speaking Trumpet, 1 Fog Horn, 6 Deck Scrubbing Brushes, 6 Paint Brushes, 1 Register Box and Brass Lock and Key, 4 Mops, 1 Cabin Sweeping Brush, 12 Paint Brushes assorted, 5 Oil Tanks (10 gallons each to be fitted where required), 1 Shark Hook, 1 Large Portable Filter for Water, 1 Teak Medicine Chest with flips of names on it and fitted with medicines according to Act of Parliament, 1 Ensign, 1 Union Jack, 1 Vane, 1 Burgee with Ship's name, 1 Set Signals (largest size), Mercantile Code and Book complete with Signal Halliards fore and aft and box on locker to hold them, 1 Private Signal.

No.72　Cabin Stores. 1 Copper Tea Kettle, 1 Tea Pot Elkington E. Plate, 1 Coffee Pot, 12 Tea Spoons Elkington E. Plate, 12 Table Spoons Elkington E. Plate, 12 Dessert Spoons Elkington E. Plate, 12 Plated Forks Elkington E. Plate, 12 Table Knives with Ivory Handles, 12 Dessert Knives with Ivory Handles, 2 Carving Knives and Forks, 1 Steel, 1 Cabin Stove with Copper Funnel and pan complete to be approved of, 1 Metal Tureen, 1 Metal Ladle E. Plate, 4 doz. Plates assorted, 4 doz. Dishes to match, 3 Metal Dish Covers, 2 Black Jacks, Wash-hand Basin and Jug, and other crockery to match to be fitted up in each state cabin, 6 Stools and 1 set of fire and hair cushions, the same to be secured to the Deck and locker under cabin, Table for Linen, and water jugs for cabin, 6 Best Percussion muskets and Bayonets, 6 Best Percussion Pistols, 12 cutlasses, 1 Cleaning Rod, 2 Nippers Key and Trunscrew, 100 Ball Cartridges, 25 of 4 lb. Priming Horn and Pricker, 2 Boxes of Caps, 24 4 lb. shot, 2 lb. of fire Gunpowder, 1 Copper Magazine with Brass Looko and Keys, 3 Pairs Handcuffs, 2 Brass Candlesticks, 1 Pair Snuffers and Tray, 4 Decanters, 1 Cabin Lamp, 2 doz. Tumblers, 2 doz. Wine Glasses, Lamps to be supplied to each room to be portable, 1 Pair Lamp Scissors, 1 Tea and Breakfast Service complete, 2 Brass Locks, 1 Teak Sideboard, 1 Pair Flour Scales, 1 Spring Balance, 1 Set Scales and weights, 1 Pair of Steel Yards, 2 Coffee Mills, 1 Candle Box, 1 Flour Scoop, 1 Flour Dredger, 1 set of Castors with 5 or 6 bottles E. Plate, 1 Fowl (sic), 1 Plate Basket, 3 Cork Screws, 1 Brush, 1 Dust Pan, 2 Fancy Bread Basket.

Cabin to be fitted up as per plan to be given and agreed upon. Hair Cushions on after lockers, Brass rings to locker lids and locks for each.

Lockers for Bread, Peas, Barley and Rice to be fitted up and lined with tin. Pantry to be properly fitted up.

Lockers that are necessary to be fitted up in cabin. Brass lights to be in each room and on each side of the forecastle as before described. Looking glass and Time-piece for Cabin. The Poop Skylight Companion and Quarter Hatch Grating over wheel gear and Hen Coops to be of Teak.

No.73　Galley. To be of Wood.

No.74　Cook's Stores. 1 Frying Pan, 1 Cook's Ladle, 1 Tormentor, 1 Cullender, 2 Dippers, 6 Saucepans, 2 Stew Pans, 1 Baker, 1 Pair of Tongs, 1 Gridiron, 3 Baking Pans, 1 Cook's Knife, 1 Sieve, 1 Ladle, 1 Cook's Lantern, 1 Cook's Axe. Any of the above to be found with Cabouse not to be supplied, Cabouse to be approved of by owner to be of the best Modern Construction. 6 Bath Bricks, 1 Cook's Saw.

No.75　The whole to be of the very best workmanship, material and finish. All wood about the decks to be of Teak and anything omitted in this specification necessary in either building or outfit to complete the vessel for sea to be supplied by the builder free of charge.

The colour of *Cutty Sark*

For the 1950s' restoration, models and paintings were studied to determine the colours the external elements of the ship should be painted. The painting by Frederick Tudgay (see pages 20–21) was the primary source and the scheme adopted varied very little from it. The scheme was repeated in the 2006–12 conservation project.

Sails on British merchant ships of the late nineteenth century were of flax canvas, sometimes with a hemp mixture. In appearance they would be grey or pale fawn.

THE INTERIOR

As part of the preparation for 2006–12, paint samples from the interior of the ship were collected by University College London for analysis. These identified 25 paint schemes: the investigators concluded there would have been more, but neglect and paint stripping in the 1950s has meant that the evidence has been lost.

Lower mast	white
Top masts and topgallant masts	varnished wood with white doublings
Lower yards, topsail yards, top-gallant yards, royal and skysail yards	black
Other yards	varnished wood
Stunsail booms	wood with black tips
Poles	white
Spanker gaff and boom	white
Bowsprit	white
Jib-boom	white over bowsprit, varnished wood elsewhere
Spencer gaff	white
Trestle trees, cross-trees, tops	white
Dolphin striker	white
Blocks	black
Lower dead-eyes and seizings	black, treated with Stockholm tar
Figurehead	white
Bobstay and bowsprit chains	black
Plank sheer	white
Name and scrollwork	gold
Deckhouses	varnished wood with white roofs

TEA CLIPPER YEARS

Although the specification called for the 'tween deck to be painted white, the evidence is that that the whole of the hold was painted with a red/brown oxide paint, a type of oil paint commonly used as a metal primer throughout the nineteenth century. There is evidence of at least six repaintings, suggesting that she was repainted for each voyage. In the fo'c's'le – where the crew had sleeping accommodation – there were traces of a limewash finish over the red oxide, which was identified as belonging to the early but not the earliest years.

1883–1922

Around the seventh time the interior was repainted, red lead primers were used and continued to be used for another six repaintings. After that two paintings were made with iron oxide. Assuming that little or no work was undertaken during the Portuguese period, this would allow for a repainting around every two years when the ship was a wool clipper. No red lead was found in the lazarette or afterpeak, suggesting that there was no repainting in these areas during the first half of the twentieth century.

1922–52

From red, the ship's interior suddenly is turned white, first with lead and then with zinc white paint. It is not certain whether this happened in Falmouth or Greenhithe. No metal primer was applied and the colour was confined to the hold – lead white paint traces were not found in the fo'c's'le, afterpeak or lazarette.

1950S' RESTORATION AND AFTER

The interior of the planking and ironwork in the 'tween deck was again painted white using titanium dioxide paint. In the lower hold, the planking was varnished and the ironwork painted white. Later, the iron framework's diagonal bracing was later picked out in red in order to distinguish it.

2006–12 CONSERVATION PROJECT

Rather than recreate the original colour scheme, it was decided to repeat that 1950s' scheme on the 'tween deck by painting both hull planks and ironwork white. In the lower hold, to emphasise the structure of the ship, the planks were left unpainted, the original ironwork painted white and all new structure – from the 1950s onwards – painted grey.

Appendix B: Crew numbers

The following table gives the number of crew who signed on at the beginning of each voyage and actually sailed (a small number of men signed on but did not turn up for the ship's departure). The effect of the reduction of the ship's rig in 1880 on crew numbers can be clearly seen.

Most of the seamen who sailed on *Cutty Sark* did so just once. They were paid off when they returned to London and had to look for another ship. But many took the opportunity of a free passage to Australia. In 1876 for example, 12 of the 16 able seamen deserted. They had to be replaced by expensive Australian seamen. The youngest were 14-year-old apprentices – the oldest a 54-year-old able seaman.

In total, 682 men are known to have sailed on *Cutty Sark* (excluding her years in Portuguese ownership). Only five were lost at sea.

TABLE 17   Crew numbers
(analysis of data in Bailey, 1989)

	1870 (1)	1870 (2)	1872 (1)	1872 (2)	1873	1874	1875	1876	1877 (1)	1877 (2)	1880 (1)	1880 (2)	1882	1883	1884	1885	1886	1887	1888	1889	1890	1891	1892	1893	1894
Master	1	1	1	1	1	1	1	1	1	1	1	1	1	1	1	1	1	1	1	1	1	1	1	1	1
First Mate	1	1	1	1	1	1	1	1	1	1	1	1	1	1	1	1	1	1	1	1	1	1	1	1	1
Second Mate	1	1	1	1	1	1	1	1	1	1	1	1	1	1	1	1	1	1	1	1	1	1	1	1	1
Third Mate									1		1				1				1	1					1
Bo'sun		1	1		1				1							1	1	1							
Steward	1	1	1	1		1	1		1					1		1	1	1	1	1	1	1	1	1	1
Cook	1	1	1	1	1	1	1	1	1	1	1	1	1	1	1	1	1	1	1	1	1	1	1	1	1
Carpenter	1	1	1	1	1	1	1	1	1	1	1	1	1	1	1	1	1	1	1	1	1	1	1	1	1
Carpenter's Mate	1	1																1							
Sail Maker	1	1	1	1		1	1	1	1	1			1					1							
Able Seaman	17	20	18	18	17	18	16	16	17	13	13	10	10	11	9	10	8	9	9	9	8	9	10	10	10
Ordinary Seaman	2	1	2	1	1	2	2	2		2		2	0		1			1							
Apprentice			1	3	1	4	4	4		4	5	5	3	5	7	6	6	5	3	3	5	9	5	4	4
Boy																				1			1	1	
TOTAL	27	30	29	29	25	28	29	29	27	26	21	23	22	19	21	25	21	24	24	18	19	24	22	21	21

Appendix C: Monthly wages for seamen

TABLE 18   Able Seamen's monthly wages according to port of engagement
(from Bailey, 1989)

	LONDON	SHANGHAI	HONG KONG	SYDNEY	MANILA	MELBOURNE	CALCUTTA	SINGAPORE	NEWCASTLE	NEW YORK
1870	£2 10s	£2 10s								
1870–71	£2 10s	£2 10s	£2 10s							
1872	£2 10s	£2 10s								
1872–73	£3									
1873–74	£3 5s			£4 5s						
1874–75	£3 5s			£5						
1875–76	£3 5s	£3 10s		£5						
1876–77	£3 5s	£3 10s		£5						
1877	£3 5s									
1877–80	£3 5s	£3 5s		£4 10s	£3					
1880	£3 5s			£4						
1880–82	£2 10s	£2 15s		£4		£4	£3	£3		
1882–83										£1 8s
1883–84	£3								£5 10	
1884–85	£3								£4 10s or £5	
1885	£2 15s									
1886–87	£2 15s	£2 15s								
1887–88	£2 10s								£4 10s	
1888–89	£2 10s			£4						
1889–90	£3			£4						
1890–91	£3 10s			£4						
1891–92	£3 10s									
1892–93	£3			£3 (?)						
1993–94	£3									
1894–95	£2 15s									

Appendix D: Log positions from four voyages

LONDON TO SHANGHAI, 1870 (FIRST VOYAGE)

Day	Date	Lat	Lon
Day 2	17th February	48°48'N	5°45'W
3	18th February	46°14'N	9°19'W
4	19th February	42°34'N	13°17'W
5	20th February	40°15'N	16°22'W
6	21st February	39°13'N	17°25'W
7	22nd February	37°24'N	18°54'W
8	23rd February	36°9'N	15°33'W
9	24th February	32°55'N	14°28'W
10	25th February	30°24'N	13°50'W
11	26th February	29°52'N	15°15'W
12	27th February	28°22'N	16°5'W
13	28th February	27°28'N	15°55'W
14	1st March	26°38'N	16°26'W
15	2nd March	24°8'N	17°22'W
16	3rd March	21°2'N	18°32'W
17	4th March	17°25'N	20°10'W
18	5th March	14°14'N	20°42'W
19	6th March	11°58'N	21°0'W
20	7th March	9°38'N	21°60'W
21	8th March	7°18'N	21°13'W
22	9th March	4°49'N	21°28'W
23	10th March	2°49'N	21°41'W
24	11th March	1°55'N	22°0'W
25	12th March	0°34'N	21°57'W
26	13th March	0°4'N	21°56'W
27	14th March	0°37'S	21°58'W
28	15th March	1°33'S	22°10'W
29	16th March	2°20'S	22°15'W
30	17th March	3°56'S	23°41'W
31	18th March	6°7'S	25°26'W
32	19th March	9°11'S	26°25'W
33	20th March	12°33'S	26°53'W
34	21st March	15°39'S	25°31'W
35	22nd March	19°5'S	24°0'W
36	23rd March	22°20'S	22°41'W
37	24th March	24°29'S	23°7'W
38	25th March	26°12'S	23°41'W
39	26th March	26°26'S	23°47'W
40	27th March	27°40'S	23°9'W
41	28th March	29°29'S	21°13'W
42	29th March	31°43'S	18°4'W
43	30th March	32°57'S	16°38'W
44	31st March	36°17'S	16°57'W
45	1st April	37°56'S	17°2'W
46	2nd April	36°52'S	15°13'W
47	3rd April	38°28'S	13°59'W
48	4th April	39°30'S	8°47'W
49	5th April	40°34'S	4°39'W
50	6th April	41°43'S	1°35'E
51	7th April	42°26'S	6°58'E
52	8th April	42°35'S	13°48'E
53	9th April	42°41'S	17°56'E
54	10th April	43°42'S	22°34'E
55	11th April	43°51'S	26°42'E
56	12th April	43°35'S	31°50'E
57	13th April	44°18'S	38°48'E
58	14th April	44°18'S	47°80'E
59	15th April	44°25'S	53°22'E
60	16th April	44°9'S	60°22'E
61	17th April	43°23'S	66°21'E
62	18th April	42°17'S	73°51'E
63	19th April	40°27'S	78°14'E
64	20th April	39°13'S	82°49'E
65	21st April	37°54'S	84°18'E
66	22nd April	36°9'S	85°37'E
67	23rd April	34°41'S	88°35'E
68	24th April	33°13'S	92°50'E
69	25th April	31°15'S	96°20'E
70	26th April	28°26'S	99°14'E
71	27th April	24°56'S	101°36'E
72	28th April	21°32'S	103°44'E
73	29th April	18°23'S	104°39'E
74	30th April	15°32'S	105°17'E
75	1st May	12°45'S	105°33'E
80	6th May	9°27'S	105°31'E
81	7th May	1°39'S	107°18'E
82	8th May	0°2'N	106°58'E
83	9th May	2°0'N	107°0'E
84	10th May	4°34'N	107°12'E
85	11th May	6°3'N	107°42'E
86	12th May	6°45'N	108°19'E
87	13th May	7°38'N	109°90'E
88	14th May	9°25'N	110°48'E
89	15th May	10°36'N	111°44'E
90	16th May	11°58'N	112°44'E
91	17th May	13°19'N	114°17'E
92	18th May	14°45'N	115°16'E
93	19th May	15°50'N	116°2'E
94	20th May	16°59'N	117°21'E
95	21st May	18°14'N	118°42'E
96	22nd May	20°12'N	119°57'E
97	23rd May	22°42'N	121°43'E
98	24th May	24°0'N	122°13'E
99	25th May	25°13'N	122°33'E
100	26th May	26°21'N	122°34'E
101	27th May	27°8'N	123°35'E
102	28th May	27°32'N	124°17'E
103	29th May	28°25'N	123°43'E
105	31st May	*Reached Shanghai*	

SHANGHAI TO LONDON, 1872

Day	Date	Lat	Lon
Day 6	22nd June	29°50'N	123°14'E
7	23rd June	27°47'N	121°58'E
8	24th June	24°58'N	119°33'E
9	25th June	22°8'N	117°30'E
10	26th June	20°27'N	114°43'E

#	Date	Lat	Long
11	27th June	18°59'N	114°58'E
12	28th June	17°42'N	115°30'E
13	29th June	15°54'N	115°19'E
14	30th June	15°7'N	114°30'E
15	1st July	14°15'N	112°25'E
16	2nd July	14°47'N	111°17'E
17	3rd July	14°31'N	110°55'E
18	4th July	13°48'N	110°58'E
19	5th July	12°59'N	110°37'E
20	6th July	11°40'N	110°35'E
21	7th July	10°58'N	110°46'E
22	8th July	8°6'N	110°55'E
23	9th July	5°19'N	111°44'E
24	10th July	3°45'N	111°19'E
25	11th July	4°70'N	109°54'E
26	12th July	3°28'N	108°10'E
27	13th July	2°27'N	107°0'E
28	14th July	0°47'N	108°6'E
29	15th July	0°12'N	108°18'E
30	16th July	1°18'S	108°16'E
31	17th July	2°54'S	107°18'E
32	18th July	4°40'S	106°55'E
33	19th July	5°45'S	106°1'E
34	20th July	6°38'S	104°37'E
35	21st July	7°42'S	103°40'E
36	22nd July	8°13'S	102°46'E
37	23rd July	9°50'S	101°16'E
38	24th July	11°2'S	99°21'E
39	25th July	12°22'S	97°0'E
40	26th July	13°30'S	93°19'E
41	27th July	14°55'S	55°S'87
42	28th July	16°33'S	82°19'E
43	29th July	18°1'S	77°12'E
44	30th July	19°18'S	72°47'E
45	31st July	20°36'S	68°50'E
46	1st August	21°14'S	65°43'E
47	2nd August	22°0'S	62°40'E
48	3rd August	23°24'S	57°30'E
49	4th August	24°26'S	52°34'E
50	5th August	25°42'S	48°0'E
51	6th August	27°26'S	43°39'E
52	7th August	28°49'S	39°54'E
53	8th August	28°40'S	38°51'E
54	9th August	29°29'S	36°36'E
55	10th August	30°38'S	33°53'E
56	11th August	33°19'S	30°43'E
57	12th August	32°48'S	29°19'E
58	13th August	34°3'S	28°70'E
59	14th August	34°6'S	28°70'E
60	15th August	34°26'S	28°1'E

this was the day the rudder was lost

#	Date	Lat	Long
61	16th August	34°13'S	28°24'E
62	17th August	34°43'S	28°25'E
63	18th August	34°58'S	28°11'E
64	19th August	34°51'S	27°58'E
65	20th August	34°38'S	27°36'E
66	21st August	34°19'S	26°58'E
67	22nd August	35°60'S	24°50'E
68	23rd August	35°41'S	20°58'E
69	24th August	35°55'S	17°55'E
70	25th August	35°24'S	17°37'E
71	26th August	35°8'S	17°28'E
72	27th August	35°3'S	17°17'E
73	28th August	34°56'S	16°56'E
74	29th August	34°1'S	16°2'E
75	30th August	33°52'S	14°54'E
76	31st August	32°33'S	14°19'E
77	1st September	30°44'S	12°24'E
78	2nd September	28°32'S	9°16'E
79	3rd September	26°28'S	6°7'E
80	4th September	24°50'S	3°48'E
81	5th September	23°15'S	1°31'E
82	6th September	21°40'S	0°28'W
83	7th September	20°11'S	1°55'W
84	8th September	18°14'S	3°36'W
85	9th September	15°38'S	6°9'W
86	10th September	12°53'S	8°46'W
87	11th September	9°56'S	11°10'W
88	12th September	7°1'S	13°26'W
89	13th September	4°22'S	15°38'W
90	14th September	2°5'S	17°15'W
91	15th September	0°7'S	18°52'W
92	16th September	2°24'N	19°41'W
93	17th September	4°10'N	19°47'W
94	18th September	6°16'N	19°43'W
95	19th September	7°27'N	19°43'W
96	20th September	7°28'N	20°37'W
97	21st September	8°21'N	21°2'W
98	22nd September	9°46'N	21°0'W
99	23rd September	10°44'N	21°2'W
100	24th September	11°22'N	21°56'W
101	25th September	11°59'N	23°7'W
102	26th September	14°9'N	25°4'W
103	27th September	16°8'N	26°47'W
104	28th September	18°48'N	28°32'W
105	29th September	21°56'N	29°56'W
106	30th September	25°14'N	31°17'W
107	1st October	27°47'N	32°5'W
108	2nd October	29°35'N	33°48'W
109	3rd October	32°9'N	34°42'W
110	4th October	35°17'N	34°10'W
111	5th October	37°41'N	31°59'W
112	6th October	39°6'N	29°19'W
113	7th October	39°45'N	24°43'W
114	8th October	40°56'N	25°7'W
115	9th October	42°29'N	21°34'W
116	10th October	42°59'N	19°25'W
117	11th October	44°20'N	16°55'W
118	12th October	45°37'N	13°26'W
119	13th October	46°10'N	10°7'W
120	14th October	47°17'N	7°12'W
121	15th October	48°1'N	5°43'W
122	16th October	50°4'N	2°24'W

Reached London

LONDON TO SYDNEY, 1885

Day	Date	Lat	Long
Day 4	4th April	48°57'N	6°18'W
5	5th April	47°16'N	8°25'W
6	6th April	46°13'N	9°20'W
8	8th April	40°43'N	12°29'W
9	9th April	37°27'N	13°52'W
10	10th April	34°30'N	16°45'W
11	11th April	33°10'N	18°47'W
12	12th April	31°50'N	19°43'W
13	13th April	29°12'N	21°2'W
14	14th April	26°46'N	22°47'W
15	15th April	24°59'N	24°20'W
16	16th April	22°9'N	26°22'W
17	17th April	18°41'N	28°7'W
18	18th April	14°38'N	28°35'W
19	19th April	11°3'N	28°30'W
20	20th April	7°15'N	27°49'W
21	21st April	4°28'N	26°38'W
22	22nd April	1°45'N	25°30'W
23	23rd April	0°16'N	26°5'W
24	24th April	0°51'S	26°25'W
25	25th April	1°41'S	26°58'W
26	26th April	3°8'S	27°34'W
27	27th April	6°12'S	28°39'W
28	28th April	9°54'S	30°24'W
29	29th April	13°3'S	32°29'W
30	30th April	16°7'S	33°57'W
31	1st May	18°46'S	34°41'W

32	2nd May	20°0'S	34°10'W		**SYDNEY TO LONDON, 1885**				49	3rd December	12°29'N	33°58'W
33	3rd May	21°9'S	33°30'W		**Day 2**	18th October	37°26'S	153°0'E	50	4th December	16°7'N	36°7'W
34	4th May	22°58'S	33°15'W		3	19th October	40°21'S	156°3'E	51	5th December	19°17'N	38°1'W
35	5th May	25°48'S	33°7'W		4	20th October	43°50'S	159°17'E	52	6th December	22°39'N	39°42'W
36	6th May	28°32'S	32°16'W		5	21st October	47°38'S	162°26'E	53	7th December	25°45'N	41°29'W
37	7th May	30°53'S	29°52'W		6	22nd October	50°22'S	167°11'E	54	8th December	28°2'N	42°21'W
38	8th May	33°8'S	25°43'W		7	23rd October	53°3'S	174°16'E	55	9th December	29°51'N	42°10'W
39	9th May	33°25'S	23°17'W		8	23rd October	54°14'S	178°13'W	56	10th December	30°38'N	41°10'W
40	10th May	33°56'S	22°42'W		9	24th October	55°20'S	170°1'W	57	11th December	31°10'N	39°55'W
41	11th May	35°11'S	21°9'W		10	25th October	55°47'S	166°24'W	58	12th December	33°42'N	40°8'W
42	12th May	37°22'S	17°42'W		11	26th October	56°38'S	162°8'W	59	13th December	35°55'N	41°2'W
43	13th May	39°6'S	13°12'W		12	27th October	57°2'S	156°43'W	60	14th December	37°9'N	40°34'W
44	14th May	40°32'S	8°19'W		13	28th October	57°46'S	149°35'W	61	15th December	38°47'N	35°52'W
45	15th May	41°49'S	3°22'W		14	29th October	58°10'S	140°38'W	62	16th December	39°20'N	31°47'W
46	16th May	42°28'S	1°55'E		15	30th October	59°8'S	134°34'W	63	17th December	39°35'N	28°32'W
47	17th May	43°10'S	8°28'E		16	31st October	59°28'S	126°32'W	64	18th December	39°42'N	39°40'W
48	18th May	43°45'S	14°38'E		17	1st November	59°51'S	120°0'W	65	19th December	41°7'N	25°46'W
49	19th May	44°24'S	19°40'E		18	2nd November	60°23'S	110°50'W	66	20th December	42°48'N	22°34'W
50	20th May	44°52'S	23°52'E		19	3rd November	60°47'S	100°23'W	67	21st December	44°54'N	17°57'W
51	21st May	45°15'S	31°18'E		20	4th November	60°21'S	93°48'W	68	22nd December	46°29'N	12°25'W
52	22nd May	45°36'S	38°31'E		21	5th November	59°13'S	86°9'W	69	23rd December	46°56'N	7°34'W
53	23rd May	46°5'S	45°38'E		22	6th November	58°47'S	82°7'W	70	24th December	48°0'N	7°40'W
54	24th May	46°52'S	50°55'E		23	7th November	58°36'S	78°7'W	71	25th December	49°4'N	7°54'W
55	25th May	46°52'S	54°3'E		24	8th November	57°30'S	71°20'W	72	26th December	48°43'N	6°12'W
56	26th May	47°15'S	58°27'E		25	9th November	56°50'S	62°55'W	73	27th December	49°0'N	4°35'W
57	27th May	47°15'S	58°27'E		26	10th November	55°9'S	55°43'W	74	28th December	49°27'N	3°51'W
58	28th May	47°22'S	67°0'E		27	11th November	52°25'S	50°24'W		*Reached London*		
59	29th May	48°2'S	69°15'E		28	12th November	49°50'S	43°32'W				
60	30th May	46°50'S	70°34'E		29	13th November	48°20'S	39°30'W				
61	31st May	46°56'S	74°43'E		30	14th November	45°6'S	34°15'W				
62	1st June	46°56'S	81°5'E		31	15th November	41°43'S	32°5'W				
63	2nd June	47°2'S	84°25'E		32	16th November	39°29'S	31°53'W				
64	3rd June	47°15'S	91°21'E		33	17th November	35°13'S	31°52'W				
65	4th June	47°32'S	99°24'E		34	18th November	34°45'S	31°28'W				
66	5th June	47°42'S	105°0'E		35	19th November	31°45'S	29°24'W				
67	6th June	47°21'S	111°15'E		36	20th November	29°31'S	29°37'W				
68	7th June	46°40'S	116°54'E		37	21st November	26°0'S	29°27'W				
69	8th June	46°0'S	119°57'E		38	22nd November	22°24'S	29°43'W				
70	9th June	45°17'S	123°55'E		39	23rd November	20°3'S	30°55'W				
71	10th June	44°56'S	127°13'E		40	24th November	17°28'S	31°40'W				
72	11th June	44°45'S	131°49'E		41	25th November	14°53'S	32°23'W				
73	12th June	44°56'S	137°51'E		42	26th November	11°19'S	32°24'W				
74	13th June	46°0'S	140°35'E		43	27th November	7°16'S	32°35'W				
75	14th June	45°20'S	144°9'E		44	28th November	3°38'S	32°16'W				
76	15th June	45°20'S	147°58'E		45	29th November	0°21'N	31°16'W				
77	16th June	44°7'S	149°38'E		46	30th November	3°5'N	30°33'W				
78	17th June	41°50'S	150°38'E		47	1st December	5°57'N	30°20'W				
81	18th June	*Reached Sydney*			48	2nd December	9°11'N	31°28'W				

A selection of figureheads from the Silver Collection, the largest collection of merchant ship figureheads in the world, displayed beneath the *Cutty Sark*. Decorating the bows of a great variety of ships, they date mostly from the nineteenth century and often depict famous figures, both contemporary and mythological, from Florence Nightingale to Sir Lancelot. Figureheads were believed to be lucky, embodying the spirit of the ship and representing its 'eyes', seeing its way through the waves.

CUTTY SARK: THE LAST OF THE TEA CLIPPERS

Recent restoration work
Gilding

In 2016, a programme of thorough research into the *Cutty Sark*'s carved bow and stern 'gingerbread' commenced, in preparation for the restoration and gilding project pictured here. Gilding describes the process of applying sheets of gold leaf to a surface, in this case *Cutty Sark*'s wooden decorative carving. Building on previous restoration work completed over the last six decades, in 2018 *Cutty Sark*'s shipkeeping team removed sixty separate pieces of the

ship's gingerbread carving from the stern, various name boards and other decorative elements of the ship's form. These were each examined, photographed and logged, before being transported to a specialist gilder, where further analysis and restorative work were carried out.

A new 'Star of India', the centrepiece of the stern gingerbread, has also been carved, which more closely adheres to its appearance in 1872. This was accomplished by meticulous

research into original designs and extant photographs of the ship from this time.

Supported by The Goldsmiths' Company, with whom the *Cutty Sark* has had a longstanding relationship, this is just one element of a programme of ongoing conservation work on the ship's gilded gingerbread that will ultimately see the ship's ornate decorative elements preserved and their appearance maintained for years to come.

Recent restoration work
Lifeboats

Cutty Sark's lifeboats were replaced regularly during their working years, having often been damaged in rough seas and stormy weather. While the 1950s replicas were originally made as shells for ornamental purposes, they were later fitted out to be seaworthy and have been involved in a number of boating regattas.

In 2016, a report on the condition of the lifeboats indicated that they were in need of conservation work. With the project supported by a number of generous donors, shipkeepers removed the boats from the Main Deck in September 2017 and delivered them into the care of apprentices working under the supervision of trained boat builders. The boats were stripped back to properly assess their condition and any issues. The port-side boat had areas of rot removed and the bottom two strakes – the planks running the length of the vessel next to the keel – were replaced in iroko, a durable African hardwood. These timbers were cut to size, steam-bent to the right shape and fitted into the stem and the stern and copper rivets were added. Following a fresh coat of paint, the ships were then returned to the Cutty Sark in March 2018, preserved for future generations to enjoy.

Bibliography

Bailey, S.F., *The Crews of the Cutty Sark*, London: Cutty Sark Society, 1989.

Bailey, S.F., *Cutty Sark Figureheads: The Long John Silver Collection*, Shepperton: Ian Allan Ltd, 1992.

Brettle, Robert E., *The Cutty Sark: Her Designer and Builder HERCULES LINTON, 1836-1900*, Cambridge: W. Heffer & Sons Ltd, 1969.

Campbell, George F., *China Tea Clippers*, New York: David McKay, 1974.

Carr, Frank G.G., *The Restoration of the Cutty Sark*, London: The Royal Institution of Naval Architects, 1966.

Crosse, John, *Thermopylae and the Age of Clippers*, Canada: Historian Publishers, 1968.

Ferguson, J. De Lancy, *The Letters of Robert Burns*, volume 2, pp. 23–24 (letter 401), 1985.

Geels, Frank W., *Technological Transitions and System Innovations: A Co-evolutionary and Socio-Technical Analysis*, Cheltenham: Edward Elgar Publishing Ltd, 2005.

Gibb, George, *Wood on Iron: Composite Construction in Shipbuilding*, Maritime Museum of British Columbia, 1996.

Longridge, C. Nepean, *The Cutty Sark: The Last of the Famous Tea Clippers*, London: Percival Marshall & Co. Ltd, 1933.

Lubbock, Basil, *The Log of the Cutty Sark*, Glasgow: James Brown & Son (2nd edition), 1925.

Lubbock, Basil, *The Colonial Clippers*, Glasgow: James Brown & Son (4nd edition), 1948.

MacGregor, David R., *The Tea Clippers: Their History and Development 1833–1875*. London: Conway Maritime Press (2nd edition), 1985.

Manil, Christian and Zbinden, Marie, *Tea Time*, Cassell & Co., 2001.

Platt, Alan and Sexton, Robert T., 'Philanthropy and the *Cutty Sark*: Capt. W.H. Dowman and Mrs Catharine Dowman, née Courtauld', *Mariner's Mirror* 95 (2009): pp. 458–73.

Platt, Alan; Waite, Simon and Sexton, Robert T., 'The *Cutty Sark*'s second keel and history as the *Ferreira*', *Mariner's Mirror* 95 (2009): pp. 8–32.

Plutarch, *Lives. Volume One*. Translated by J. Dryden. Little Brown: Boston, 1910.

Rose, Sarah, *For All the Tea in China: Espionage, Empire and the Secret Formula for the World's Favourite Drink*, London: Hutchinson, 2009.

Smith, Edgar C., *A Short History of Naval and Marine Engineering*. Cambridge: Babcock & Wilcox, 1937.

Short, Douglas, '"Robert Burns", "Tam O'Shanter" and the Authorship of "Duncan Macleerie"', *Studies in Scottish Literature*, 13:1:32–42 (1978).

Steele, Gordon, *The Story of the* WORCESTER, London: George G. Harrap & Co. Ltd, 1962.

Villiers, Alan, *The Cutty Sark: Last of a Glorious Era*, London: Corgi, 1955.

Index

Page references in *italics* refer to an illustration or to the item's inclusion in a table

THE CUTTY SARK: THE LAST OF THE TEA CLIPPERS

Author's Acknowledgements

I would like to thank all those who researched the history of this fascinating ship and on whose work I have drawn. I am grateful to Diana Cashin, Jake Motley, Alan Platt, Simon Waite and Fred Walker for their advice in a number of areas, and to Shirley Eaton, Claire Durrant and Sabrina Zakaria for their heroic recording of the conservation project. Tina Warner and David Westwood did an exceptional job in capturing the magnificence of the conserved ship in photographs. Pieter van der Merwe, as always, improved the text considerably by his editing, as did Christopher Westhorp and the very patient Kara Green.

Particularly large debts are owed to two people. First to Jessica Lewis, the Curator of *Cutty Sark*, for help and support over many years including advice and all the picture research for this book. And secondly to my friend Richard Doughty, the Director of the Cutty Sark Trust, who saw through, from beginning to end, one of the most complex and taxing conservation projects ever undertaken.

Picture Credits

Cutty Sark was conserved and re-opened to the public in 2012 with the support of: